**Automated Generation of Model-Based
Knowledge-Acquisition Tools**

Mark A. Musen
Medical Information Sciences Program
Stanford University School of Medicine

Automated Generation of Model-Based Knowledge-Acquisition Tools

CB777   232

Pitman, London

Morgan Kaufmann Publishers, Inc., San Mateo, California

PITMAN PUBLISHING
128 Long Acre, London WC2E 9AN

A Division of Longman Group UK Limited

© Mark A. Musen 1989

First published 1989

Available in the Western Hemisphere from
MORGAN KAUFMANN PUBLISHERS, INC.,
2929 Campus Drive, San Mateo, California 94403

ISSN 0268-7526

British Library Cataloguing in Publication Data

Musen, Mark A.
  Automated generation of model-based
  knowledge-acquisition tools.—(Research
  notes in artificial intelligence, 0268-7526).
  1. Expert systems.
  I. Title.
  006.3'3

ISBN 0 273 08812 2

Library of Congress Cataloging in Publication Data

Library of Congress Catalog Card Number: 89-045585

ISBN 1 55860 090 6

Reproduced and printed by photolithography
in Great Britain by Biddles Ltd, Guildford

Contents

List of Figures

List of Tables

Preface

This book, like many in the *Research Notes in Artificial Intelligence* series, is based on an investigation done as part of a doctoral dissertation. I have expanded and updated the original material, although the emphasis on the doctoral research remains. What is unusual about this work, perhaps, is that the dissertation was not submitted to a computer-science department, but rather to an interdisciplinary program at Stanford University in Medical Information Sciences. The thesis of the dissertation—and of this book—represents a fundamental contribution to the field of artificial intelligence (AI). At the same time, the research that I performed has, I believe, important implications both for the rapidly evolving discipline of medical informatics and for clinical medicine. Whereas this book addresses the general problem of knowledge acquisition for expert systems, the knowledge-acquisition tools that I describe should be useful in a wide range of clinical applications. Thus, it is likely that readers of quite varied backgrounds will be interested in this book.

I have tried to make my presentation as nontechnical as possible, and I have used footnotes liberally to define each essential concept that might be novel either to computer scientists unfamiliar with medicine or to clinicians unfamiliar with AI. I hope that the result is a book that is accessible to an interdisciplinary community of researchers.

The work that I describe in this book developed within the ONCOCIN project at Stanford University. Under the direction of Ted Shortliffe and Larry Fagan, some 50 students and full-time programmers have contributed to the design, implementation, and evaluation of ONCOCIN during the past decade. Whereas I have built on the work of all the members of the ONCOCIN team, my research would have been impossible had I not received sound advice, encouragement, and program code from the following talented people: Dave Combs, Samson Tu, Cliff Wulfman, Michael Kahn, Jay Ferguson, Christopher Lane, and Joan Walton.

Ted Shortliffe served as my principal advisor during my doctoral studies, helping me to clarify my ideas and to present them understandably. Bruce Buchanan, Peter Rudd, and Larry Fagan also participated on my dissertation reading committee. I am grateful to all of them for their help and for their support.

Many friends and coworkers encouraged me in my research and made suggestions regarding previous drafts of this book. Glenn Rennels, Michael Kahn, Curt Langlotz, and Johan van der Lei provided especially helpful advice.

Lyn Dupré offered excellent editorial suggestions. Lynne Hollander assisted with the preparation of the final manuscript.

The research that I describe in this book was funded by grants LM-07033 and LM-04420 from the National Library of Medicine, and by support from the Henry J. Kaiser Family Foundation. Computing and text-processing facilities were provided by the SUMEX-AIM resource under NIH grant RR-00785, and through gifts from Xerox Corporation and Corning Medical. Darlene Vian and Trudy Haley administered the funds that made it all possible.

My family, my parents, and my friends have given me enormous inspiration and support throughout my career. My wife, Elyse, and our young son, Jay, continue to help me to put everything into perspective. Jay was born just as the research described in this book was coming into fruition; and it is Jay, who shows me on a daily basis what knowledge acquisition is all about, to whom I dedicate this work.

Abstract

To construct knowledge-based systems, developers must create models of the problem-solving behavior of experts. This modeling process, termed *knowledge acquisition,* is laborious, and thus impedes the dissemination of expert-systems technology. This book demonstrates ways in which computer-based tools can accelerate knowledge acquisition by aiding system builders in the creation and application of expert models.

In many application areas, there are related tasks for which advice systems might be useful, and for which only one general model is needed. One such domain is that of clinical trials—formal medical experiments in which alternative therapies are compared. Although different clinical trials require different treatments, in various medical specialties there are *classes* of clinical trials to which the same generic model of treatment planning applies. In addition to similarities among the *tasks* to be performed, the computational *methods* that an expert system might apply to carry out those tasks are the same.

This book presents a methodology to facilitate knowledge acquisition for advice systems in domains where end users require multiple, but related, knowledge bases. System builders use computer-based tools to create models of the tasks to be performed. Once those task models are designed, then other computer-based tools are generated automatically to allow application specialists to enter directly the details of particular tasks. I have demonstrated this methodology in a system called PROTÉGÉ, which helps its users to build models for tasks that can be solved by successive refinement of skeletal plans. In the domain of clinical trials, system builders use PROTÉGÉ to create models of particular classes of treatment plans. PROTÉGÉ then produces custom-tailored, graphical tools with which expert physicians define the details of particular clinical trials within each class. The physicians' specifications are automatically translated into the knowledge base of an expert system.

The methodology separates the problem of modeling an application area from that of extending that model to enter content knowledge. This division of labor expedites the creation of advice systems for application areas in which multiple large knowledge bases are required for analogous domain tasks.

1 Introduction

Computer programs that contain the knowledge of human experts and offer advice on the basis of that knowledge (*expert* or *knowledge-based* systems) are a major focus of research in artificial intelligence. In recent years, as the clinical literature has begun to pay increasing attention to medical software (Huth, 1984; Watts, 1986), tools for developing knowledge-based systems have independently become available commercially. Although there are dozens of products that have been used to build advice programs in nonmedical areas, and although the need for decision-making assistance in many areas of medicine is widely recognized, there currently are no knowledge-based systems in widespread use by physicians.

There is a multitude of reasons for slowness in the transfer of expert-systems technology from research laboratories to the clinical setting. Many medical applications require basic advances in automated temporal or spatial reasoning that have not yet been achieved. Other applications must wait for improved integration of computers into physicians' daily routines. Even when the technological and sociological barriers are surmountable, one final problem remains, regardless of the application domain: Building expert systems is a laborious and time-consuming undertaking. In this book, I describe a new methodology to assist in the construction of large expert-system knowledge bases that have practical utility.

1.1 Knowledge Acquisition

Workers in artificial intelligence (AI) have identified the "knowledge-acquisition bottle-neck" as a central problem (Feigenbaum, 1984). Knowledge acquisition—the process whereby computer scientists (called *knowledge engineers*) interview experts in a given application area and attempt to encode the experts' specialized knowledge in a computer program—is widely recognized as a principal obstacle in the development of knowledge-based systems.[1] In this book, I describe a computer-based tool, PROTÉGÉ, that facilitates knowledge acquisition for certain classes of knowledge-based systems. PROTÉGÉ is neither an expert system itself nor a program that builds expert systems directly; instead, PROTÉGÉ is a tool that helps users to build *other tools* that are custom-tailored to assist with knowledge acquisition for expert systems in specific application areas.

The expert systems that PROTÉGÉ helps to build perform their problem solving using a method called *skeletal-plan refinement* (Friedland and Iwasaki, 1985). Such systems decompose a problem's abstract (skeletal) solution into one or more constituent plans that are each worked out in more detail than the more abstract plan. These constituent plans, however, may themselves be skeletal in nature and may require further distillation into subcomponents that are more fleshed out. The refinement process continues until a concrete solution to the problem is achieved.

There are many application tasks to which the method of skeletal-plan refinement applies. In my research, I have concentrated on the area of *clinical trials*—formal medical experiments in which patients are treated in accordance with predefined guidelines called *protocols*. PROTÉGÉ allows knowledge engineers to build tools that physicians can then use to enter knowledge about individual protocols. The knowledge of the protocols is in turn used by expert systems that provide treatment advice. PROTÉGÉ, however, contains no knowledge of medicine or of clinical trials. The program should therefore be useful in domains outside of medicine where tasks can be solved using the method of skeletal-plan refinement. Nevertheless, all experiments with PROTÉGÉ to date have been performed in the context of the ONCOCIN project at Stanford University (Shortliffe, 1986), and have concentrated on the issues of providing decision support for physicians caring for

---

[1] The terms *knowledge acquisition* and *knowledge engineering* are, for our purposes, interchangeable. The expression *knowledge acquisition* often connotes more the interviewing and elicitation of knowledge from experts, whereas *knowledge engineering* stresses the encoding of an expert's knowledge within a computer program. Many authors use the term *knowledge acquisition* to refer to all work involving machine learning, not just to knowledge engineering. In this book, only the more restricted interpretation is intended.

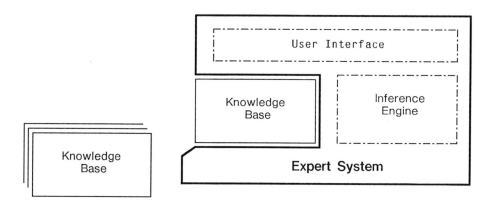

Figure 1.1: Components of an Expert System

Expert systems generally can be thought of as containing an *inference engine* and a separate *knowledge base* about which the inference engine performs reasoning. There also must be a *user interface* that channels information between the inference engine and the advice-system user. When new knowledge bases are substituted into the expert system, the inference engine can reason about whatever domain knowledge is supplied; there is no need to reprogram the inference engine or user interface.

patients enrolled in research protocols. I accordingly have limited my discussion in this book to PROTÉGÉ's documented utility for creating knowledge-entry tools for clinical-trial applications.

Before introducing PROTÉGÉ itself in more detail (Section 1.2), I shall provide essential background information that is required to clarify the methodology.

1.1.1   Creating a Knowledge Base

An important design goal for knowledge-based systems is to maintain a clear division between a system's knowledge about a particular application area and the general inference mechanism required for reasoning about that knowledge (Figure 1.1). Although the idea dates back to early work in AI (McCarthy, 1968), the advantages of separating *knowledge* from *inference* became clear in the mid-1970s with the development of programs such as MYCIN—a program that recommended therapy for presumptive bacteremia and meningitis (Buchanan and Shortliffe, 1984). Using a program called EMYCIN—a general-purpose *inference engine* representing the essential features of MYCIN, stripped of the infectious disease knowledge—a person could develop different knowledge bases for expert systems in a variety of domains (van Melle, 1979). Thus, a knowledge base for disorders of blood coagulation, when added to EMYCIN, produced an expert system called CLOT (Bennett and Engelmore, 1984). Substituting knowledge about pulmonary-function testing created PUFF (Aikins et al., 1983). Furthermore, there was nothing about EMYCIN that was intrinsically medical; entry of a knowledge base describing a computer program for structural-engineering analysis made SACON (Bennett and Engelmore, 1984).

A number of EMYCIN derivatives and numerous other expert system *shells* are now readily available; many are commercial products (Bundy, 1986; Gevarter, 1987). Most of these shells provide special editors to assist the user in entering and reviewing the contents of new knowledge bases. Many small advice systems have been developed by physicians or medical students using such shells (Mulsant and Servan-Schreiber, 1984; Tuhrim and Reggia, 1986). However, robust expert systems of sufficient scope and power to be useful clinically have rarely been developed by medical personnel working alone. The traditional paradigm still prevails: Mature consultation programs represent the work of knowledge engineers who have encoded the knowledge of experts.

Even when highly experienced knowledge engineers attempt to elicit expertise from authorities in a particular domain, the work needed to build knowledge-based systems can be extensive. In the case of ONCOCIN (Shortliffe et al., 1981), a system that advises physicians regarding the treatment of patients with cancer, over 2 years elapsed before the investigators completed an acceptable prototype.[2] CLOT, a demonstration project that dealt with a highly constrained domain and that contained only 63 rules, required about 60 person-hours (Bennett and Engelmore, 1984). The developers of Blue-Box, a prototype advice system for treating depression, needed about 300 person-hours to build a knowledge base of approximately 200 rules (Mulsant and Servan-Schreiber, 1984). (Had the knowledge engineers not been medical students already familiar with the problem area, knowledge acquisition for Blue-Box presumably would have been even more laborious.)

Reports on the time required to build large commercial expert systems are difficult to

---

[2]Not all of this time was devoted to knowledge engineering; the first ONCOCIN programmers also built major extensions to the EMYCIN shell.

obtain, as such information generally is proprietary. Nevertheless, knowledge acquisition is most often cited as the principal bottleneck by industry as well. For example, COMPASS, an expert system for maintenance of telephone switching systems used at GTE (Prerau, 1987), contains approximately 500 LISP functions, 400 if–then rules, and 1000 objects in the KEE knowledge-representation language. In designing COMPASS, GTE had to assign a senior switching services supervisor to spend 25 percent of his time working with a knowledge-engineering team for over 2 years.

Commercial expert systems that are now marketed by AI start-up companies typically required between 20 and 50 person-years to develop (Spang, 1987). The cost of building knowledge-based systems, even when experienced professionals undertake the project, can thus be staggering. For example, Syntelligence (Sunnyvale, California) spent between \$8 and \$9 million on knowledge engineering for a very large expert system that evaluates risk assessment for insurance underwriters (Spang, 1987).

1.1.2   A Case Study: The ONCOCIN System

In recent years, workers in AI have built a number of computer-based tools to assist in the knowledge-acquisition process. I shall review many of these programs in Chapter 3. An appreciation for how such tools can assist in the construction of expert systems can best be achieved by way of an example. In this section, I shall briefly describe both ONCOCIN, an expert system that provides advice concerning the treatment of patients with cancer, and OPAL, a computer-based tool that allows physicians to enter new cancer-treatment plans into the ONCOCIN knowledge base. I developed PROTÉGÉ, the system that I present in this book, to generalize the lessons learned in the development of OPAL.

ONCOCIN, which I shall discuss in detail in Chapter 5, contains a knowledge base of standardized oncology treatment plans (*protocols*), an inference engine (the *Reasoner*), and a user interface (the *Interviewer*). ONCOCIN applies its knowledge of cancer protocols to arrive at therapy recommendations for specific patients who are being treated according to these predetermined guidelines. The ONCOCIN Interviewer displays a spreadsheet (or *flowsheet*) that physicians use to enter time-oriented data concerning individual patients (Figure 1.2). Each time a physician consults the program, ONCOCIN uses its knowledge

Cover Sheet								
Mass / X-ray								
Disease Activity								

Hematology

WBC x 1000	3,5	6,4	6,3	6,2	5,1	3,3	3,2
% polys							
% lymphs							
PCV	27,3	27,6	25,7	26,5	24,3	30,6	
Hemoglobin	9,4	9,5	8,8	9	8,2	10,4	
Platelets x 1000	294	42	61	141	323	241	249
Sed. Rate							

CHEMOTHERAPY (includes non-cytoxic drugs)

BSA (m2)							
Arm assignment							
Combination Name	POCC	VAM	VAM	VAM	POCC	POCC	VAM
Cycle #	2	3	3	3	3	3	4
Subcycle	B				A	B	
Visit type	TREAT	DELAY	DELAY	TREAT	TREAT	TREAT	TREAT
Procarbazine 100 MG/M2	200				200	200	
Vincristine 1,5 MG/M2	2,0				2,0	2,0	
Cytoxan 600 MG/M2	1300				1300	1300	
CCNU 60 MG/M2	0				130		
VP16 75 MG/M2				130			130
Adriamycin 50 MG/M2				80			85
Methotrexate 30 MG/M2				45			0
Cum. Adriamycin (mg/m2)				130			167

Radiotherapy								
Symptom Review								
Toxicity								
Physical Examination								
Chemistry								
To order: Labs and Procedures								
To order: Nuclear Medicine and Tomography								
Scheduling								

Time

Day	31	24	1	8	29	5	26
Month	Mar	Apr	May	May	May	Jun	Jun
Year	86	86	86	86	86	86	86

Figure 1.2: The ONCOCIN Interviewer

The ONCOCIN system contains a knowledge base of cancer protocols, an inference engine called the *Reasoner*, and a user interface called the *Interviewer*. The Interviewer displays a graphical flowsheet that physicians use to enter data about patients who have cancer, and that the Reasoner uses to present its treatment recommendations to the physicians.

RULE 041

To determine whether the patients platelet count is too low
  for therapy to be given in VBM, in B-cycle MOPP,
  in B-cycle PAVE, in B-cycle C-MOPP, in CMF,
  or in CMFVP:

If: Platelet count (in thousands) is less than 50

Then: Conclude that the patient's platelet count is too low for
  therapy to be given

Figure 1.3: Rule from Prototype Version of ONCOCIN

This is one of 366 production rules that were manually encoded for the prototype
version of the ONCOCIN system. The rule was originally entered as a data structure
in the LISP programming language. The text that appears in the figure represents
an English translation. The rule states that, when certain drug combinations are administered to the patient, ONCOCIN should abort treatment whenever the patient's
platelet count falls below 50,000 per cubic millimeter.

of the protocol to which the patient has been assigned in conjunction with patient data
entered into the Interviewer to arrive at recommendations for treatment. (If a physician
disagrees with ONCOCIN's advice, he can, of course, disregard the program's suggestions.)

Knowledge acquisition for ONCOCIN requires entering the specifications for these
cancer-treatment protocols into the system's knowledge base. In the current version of
ONCOCIN, most of this knowledge is entered using the automated tool called OPAL
(Musen et al., 1988a). For the prototype version of ONCOCIN described by Shortliffe
et al. (1981), however, knowledge engineers had to type in all the knowledge by hand.

In the ONCOCIN prototype, much of the knowledge was encoded using if–then *production* rules such as the one in Figure 1.3. Such rules produce conclusions if specified
conditions are satisfied. The rule in Figure 1.3, for example, asserts that ONCOCIN should
abort the administration of the indicated combinations of drugs (called *chemotherapies*) if
the patient's platelet count falls below 50,000 per cubic millimeter. The prototype version
of ONCOCIN required 366 such production rules (and scores of other data structures) to

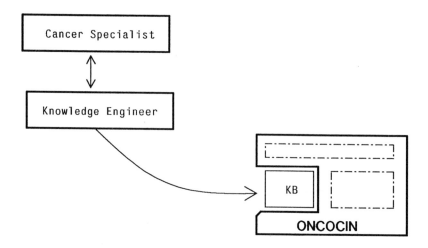

Figure 1.4: Knowledge Entry into the ONCOCIN Prototype

In the prototype version of ONCOCIN, cancer protocols were entered into the system by knowledge engineers who, in consultation with cancer specialists, programmed if–then rules and other data structures into the knowledge base.

define 24 oncology protocols. (Many of the treatment plans in the original knowledge base were similar, and shared a large proportion of their rules.)

In developing the ONCOCIN prototype, knowledge engineers collaborated with physicians who were experts in administering cancer therapy. The experts explained the particular cancer protocols to the knowledge engineers, who then encoded the necessary production rules and other knowledge-base components in LISP (Figure 1.4). The physicians could then observe the prototype's performance on test cases to determine whether the rules that had been entered resulted in appropriate therapy recommendations. Using this traditional knowledge-engineering approach, ONCOCIN's initial developers required several weeks or even months to encode each new cancer protocol.

In view of the dozens of cancer-treatment plans that physicians wanted to have available in ONCOCIN's knowledge base, the labor required for knowledge entry using traditional methods was unacceptable to physicians and knowledge engineers alike; encoding all the protocols this way would have taken years. In searching for a means to expedite the knowledge-acquisition process, it became apparent that there were important similarities

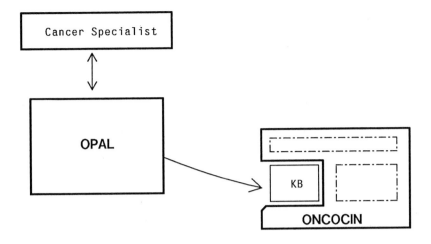

Figure 1.5: Knowledge Entry into OPAL

OPAL is a computer-based knowledge-acquisition tool that allows physicians to enter new oncology protocols directly. OPAL automatically constructs the rules and other data structures that are required to run ONCOCIN consultations from the physician's entries, and transfers those knowledge-base components to ONCOCIN.

among all the oncology protocols that were then represented in the ONCOCIN knowledge base. These similarities formed the basis for a general *model* of oncology protocols—a model that could be used to drive the computer-based tool called OPAL (Musen et al., 1987).

OPAL, which I shall discuss in Chapter 6, allows oncology experts to enter cancer protocols into ONCOCIN's knowledge base *directly* (Figure 1.5). Instead of typing individual production rules, the physicians themselves describe complete cancer protocols by filling out special-purpose graphical forms (such as the one in Figure 1.6). The physicians make selections from pop-up menus[3] to fill in the various predefined blanks. Another portion of OPAL allows the oncologists to draw flowchart diagrams that describe a given protocol's sequence of chemotherapy and radiotherapy treatments. Thus, rather than relying on knowledge engineers to enter LISP rules (as in Figure 1.3), physicians themselves use OPAL to fill in the blanks of the various graphical forms and to draw flowcharts to define

---

[3]A *pop-up menu* is a list of choices that the system displays on the workstation screen when the user requests to make an entry.

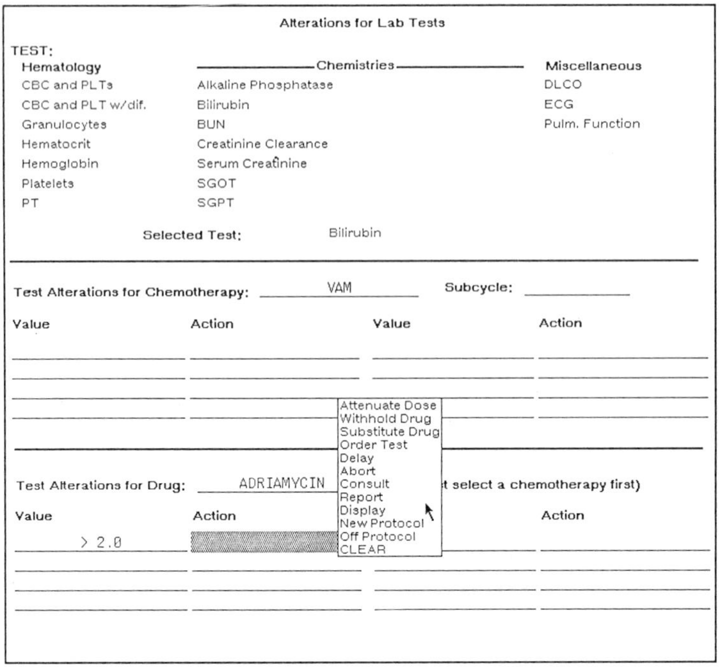

Figure 1.6: OPAL: A Knowledge-Acquisition Tool for Oncology Protocols

OPAL uses a model of the general concepts it expects to find in oncology protocols to acquire specific treatment plans from physicians. OPAL uses a number of graphical forms in which physicians fill in the blanks to define relevant information. In this form, the physician is specifying how therapy should be modified if the level of bilirubin in a patient's blood is elevated to more than 2.0 mg/dl.

new cancer treatment plans. The specifications they enter into OPAL are then automatically converted to the internal knowledge representations used by the current version of ONCOCIN.[4]

Because the concepts that appear in OPAL are familiar to oncologists, knowledge engineers are not required as intermediaries in the knowledge-entry process. Cancer specialists by themselves can enter complete protocols into OPAL in a few hours. In 1986, 36 cancer protocols were added to the ONCOCIN knowledge base using this program.

OPAL is a member of the class of computer programs that I shall refer to as *knowledge*

---

[4]As I shall discuss in Chapter 5, the present ONCOCIN system (Tu et al., 1989) has evolved considerably from the prototype described by Shortliffe et al. (1981).

editors. Knowledge editors are tools that allow users to enter and to refine the contents of expert-system knowledge bases—much as text editors allow users to enter and to refine the contents of textual documents. I shall discuss knowledge-editing programs in depth in Chapter 3.

OPAL is specialized for the oncology domain. The reason oncologists find so much of OPAL to be intuitive is that each of the graphical forms deals with concepts that relate directly to cancer therapy. The form in Figure 1.6, for example, anticipates that cancer specialists will want to adjust their patients' treatment on the basis of certain laboratory tests; the form has blanks that display the names of antitumor-drug combinations (chemotherapies) and individual drugs (in this case, a chemotherapy called *VAM* that contains the drug *Adriamycin*[5]); the adjustments to treatment that the user can select include options such as attenuating (decreasing) the dose of a drug or aborting the administration of a chemotherapy. All these oncology-specific notions are programmed into the form and cannot be changed easily.

Although OPAL makes it convenient for oncologists to enter plans for treating cancer, the program is of no value to other specialists, such as endocrinologists who might want to enter plans for managing thyroid disease or to cardiologists who might want to enter plans for controlling heart failure. The knowledge of oncology that is inherent in OPAL—which makes the program ideal for entering cancer protocols—prevents the program from being useful outside of the oncology domain. But what if the oncology knowledge in OPAL could be changed? Knowledge engineers could then build versions of OPAL that could acquire treatment plans for thyroid disease, heart failure, or a host of other medical problems. ONCOCIN could then offer therapy advice for clinical trials *other than those in oncology.* More important, physicians in other medical disciplines could inherit the same knowledge-engineering advantages that oncologists now receive from OPAL.

Adapting the present implementation of the OPAL editor to other application areas would be difficult. In OPAL, the various graphical forms and their blanks cannot be

---

[5]Adriamycin is a formulation of the generic drug *doxorubicin* that is distributed by Adria Laboratories (Columbus, Ohio). In the text of this book, trade names for drugs are capitalized, whereas generic names are printed in all lowercase characters. The computer output that appears in the figures, however, tends not to make this distinction.

11

changed without reprogramming. The layout of the forms, the possible values that users can enter, and the *meanings* that the program ascribes to those values are all embedded in program code that would have to be completely rewritten if OPAL were to be applied in a new discipline such as cardiology. It is possible, however, to imagine a program like OPAL that could make these application-dependent assumptions *explicit* and readily accessible. The creation of OPAL-like knowledge editors for new problem areas would become a manageable task: A knowledge engineer could change the application domain of the editor by changing these explicit assumptions. At the same time, making conspicuous the application-dependent assumptions in the knowledge editor would allow knowledge engineers to *edit* those assumptions easily by using a specially designed tool. Such an approach would facilitate the creation of programs like OPAL for many different areas of medicine—and for many nonmedical application areas as well.

This strategy forms the foundation for PROTÉGÉ—a program that knowledge engineers use to define and to edit the application-dependent assumptions in knowledge-editing programs like OPAL (Figure 1.7). With PROTÉGÉ, knowledge engineers create new knowledge editors that are custom-tailored for particular tasks. Each knowledge editor then is used by application experts to create knowledge bases for advice systems in the particular experts' specialty. In the next section, I shall show how PROTÉGÉ allows construction of a knowledge-acquisition tool for oncology that replicates much of the functionality of OPAL. In Chapter 9, I shall demonstrate how the methodology can be used in other domains as well.

1.2 An Overview of the Methodology

PROTÉGÉ generates graphical knowledge-editing tools that can be used by physicians to create knowledge bases for *e-ONCOCIN*—an expert-system shell that represents the *essential* features of ONCOCIN, without the oncology knowledge base. The e-ONCOCIN program, unlike ONCOCIN, makes no suppositions about the care of cancer patients. Any oncology knowledge that might be in an e-ONCOCIN system must be entered explicitly through PROTÉGÉ.

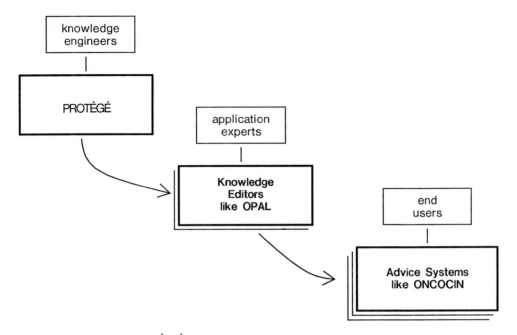

Figure 1.7: PROTÉGÉ: An Architecture for Generating Advice Systems

PROTÉGÉ is used to generate knowledge editors tailored for various *classes* of planning tasks (for example, classes of clinical trials). Experts in a particular application area use the knowledge editors created by PROTÉGÉ to develop knowledge bases that encode *specific* planning tasks (for example, particular clinical-trial protocols). End users consult with the resulting knowledge-based systems to obtain recommendations concerning appropriate planning actions (for example, how to apply a particular protocol to a particular patient situation).

PROTÉGÉ and the knowledge editors that it produces display knowledge using a graphical syntax. Knowledge is presented as two-dimensional images—typically, rectangular forms that have predefined blanks, as in OPAL. An additional component of the PROTÉGÉ-generated editors is an icon-based language that allows users to construct flowcharts that represent the fixed procedures that e-ONCOCIN should follow for particular clinical trials. (This visual programming language is much like the one in OPAL that oncologists use to specify the sequence of chemotherapies and radiation treatments in cancer protocols.) In all the programs that I shall describe, users enter and change knowledge via direct manipulation of the images on a workstation screen by means of a mouse pointing device. When possible, users specify selections via pop-up menus or other

13

software input mechanisms; keyboard entries are minimal.

Figure 1.8 shows a typical graphical form that a knowledge engineer[6] might fill out using PROTÉGÉ. With this form, the knowledge engineer describes the kinds of input data that could cause e-ONCOCIN to modify its treatment recommendations for patients enrolled in clinical trials in a particular application area. In this example, the application area is cancer therapy. The knowledge engineer has specified previously that such clinical trials have a class of input data called *chemistry data*. The form in Figure 1.8 shows the data items that the PROTÉGÉ user has determined are relevant in the chemistry data class—laboratory tests that measure the concentration of various substances in the blood such as *glucose, sodium, potassium,* and so on. The knowledge engineer must enter additional information about each data item, as I shall describe in Chapter 7.

The knowledge entered into the forms at the PROTÉGÉ level shapes the appearance and behavior of the knowledge editor that PROTÉGÉ generates. At the knowledge-editor level, physicians enter knowledge that pertains to individual clinical trials within the class that was defined using PROTÉGÉ. Thus, if a knowledge engineer uses PROTÉGÉ to describe oncology protocols in general, PROTÉGÉ creates a custom-tailored editor that physicians can use to describe particular protocols to treat patients with cancer. The editor for oncology protocols that PROTÉGÉ generates, in fact, looks much like OPAL. Figure 1.9, for example, shows one of several knowledge-editor forms that PROTÉGÉ produces for this domain. The form, which bears the heading *"Chemistry,"* lists all the blood-chemistry tests declared by the knowledge engineer at the PROTÉGÉ level as shown in Figure 1.8. In Figure 1.9, the user has chosen to enter rules based on abnormalities in the patient's bilirubin. Thus, the system highlights the word *bilirubin* at the top of the form. Using the pop-up menu, the clinical-trial expert is about to declare that, if a patient's bilirubin is greater than 2.0, the dose of Adriamycin in VAM chemotherapy

---

[6]In this book, I shall simplify the discussion by using several conventions. First, I shall refer to the PROTÉGÉ user consistently as a *knowledge engineer*, although a more typical scenario is a knowledge engineer and an application specialist (generally, a physician) using PROTÉGÉ together. Second, I shall always use masculine pronouns when referring to the knowledge engineer; conversely, I shall use feminine pronouns when referring to an application specialist. No presumptions about the actual gender of these people are implied. Third, although both application specialists and knowledge engineers may use the knowledge-editing programs produced by PROTÉGÉ, I shall consistently refer to users of these knowledge editors as *application specialists*.

CHEMISTRY   CONTINUOUS   BILIRUBIN   [Finished]
Data Class   Data-Type Class   Selected Data Item

CALCIUM ▷	SGOT ▷	▷	▷
PHOSPHORUS ▷	SGPT ▷	▷	▷
BUN ▷	SODIUM ▷	▷	▷
URIC ACID ▷	POTASSIUM ▷	▷	▷
GLUCOSE ▷	CHLORIDE ▷	▷	▷
TOTAL PROTEIN ▷	CO2 ▷	▷	▷
ALBUMIN ▷	CREATININE ▷	▷	▷
BILIRUBIN ▷	▷	▷	▷
CHOLESTEROL ▷	▷	▷	▷
ALK PHOSPHATASE ▷	▷	▷	▷
LDH ▷	▷	▷	▷

Figure 1.8: Sample PROTÉGÉ Form

This form allows the PROTÉGÉ user to enter the individual data items within a *data class* that can influence treatment. In this case, the form shows potential *chemistry* data in the oncology domain. These data are used to construct the OPAL-like form in Figure 1.9..

should be attenuated by 50 percent. The data items shown at the top of the form (sodium, potassium, bilirubin, and so on), the various actions listed in the menu (for example, attenuate the dose of a drug or delay chemotherapy), the fact that the bilirubin value should be entered as a positive real number (rather than as an integer or as some other type of data), and the context in which the physician's rule should be relevant (in this case, when administering a drug within a chemotherapy) are all derived from specifications that the knowledge engineer entered into PROTÉGÉ using various graphical forms. Unlike the OPAL form in Figure 1.6, these oncology-specific assumptions are not built into the knowledge editor, so they can be revised easily at the PROTÉGÉ level.

By filling out forms such as the one in Figure 1.9, an expert physician uses the editor produced by PROTÉGÉ to describe individual clinical trials. The knowledge editor then converts the expert's specifications into an e-ONCOCIN knowledge base, creating

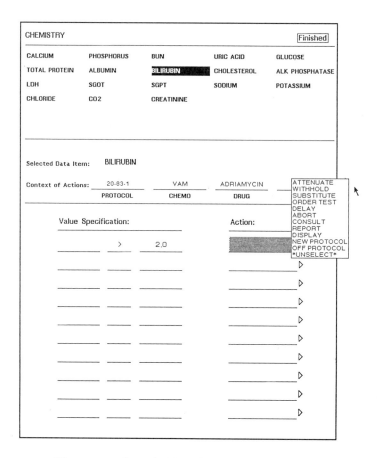

Figure 1.9: Sample Knowledge-Editor Form

This form allows application specialists to define the mapping between particular conditions that are entered into e-ONCOCIN and appropriate actions. In this example, for a certain oncology protocol, the physician is indicating what to do if a patient's serum bilirubin level is greater than 2.0 mg/dl. The appearance and behavior of this graphical form are derived from the specifications entered using PROTÉGÉ. Compare this form with the corresponding OPAL form in Figure 1.6.

the necessary production rules and other internal representations. The knowledge base allows e-ONCOCIN to provide treatment recommendations for patients who are enrolled in the clinical trials described by the expert. Each time a user requests a consultation, e-ONCOCIN can invoke its knowledge of the appropriate clinical trial to offer therapy advice consistent with a patient's current condition. As in the original ONCOCIN program, the physician who uses e-ONCOCIN enters the data that describe the state of the patient; e-ONCOCIN, in turn, recommends the therapy mandated by the protocol.

In summary, knowledge engineers use PROTÉGÉ to describe a clinical-trial application area. PROTÉGÉ then generates a custom-tailored knowledge-editing tool that physicians use to define specific clinical studies. The PROTÉGÉ-generated editor then produces knowledge bases that e-ONCOCIN uses to offer treatment advice for particular patients who are enrolled in one of those trials. The approach allows knowledge engineers to construct knowledge editors for new application areas rapidly, without the need for custom programming. The availability of these special-purpose tools permits domain experts, on their own, to develop new e-ONCOCIN knowledge bases for a variety of clinical-trial applications.

1.3   Conceptual Models

Although many computer-based tools for knowledge acquisition have been reported in the AI literature, it often is difficult to pinpoint the specific contributions of each one. Many articles have emphasized detailed descriptions of new knowledge-acquisition programs without attempting to explain how each system relates to all the others. In Chapter 3, I propose a taxonomy for knowledge-acquisition tools that is based on the manner in which these programs present the contents of a knowledge base to their users. My classification scheme centers on a program's *conceptual model*—the terms and relationships that a program uses to establish the semantics of a user's entries.

A conceptual model allows the user of a computer program to understand the meaning of the messages that the program produces and the nature of the data on which the program operates. For example, it would be impossible to use a spreadsheet program such as VisiCalc or Lotus 1-2-3 without appreciating the simple, but powerful, conceptual model that ascribes meaning to the rows and columns in the grid. Without such a conceptual model, a spreadsheet is merely a collection of numbers and boxes. With such a model, a spreadsheet contains *cells* and *columns* and *rows* that have positional and functional interrelationships.

If a user who had never before seen a spreadsheet program wanted to discover VisiCalc's conceptual model, he could not expect to find an obvious set of terms and relationships by glancing at VisiCalc's program code. The developers of VisiCalc had no need to make the conceptual model explicit within the program itself. (The model is well described in the user manual, however.) Similarly, it would be difficult to examine the program code for OPAL and thus to discover a clear set of terms and relationships that define protocols in the oncology domain—but such a model is there, nonetheless. (I shall discuss OPAL's conceptual model in Chapter 6.)

In the knowledge editors created by PROTÉGÉ, the conceptual models are made explicit. By using a set of conceptual terms and relationships stored in a relational database, PROTÉGÉ creates knowledge-acquisition tools with models that are tailored for particular application areas. The terms and relationships that define the nature of clinical trials in oncology may look nothing like the terms and relationships that define the nature of clinical trials in psychiatry. But because the conceptual models are conspicuously represented in the database, PROTÉGÉ can readily generate knowledge editors that incorporate the desired semantics.

The conceptual model in PROTÉGÉ itself is derived predominantly from a set of terms and relationships that define a model for the refinement of skeletal plans that take place over discrete time intervals. This conceptual model reflects e-ONCOCIN's problem-solving method (specifically, the manner in which e-ONCOCIN constructs a treatment plan). The data that knowledge engineers enter into PROTÉGÉ are used to construct the application-specific conceptual models for the editors that PROTÉGÉ generates.

In this book, I emphasize the importance of the conceptual models that shape all knowledge-editing programs. Moreover, I present a methodology that enables these conceptual models to be made explicit and to be edited. Because each conceptual model precisely defines the notions that application specialists may (and may not) enter into an expert system's knowledge base, PROTÉGÉ elucidates the assumptions that system builders make about the world. This approach allows knowledge engineers and domain experts to concentrate on the models that they construct and to recognize the strengths and limitations of those models. In generating custom-tailored tools to help system designers to build better models, PROTÉGÉ can facilitate the creation of advice systems for a variety of applications.

1.4   A Guide to the Reader

PROTÉGÉ, as a "tool to produce tools to produce tools," can be difficult to understand without substantial background information. The first six chapters of this book provide that foundation.

In **Chapter 2**, I describe the process of knowledge engineering and explore several of the reasons that knowledge acquisition is difficult. Much of the discussion reviews work in cognitive science and social psychology relating to the way in which experts apply and communicate their knowledge. Although I have not performed psychological experiments for this book, I do show how the methodology that I advocate addresses the cognitive and linguistic barriers to knowledge acquisition that have been identified by other researchers.

In **Chapter 3**, I review both traditional and computer-based methodologies for knowledge acquisition. I describe previous automated tools to elicit knowledge from experts, using a taxonomy that emphasizes the conceptual models presented by these knowledge-acquisition programs. I also discuss a model for *learning systems* that investigators have applied in the machine-learning community—a model that provides a useful perspective on the research that I describe here.

In **Chapter 4**, I present background information on the application domain explored in this research—controlled clinical trials. I discuss previous approaches to providing computer-based assistance to physicians cooperating in such trials, and speculate on how the knowledge editors generated by PROTÉGÉ could aid researchers in the design and implementation of new clinical studies. It is not essential to read this chapter to understand PROTÉGÉ's contributions to AI. Nevertheless, an appreciation for the practical aspects of the problem domain in which I have applied PROTÉGÉ will make the examples of the program's operation that I present in later chapters more comprehendible.

In **Chapter 5**, I describe the ONCOCIN expert system for clinical trials in oncology, and present ONCOCIN's methods for knowledge representation and the program's inference mechanism in detail. Because PROTÉGÉ is designed to create knowledge editors that may in turn be used to define a knowledge base for *e-ONCOCIN*, a slightly modified version of ONCOCIN in which the oncology knowledge has been removed, this chapter is required reading for those people who wish to understand the details of my research.

In **Chapter 6**, I discuss OPAL, an interactive program that acquires knowledge of oncology clinical trials for ONCOCIN. Because the knowledge editors generated by PROTÉGÉ are based on techniques that were first derived in the construction of OPAL, this chapter provides a concrete example of the functionality that PROTÉGÉ seeks in the knowledge editors that it produces. In the following two chapters, I show how PROTÉGÉ constructs a new knowledge editor, called p-OPAL, that has much the same behavior as that of the original OPAL program.

In **Chapter 7**, I describe PROTÉGÉ in detail, including both the implementation of the system and the model of problem solving that knowledge engineers use to define clinical-trial application areas.

In **Chapter 8**, I show how a task model entered by a knowledge engineer into PROTÉGÉ can be used for the automatic construction of a custom-tailored knowledge-acquisition system. PROTÉGÉ uses the model of the oncology domain that provides the examples in Chapter 7 as the conceptual model for a new knowledge editor, p-OPAL, which I describe in this chapter.

In **Chapter 9**, I seek to demonstrate that my methodology—previously illustrated solely in the setting of oncology clinical trials—can be used to create a knowledge editor and e-ONCOCIN advice system for an entirely different medical domain. Using the field of clinical trials for hypertension, I trace the generation of an advice system from the PROTÉGÉ level, where the application area is described; to HTN, a knowledge-editing program that PROTÉGÉ creates for hypertension clinical trials; to e-ONCOCIN, which provides advice regarding patients enrolled in the trials defined using HTN. The use of PROTÉGÉ to produce an advice system in a different application area (namely, hypertension) shows the viability of the methodology as well as the potential generality of e-ONCOCIN.

In **Chapter 10**, I summarize the important lessons of this research. I point out its limitations, while placing PROTÉGÉ, and other work on knowledge acquisition, in perspective. I identify key topics for further work and speculate about the potential applicability of the PROTÉGÉ approach to the creation of knowledge editors that are custom-tailored for generic problems that cannot be solved using the method of skeletal-plan refinement.

2 The Knowledge-Acquisition Bottleneck

In this chapter, I discuss the problem of knowledge acquisition for expert systems. I describe the work required to construct a knowledge base, and identify reasons why knowledge acquisition is difficult. The barriers that emerge range from the limitations of current knowledge-representation languages to the elusive nature of human expertise itself. All methodologies for knowledge acquisition must face these obstacles. In the final section of this chapter, I foreshadow how the barriers are confronted by PROTÉGÉ.

2.1 Building a Knowledge Base

Buchanan and others (1983) have divided knowledge acquisition into six discrete stages (Figure 2.1). Although actual expert systems are rarely developed in such a well-structured manner (the individual steps frequently overlap), the model captures the important elements of knowledge-base construction. The stages of knowledge acquisition are as follows:

1. **Identification:** Important aspects of the application are defined. The nature of the problem to be solved, the data that bear on that problem's solution, and the goals for the completed expert system are established by the domain expert working with the knowledge engineer. The identification stage thus determines the expert system's task.

2. **Conceptualization:** The key concepts and relationships in the domain are made explicit. The knowledge engineer establishes the linguistic terms used by application

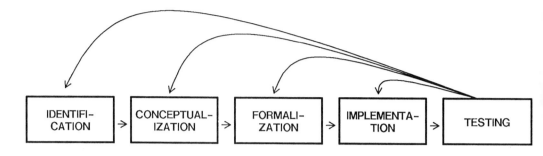

Figure 2.1: Stages of Knowledge Acquisition

Knowledge acquisition involves identifying the task, conceptualizing the knowledge, developing a formal representation, implementing a prototype, and testing the working system. Frequent revisions of the expert system commonly are dictated by errors that may have been introduced during any of the first four stages of knowledge acquisition. (Source: Adapted from Buchanan et al., 1983, p. 139)

specialists to describe features of the domain, and attempts to define the concepts that those terms represent. The knowledge engineer determines what types of data are available, what hypotheses can be inferred from the data, and how hypotheses lead to solutions. The future system's behavior is defined, ideally, independent of whatever shell might eventually be used to encode the elicited knowledge. The conceptualization stage entails what Newell (1982) calls *knowledge-level analysis,* discussed further in Section 3.1.1.

3. **Formalization:** The knowledge engineer selects an appropriate tool for building the expert system and begins exploring ways of representing the required knowledge in terms of the language provided by the particular shell. For example, if the knowledge engineer decides from the conceptualization step that EMYCIN might serve as a useful tool with which to develop the system, formalization of the knowledge requires establishing how the concepts and relationships in the domain might translate into EMYCIN parameters, contexts, and rules (van Melle, 1979). By defining a mapping between abstract knowledge and a particular knowledge-representation framework, the knowledge engineer determines the preliminary specifications needed to build the knowledge base.

4. **Implementation:** The knowledge needed for the application task is encoded using the representational framework of the selected expert-system shell. The resulting knowledge base, when processed by the shell's inference engine, yields an operational advice system.

5. **Testing:** The knowledge engineer and domain expert validate the knowledge base by observation of the system's performance on test cases. If they note aberrant behavior, they must trace the source of the problem.

6. **Revision:** The knowledge engineer may then have to redesign and reimplement the system. When finally presented with a program the behavior of which they can observe and comment on, domain experts often discover incorrect knowledge. Some errors may represent incorrect "facts," whereas others may be traceable to problems in either the identification or conceptualization steps. Errors of the latter type, not surprisingly, may demand substantial human effort to rectify.

Knowledge acquisition is clearly labor-intensive and often is highly iterative, due to the frequent need to reconceptualize, to redesign, and to reimplement portions of the knowledge base. Although careful attention to details at the conceptualization stage should obviate much of the need for repetitive prototyping (Breuker and Wielinga, 1987), in practice knowledge engineers and the domain experts with whom they collaborate seldom "get things right" the first time. The next section explores some of the reasons why this is so.

2.2   Obstacles to Knowledge Acquisition

The process of knowledge acquisition was identified as a central concern in the creation of advice systems over 20 years ago, during the development of programs such as DEN-DRAL (Buchanan et al., 1969). Since that time—as interest in encoding expert knowledge within computer programs has increased almost exponentially—various investigators have proposed explanations of why building a knowledge base is so difficult. Some authors attribute the problem to the lack of a formal theory for knowledge engineering (for example, Breuker and Wielinga, 1987), stressing the need to establish more principled methodologies

that can be used by system builders. Others point to the impalpable nature of human expertise, claiming that the limited ability of experts to introspect on their problem-solving
behavior and the difficulty of encoding their behavior within a computer may represent
insurmountable barriers to the creation of truly "expert" systems (Dreyfus, 1981). This
section reviews the primary barriers to knowledge acquisition. The nature of expert knowledge, the problems associated with communicating knowledge, and the limitations of our
languages for encoding knowledge within computers all contribute to the difficulties of
knowledge engineering.

2.2.1 The Psychology of Expertise

Human cognitive skills appear to be acquired in three generally distinct phases of learning
(Fitts, 1964). Initially there is the *cognitive* stage, in which the actions that are appropriate
in particular circumstances are identified, either as a result of direct instruction or from
observation of others. In this stage, learners often rehearse verbally information needed
for execution of the skill. Next comes the *associative* phase of learning, in which the
relationships noted during the cognitive stage are practiced and verbal mediation begins to
disappear. With repetition and feedback, the person begins to apply the actions accurately
in a fluent and efficient manner. Then, in the final *autonomous* stage, the person "compiles"
(Neves and Anderson, 1981) the relationships from repeated practice to the point where
she can perform them without conscious awareness. Suddenly, the person performs the
actions appropriately, proficiently, and effortlessly—"without thinking." The knowledge
has become *tacit* (Fodor, 1968).

Problems of Tacit Knowledge

Philosophers have long made a distinction between the concepts *knowing how* and *knowing
that* (Ryle, 1949). In recent years, it has become abundantly clear to cognitive psychologists that *knowing how* generally involves tacit knowledge, whereas *knowing that* requires
knowledge accessible to consciousness (Fodor, 1968). Tacit knowledge governs activities
that are skilled, smooth, and efficient—behaviors that are neither easily separated into
their components nor easily modified. The knowledge of which we are conscious, on the

26

other hand, can be inspected, abstracted, and applied in totally novel contexts—albeit without the deftness associated with skilled behavior.

Workers in AI have noted an analogous distinction in the ways that knowledge can be encoded (represented) in a computer. *Procedural* knowledge representations, in which the knowledge is incorporated within actual programs, offer the fastest and most efficient problem-solving performance, tailored specifically for predefined tasks. Alternatively, *declarative* representations encode knowledge as *facts* using data structures. Declarative representations are less efficient during problem-solving because they have to be *interpreted* by a general-purpose program that examines the data structures and behaves in accordance with the values that have been stored. Yet declarative representations have the advantage that knowledge is encoded such that it can be viewed by multiple programs and accessed for a variety of uses (Winograd, 1975). The knowledge bases with which we are concerned in this book therefore are encoded declaratively. A number of psychologists, struck by the correspondences between human expertise and knowledge representation in AI, have begun to refer to tacit, compiled knowledge in humans as *procedural;* knowledge available to consciousness, on the other hand, is considered *declarative* (Jacoby and Witherspoon, 1982; Rumelhart and Norman, 1983; Cohen, 1984; Anderson, 1987).

Although there may not be consensus regarding how knowledge is encoded physiologically in human memory (Rumelhart and Norman, 1983), the evidence that problem solving by experts involves some degree of tacit knowledge has enormous implications for those researchers concerned with knowledge acquisition for expert systems. As humans become experienced in an application area and repeatedly apply their know-how to specific tasks, their declarative knowledge becomes procedural. Experts lose awareness of what they know. Consequently, the special knowledge we would most like to incorporate into our advice systems often is the knowledge about which experts are least able to talk. Johnson (1983) has identified this phenomenon as "the paradox of expertise."

The paradox is confirmed by experimental data from the psychology literature (for example, Slovic, 1969), as well as by much anecdotal experience. Johnson (1983), for example, reports that he once enrolled in courses at the University of Minnesota Medical School as part of his investigation of the process of medical diagnosis. At the same time,

Johnson also had the opportunity to study a medical colleague (one of his teachers) caring for patients on the hospital wards. Johnson compared the physician's observed clinical behavior with the diagnostic methods his colleague was teaching in the classroom. To Johnson's surprise, the medical-school professor's behavior in practice seemed to contradict the clinical strategies that the teacher professed. When confronted with these observations, Johnson's subject responded:

> Oh, I know that, but you see I don't know how I do diagnosis, and yet I need to teach things to students. I create what I think of as plausible means for doing tasks and hope students will be able to convert them into effective ones. (Johnson, 1983, p. 81)

The clinician claimed to have no declarative knowledge of his diagnostic methods. His procedural knowledge was completely tacit, yet he attempted to reconstruct a plausible explanation of his behavior for the purposes of instructing his students. Unfortunately, what is plausible often may be incorrect (Nisbett and Wilson, 1977; Cleaves, 1987). Although Johnson's colleague had faith that his students would ultimately develop their own effective problem-solving skills, expert systems lack such power to improve their own performance. Current systems know only what is encoded in their knowledge base.

The problem for knowledge engineers is that experts do not introspect reliably. Although people may have some declarative knowledge of the extent of their procedural memory (Flavell and H. M. Wellman, 1977), the two types of memory appear to be handled quite separately by the nervous system. For example, Cohen (1984) has investigated patients with neurologic amnesia to learn more about the mechanisms of human memory. In one experiment, 12 such patients were taught how to solve the Tower of Hanoi puzzle.[1] The patients with amnesia became proficient at the task just as quickly as did the control

---

[1] The Tower of Hanoi puzzle has been used as the substrate of a number of investigations into human problem solving (for example, Simon, 1975). The puzzle consists of three vertical poles and a number of doughnut-shaped disks of different sizes that fit onto the poles. Initially, all the disks are stacked to form a pyramid on one of the poles, the largest disk on the bottom. The goal is to move all the disks onto the third of the three poles such that (1) only one disk is moved at a time and (2) no disk is ever placed on top of a disk smaller than itself. In solving the puzzle, intermediate stacking of disks on the three poles is permitted (and indeed is necessary). When five disks are to be transferred, the solution is attainable in a minimum of 31 moves.

subjects, and they learned rapidly to perform the necessary sequences of moves "without thinking." However, despite their obvious acquired expertise at solving the Tower of Hanoi problem, *not one of the amnesia patients would ever state that he was familiar with the puzzle or knew its solution!* As in Johnson's anecdote, *knowing how* was orthogonal to *knowing that.*

In normal subjects with intact declarative memory, the distinction between procedural knowledge and declarative knowledge becomes even more important. Whereas declarative memory may continue to hold traces of knowledge that later is compiled procedurally, the declarative knowledge may well be imperfect. Nisbett and Wilson conducted extensive surveys of the evidence that suggests that people have "little or no introspective access to higher order cognitive processes" (Nisbett and Wilson, 1977, p. 231). In experimental situations, subjects have been shown to be frequently (1) unaware of the existence of a stimulus or cue influencing a response, (2) unaware that a response has been affected by a stimulus, and (3) unaware that a cognitive response has even occurred. Instead, subjects give verbal reports of their cognition based on prior causal theories from their declarative memory. These prior theories may or may not be accurate. In a given situation, a subject's verbal report of cognitive behavior is likely to be accurate only if the influential stimuli are salient enough to be *available* in declarative memory (Tversky and Kahneman, 1974). The stimuli also must be plausible causes of the response and must not be accompanied by other available, plausible, noninfluential factors (Nisbett and Wilson, 1977).

Despite our confident attempts at introspection, compiled knowledge is not accessible to our conscious awareness. We offer plausible (and often incorrect) explanations of our behavior because we are immersed in a culture that has taught us, paradoxically, that accurate introspection is somehow possible (Lyons, 1986). System builders therefore must seek ways to acquire expert knowledge using techniques that do not force experts to answer questions that these experts cannot answer reliably (Ericsson and Simon, 1984; Cleaves, 1987; Cooke and McDonald, 1987). It is an important theme of my research to develop knowledge-acquisition tools that ask the right kinds of questions.

Task-Specific Representations

An additional point regarding the nature of expertise suggests that knowledge engineering will always be troublesome: The portion of expert knowledge that is not declarative appears to be compiled in a task-specific manner. Knowledge engineers will invariably experience difficulty when they attempt to capture the specialized problem-solving methods of experts using general-purpose computational strategies.

As I discussed previously, the reasoning portion of expert systems can be viewed as consisting of two components: a declarative knowledge base and a procedural inference engine. The inference engine assumes a particular method of problem solving (for example, a method such as selecting a solution from a pre-enumerated set or assembling a solution from component parts). The knowledge base, on the other hand, captures information about the domain task (for example, choosing antibiotics for meningitis or designing an experiment in molecular genetics) in a manner such that the problem-solving method of the inference engine can be applied (Clancey, 1985). During the conceptualization stage of the knowledge-acquisition cycle, the knowledge engineer explores computational methods for problem solving that can be applied to the expert's task. Eventually, the knowledge engineer defines the task in terms of one or more of these general methods (Chandrasekaran, 1986; Bylander and Chandrasekaran, 1987).[2]

But this is not how experts seem to think. Although the cognitive phase of skill acquisition is marked by the application of general problem-solving procedures to declarative domain knowledge (as is done in current expert systems), knowledge compilation qualitatively changes the manner in which people reason. In the phase of automaticity, problem-solving knowledge become specialized for particular tasks and for particular contexts within those tasks (Anderson, 1987).

More specialized problem-solving methods are required because the way experts tend to represent tasks is different from the way novices do. The cognitive structures used to model the elements of the task, the interrelationships among those elements, and the

---

[2]The vocabulary in the AI literature is not standardized. Generally, we speak of an application *task* as a problem to be solved. A *task* thus represents a definition of a problem (for example, determining therapy for meningitis) without reference to how that problem is to be solved. A *method* is a computational strategy that is applied to a task. Chandrasekaran (1986) refers to the latter as a *generic task*.

goals of problem solving all become more abstract with increasing expertise. In studies of expert chess players (de Groot, 1965; Chase and Simon, 1973), electronics engineers (Egan and Schwartz, 1979), card players (Charness, 1979), physicists (Chi et al., 1981), and physicians (Norman et al., 1979; Coughlin and Patel, 1985; Patel et al., 1986), similar results have been obtained. Unlike novices, experts tend to decompose tasks into larger, more aggregated *chunks* of greater problem-solving relevance. It appears that experts invoke highly specialized, task-specific, context-specific methods that operate on these chunks during problem solving (Anderson, 1987).

Because the application area explored in this book is that of clinical trials, expert problem-solving in medicine is particularly relevant. A number of psychological studies of medical diagnosis have appeared in the literature, and all have reached the same conclusion: Physicians formulate hypotheses early in the clinical encounter and use a hypothetico-deductive reasoning method to rule out unlikely hypotheses and to pursue probable diagnoses (Elstein et al., 1978; Neufeld et al., 1981; Kassirer et al., 1982). No other general problem-solving strategy has been identified in either experienced or inexperienced diagnosticians, in successful or unsuccessful diagnosticians. At first glance, the identification of a seemingly universal, general-purpose clinical strategy would appear to be at odds with evidence that experts use task-specific, context-specific reasoning methods. Yet all "interesting" problem solving by experts tends to require *both* compiled procedures and the application of general methods to declarative knowledge (Shiffrin and Dumais, 1981). As Feltovich and Barrows contend, "the consistent characteristics of clinical reasoning which have been identified, beyond hypothetico-deduction, do not point to a singular, homogeneous process to be taught or understood" (Feltovich and Barrows, 1984, p. 131).

More detailed analysis of clinical reasoning leaves many unanswered questions. If hypotheses are formed early, from where exactly do the hypotheses come? How are promising hypotheses distinguished from poor ones? How are good hypotheses pursued? Studies of medical problem solving show that competence at diagnosis is surprisingly task-dependent; skill in one topic area is in no way predictive of skill in another (McGuire, 1985). In fact, like expertise in other domains, medical acumen appears to be largely a function of task-specific knowledge. General problem-solving abilities appear relatively unimportant (Feltovich and

Barrows, 1984; McGuire, 1985).

There is rarely a simple problem-solving strategy behind an expert's reasoning. In fact, there is seldom even a small set of strategies; each subtask encountered during problem solving may have its own compiled methods. As a result, knowledge engineers cannot simply elicit an expert's general reasoning method and select an appropriate inference mechanism for the task at hand; no generally applicable method will ever emerge. For example, although we can describe the organism-identification task of MYCIN in terms of the heuristic classification method (Clancey, 1985) and the disease-diagnosis task of INTERNIST-1 in terms of hypothetico-deduction[3] (Miller et al., 1982), medical experts certainly do not perform such tasks purely in these stereotyped manners. Yet MYCIN and INTERNIST-1 were successful programs because their developers were able to capture declarative knowledge such that these general reasoning methods could be applied. Even when the knowledge needed to solve a task was available to the consciousness of the expert, the knowledge had to be molded into a form compatible with some generic reasoning strategy. The intellectual effort required to create a mapping between an expert's task-specific knowledge and the computer's method-specific representation for that knowledge is a likely cause of the knowledge-acquisition bottleneck.

Content versus Process

Educational psychologists frequently make a distinction between teaching students specific facts about a topic (*content knowledge*) and teaching them knowledge of problem solving using those facts (*process knowledge*). The medical-education literature, in particular, is replete with discussion of the relative importance of process and content in clinical problem-solving (McGuire, 1985), as though the two types of knowledge were separable.

From the preceding discussion, it should be clear that successful problem solving by experts is dependent on large amounts of content knowledge. Although experts may be explicitly taught abstract process knowledge as novices (like the medical students in Johnson's anecdote), general methods of problem-solving ultimately are replaced by more task-

---

[3]Smith (1985) would use the expression *abductive assembly* to describe the method used by INTERNIST-1.

specific mechanisms (Anderson, 1987). Process knowledge becomes content-dependent. When experts are asked to verbalize their problem-solving strategies, they may well articulate the general process knowledge they were taught as novices, rather than the tacit methods that they actually use (Johnson, 1983; Lyons, 1986).

The distinction between content and process is consequently of great importance for elicitation of knowledge from domain experts. When experts discuss their process knowledge, what they report may not be an accurate reflection of their true problem-solving strategies. Furthermore, whatever those strategies are, they are likely to be heavily dependent on context. If it is our goal to allow experts to transfer their knowledge directly into the knowledge base of a computer, we may prefer that they enter only their *content* knowledge. *Process* knowledge must be treated with greater circumspection.

2.2.2 Miscommunication

People who develop expert systems often emphasize the communication difficulties that beset application specialists and knowledge engineers (Davis, 1976; Buchanan et al., 1983). At least initially, the experts in the application area and the computer scientists building the knowledge base rarely speak the same language.

To represent the relevant knowledge in the computer, knowledge engineers must familiarize themselves with the domain of application. In some ways, the knowledge engineers must become experts. They must learn a new vocabulary and, perhaps, a new way of looking at problems. In the traditional view of knowledge-engineering, knowledge is said to flow from the domain expert to the knowledge engineer to the computer (Feigenbaum, 1984). In this light, the accuracy of the knowledge base depends on the effectiveness of the knowledge engineer as an intermediary. Construction of optimum knowledge bases requires the knowledge engineer to understand the application area at a sufficient level of detail.

Psychological studies of comprehension in medicine (Patel et al., 1984) and in other fields (Miyake and Norman, 1978) suggest that a person's prior knowledge of an application area is critical for assimilating new information correctly and for recognizing the need to clarify areas of misinterpretation. Knowledge engineers must either make an effort to learn the expert's problem area or risk suffering the consequences of misunderstanding what the expert is trying to convey.

Communication of knowledge is perceived as a stumbling block by domain experts as well. As discussed previously, much of an expert's knowledge is tacit and thus is impossible to articulate; the knowledge that *is* articulated, although plausible, may not be correct. Furthermore, because experts typically do not understand programming, they have little appreciation for what knowledge might be relevant for computer-based models of their behavior: They do not know what information they should volunteer.

The precision, explicitness, and consistency with which knowledge must be programmed may be at odds with the way experts talk about their fields—even in highly formalized application areas (Musen et al., 1986). This apparent lack of consistency does not necessarily mean that domain experts are capricious or irrational. Rather, these discrepancies point out fundamental differences between the way people and computers process information, and indicate that much of human cognition—including the use of language—is influenced by factors that are unavailable to consciousness. Knowledge engineers cannot *a priori* expect domain experts to explain their specialized knowledge in precise, unambiguous terms, as no spoken language (including jargon) contains invariant definitions for what the words denote.

The issue has been explored in depth by Winograd and Flores (1986). In their view, a primary objective of knowledge acquisition is the explicit construction of a *systematic domain*—a formal description of the expert's task in terms of words that have unequivocal, agreed-on meanings. The systematic domain is created during the interactions of the expert and the knowledge engineer. Until these people identify the relevant concepts, label them, and decide unambiguously what the labels mean, it is impossible for domain experts to relate their knowledge in a consistent fashion. Thus, in the MYCIN domain, the use of terms such as "compromised host," "sterile site," and "significant organism" allowed both infectious-disease specialists and computer scientists to speak without confusion about the contents of the knowledge base and the behavior of the program. Equally important, these systematic terms allowed users to interact with MYCIN and to understand the intention of the questions the program asked. Knowledge acquisition "is often described as a process of 'capturing' the knowledge that experts already have and use. In fact, it is a creative design activity in which a systematic domain is created, covering certain aspects of the professionals' work" (Winograd and Flores, 1986, p. 175). In this perspective, knowledge acquisition is difficult not because experts and knowledge engineers do not speak the same language, but rather because they must work together to create a language.

2.2.3 Knowledge Representation

In addition to the cognitive and linguistic barriers, there is the issue of how knowledge is encoded in the computer. Knowledge acquired from a human expert cannot be captured within a knowledge base if the representation language to be used lacks sufficient expressive power. McCarthy and Hayes (1969) introduced the notion of *epistemological adequacy* as the ability of a knowledge-representation formalism to express the facts that a person knows about some aspect of the world. Since that time, substantial work in AI has concentrated on the development of representation languages that are epistemologically adequate for various types of problems (Brachman and Levesque, 1985).

Knowledge-representation languages and, as a result, tools for building expert systems, differ in the ease with which they can describe particular concepts. The differences are often not so much a matter of epistemological adequacy as of what some workers in AI have called *transductional adequacy*. With current tools, certain abstractions will always be easier to represent than others are.[4]

A classic example of this phenomenon is described in the book *Building Expert Systems* (Waterman and Hayes-Roth, 1983). In 1980, teams of experienced knowledge engineers, each well versed in the use of a particular expert-system shell, were assembled as part of a workshop on expert systems. Each team spent three days developing a prototype expert system designed (1) to classify possible toxic spills at Oak Ridge National Laboratory and (2) to identify and apply an appropriate strategy to contain such a spill within the intricate drainage system installed at that site. Two domain experts were brought in specifically for this experiment, and written documents also were made available to the knowledge

---

[4]Knowledge representations also differ in their computational efficiency, a property that McCarthy and Hayes (1969) dubbed *heuristic adequacy*. Levesque and Brachman (1985) provide an excellent discussion of some of these computational issues, which are distinct from the psychological concerns I am raising here.

engineers. Prior to the workshop, not one of the participants knew what the application area would be.

Although this was not a well-controlled experiment, the results were illuminating. The spill-containment task had been delineated in advance by one of the workshop organizers, yet each knowledge-engineering team interpreted that task somewhat differently. The exercise showed that knowledge engineers, when using preselected formalisms for knowledge representation, may model *different aspects of the same task* on the basis of what is easy to express in the given representation language. For example, tools such as EMYCIN, KAS (Reboh, 1981), and EXPERT (Weiss and Kulikowski, 1979) lacked facilities to model interrelationships among objects directly, and thus the Oak Ridge drainage-system network could not be described explicitly. The EMYCIN team consequently downplayed the subtask of applying a containment strategy for a spill; the team using KAS avoided that part of the problem entirely; the EXPERT team implemented a strategy for spill containment, but did so using a FORTRAN program invoked by the expert system. As not one of the knowledge-engineering teams worked with a language that could explicitly represent the passage of time, temporal constraints were ignored in all the systems (Waterman and Hayes-Roth, 1983).

Just as human thought is limited by our language and by our mental models of the world (Greeno, 1983), the knowledge bases of expert systems are restricted by the expressiveness of our computer languages for knowledge representation and by our cleverness in using them.

2.3   Knowledge Acquisition as Modeling

Current expert systems make major assumptions about their task domains; they become "brittle" when reasoning about unusual cases, and are unable to arrive at a reasonable conclusion. It would be incorrect to conclude that the epistemological inadequacies of our representation languages are primarily responsible for our systems' failures. Our knowledge bases often are imperfect for more fundamental reasons.

Knowledge bases are *models* (Clancey, 1986; Regoczei and Plantinga, 1987; Morik,

1987). Like all abstractions of reality, they are approximate. They are unavoidably selective in what they contain. In the study reported by Waterman and Hayes-Roth, for example, it would be misleading to say that the KAS team did not implement a spill-containment strategy *because* it was difficult to represent the necessary knowledge. After all, the team using EXPERT was faced with the same task, and they ended up solving the problem with FORTRAN. Rather, we should simply conclude that the KAS team chose not to model that portion of the problem. We should not say that the KAS program was less expert than was any of the others; it merely incorporated a different model. All models are imperfect approximations.

When an expert system fails often or is brittle, the knowledge base is a model that makes too many simplifying assumptions. System builders often maintain that the way to overcome brittleness in expert systems is simply to add more knowledge (Lenat et al., 1986). Such a response, however, begs the question of exactly what knowledge should be added. It may be more helpful to view the problem as the need to develop a different or more comprehensive *model* of the application area.

As a consequence of interacting with an expert, knowledge engineers develop their own mental models of the application area. Although the knowledge engineers and experts tend to have very different models at the outset, they eventually reach a compromise through a process of convergence that Regoczei and Plantinga (1987) refer to as *harmonization*. Harmonization is possible primarily because knowledge engineering forces all parties to commit their mental models to a fixed, publicly examinable form—typically the emerging knowledge base. Both the experts and the system builders continually revise their mental models of the domain as the system is constructed. The experts must work to fill in the large gaps where their knowledge is tacit. The knowledge engineers constantly struggle to revise their naive theories of how the experts solve problems.

Previously, I have described knowledge acquisition as the transfer of expertise from an expert to a knowledge engineer to a knowledge base. Such a view, however, is misleading. The model of expertise encoded in the knowledge base is not simply transferred from one locus to another. It is *created*. Much of the expert's mental model is initially fragmented and tacit; the flaws must be filled in and the compiled knowledge must be made declarative. There is initially no language with which the knowledge engineer and expert can speak unambiguously; they must construct a systematic domain and must use it to build the model. Knowledge acquisition clearly involves more than knowledge transfer. It is a dynamic and inventive activity. Like all processes that require creativity, knowledge acquisition is difficult (Brooks, 1987).

2.4 Addressing the Obstacles

Given all these impediments to knowledge acquisition, we can appreciate why observers such as Dreyfus (1981) are pessimistic about the possibility of building comprehensive expert systems. The obstacles are inherent in the nature of human cognition, of human language, and of the creative process itself. Dreyfus is correct; these problems will not go away. In this book, I suggest mechanisms by can they can be confronted and contained.

2.4.1 Domain Considerations

The methodology that I propose is relevant in only certain application areas. The technique assumes that the domain involves a number of similar tasks, each of which can be modeled as a singular knowledge base. Although the content of each task-specific knowledge base is different, the general form is homologous. Thus, the same inference engine can be applied in each case. I refer to such knowledge bases as *congeners.*

There appear to be many application areas where people might want to construct multiple, related knowledge-bases. For example, the literature describes systems for developing knowledge-base congeners to troubleshoot electronic instruments, where each knowledge base contains a model of a different device (Freiling and Alexander, 1984); to advise on the use of data-analysis programs, where each knowledge base contains a model of a different statistical routine (Gale, 1987); and to administer cancer chemotherapy, where each knowledge base contains a model of a different oncology treatment plan (Musen et al., 1987). Other domains, such as those involving process-control applications or repetitive design problems, also would be applicable.

PROTÉGÉ creates other knowledge-acquisition programs, which in turn are used to develop individual knowledge bases. The notion of a knowledge-acquisition program that generates yet other knowledge acquisition programs may seem redundant if not unduly complex. PROTÉGÉ, however, is quite unlike the knowledge editors that it generates, and therein lies the advantage of the methodology.

2.4.2 A Strategy for Knowledge Acquisition

I have noted a number of issues that influence the problem of knowledge acquisition:

- Process knowledge often is tacit and therefore is unreliably reported by experts

- Task-specific inference mechanisms may be difficult to convert to more general methods

- Systematic domains of discourse must be created before experts, knowledge engineers, and users can understand the knowledge unambiguously

- Knowledge-representation languages may not easily express important conceptual relationships

Most important, each of these items contributes to the more general observation that creating complex models *de novo* is a demanding intellectual activity. Accordingly, success at knowledge acquisition should depend on (1) the properties of the world being modeled and (2) the properties of the modeling language being used.

This book advocates a divide-and-conquer approach to facilitate knowledge acquisition from experts in those domains that require multiple, related knowledge bases. The argument is straightforward. A knowledge-acquisition tool such as PROTÉGÉ should be used to develop a systematic domain and a general model of the application area—the part of knowledge acquisition that is inherently difficult. Once PROTÉGÉ has assisted the knowledge-engineering team in building the general model, constructing a working knowledge base for a given task becomes a matter of adding task-specific content knowledge. PROTÉGÉ generates application-specific knowledge editors expressly for this purpose.

PROTÉGÉ consolidates the difficult modeling problems of knowledge acquisition. The program allows construction of a model of the application area that is complete except for the content knowledge required to specify particular tasks. The necessary task-specific content thus must be added later. Because experts typically can articulate their declarative knowledge of content in a reliable manner, this last stage of knowledge-base construction can be performed by domain experts working alone. Experts and knowledge engineers thus use PROTÉGÉ to construct a generic model; PROTÉGÉ then creates a knowledge-acquisition tool, based on the model, with which the experts can independently and reiteratively enter content knowledge for different application tasks. Separation of knowledge acquisition into these two phases, and provision of specific tools and modeling languages for each phase, should greatly facilitate development of expert systems in selected application areas.

3 Methodologies for Knowledge Acquisition

For many years, the process of building expert systems has been considered an "art" (Feigenbaum, 1977), and has been associated with considerable folklore. Nevertheless, principles of knowledge engineering have started to emerge recently. An important advance was Allen Newell's (1982) observation that knowledge is a capacity for *behavior* distinct from whatever symbols are used to represent that behavior in a computer. Other investigators have built on Newell's work to characterize generic methods of problem solving that are independent of specific inference engines and of specific application areas (Clancey, 1985; Chandrasekaran, 1986). In this context, knowledge engineering can be viewed as a modeling process in which an abstraction of some task in the world (an application problem to be solved) is described in terms of one or more of these general problem-solving methods (domain-independent strategies for arriving at a solution). The methods, when applied to the task description, generate appropriate actions. But how should a task be described in the first place? How does a system builder select a problem-solving method? What is the proper mapping between a method and a task? Much more work is required before a stronger, more applicable theory can be developed; nevertheless, important principles still can be inferred from the current literature. This chapter reviews methodologies for knowledge acquisition and provides a framework in which to understand PROTÉGÉ.

3.1 Knowledge Specification

Knowledge engineering traditionally is highly iterative. Prototype systems are designed; their behavior is observed by domain specialists; then new prototypes are created as errors are detected. Many knowledge engineers advocate beginning this build–test–rebuild cycle almost immediately (Buchanan et al., 1983). In fact, Doyle (1985) suggests that the hallmark of AI programming is a process called *incremental reformulation,* where knowledge engineers continually redesign the contents of knowledge bases as application tasks become better understood. Doyle argues that the primary advantage of AI programming is that the behavior of a final program does not need to be specified in advance, but can evolve in response to the system's performance on test cases. The assumption is that it is difficult to foresee the implications and interactions of knowledge-base elements *a priori,* and that the specification of complex systems cannot be separated from the systems' implementation (Swartout and Balzer, 1982).

Many authors, however, maintain that construction of expert systems is not different from the development of other large pieces of software, and that the principles of structured software engineering that now pervade the rest of the computer industry ought to apply to AI systems as well. Such critics do not believe that incremental reformulation of an expert-system knowledge base is desirable. They suggest that concurrent specification and implementation of a knowledge-based system in some ways implies that the *implementation* and the *knowledge* are the same. The notion of incremental reformulation suggests that, when a program fails on a test case, the knowledge in the program needs to be "fixed"; correcting the knowledge may thus mean adding a rule, restricting the circumstances in which a rule may fire, or fixing a typo.

3.1.1 The Knowledge Level

An important perspective articulated by Newell (1982) is that knowledge is an abstraction that can be separated from the symbols that are used to represent the knowledge. Knowledge is a set of goals and the behaviors potentially needed to achieve those goals. Knowledge itself can never be written down; it can only be observed as an activity. Whereas we can compose rules or statements in logic to represent knowledge, such notations can capture the *behavior* we intend only when some separate *process* is applied. Thus, without an appropriate inference engine, there is no "knowledge" in our knowledge bases.[1]

This distinction between *knowledge* and the *symbols used to represent knowledge* often has been blurred by workers in AI. The distinction may be difficult to appreciate intuitively, particularly because so much of human language and cognition appears to be based on the manipulation of symbols. The following analogy therefore may be helpful. Consider the symbols reproduced in Figure 3.1, which represent a portion of a Bach violin concerto. The symbols themselves are not *equivalent* to the concerto; the music can be appreciated only when a violinist applies a particular process to these notations, generating a sequence of sounds. The notations in Figure 3.1 specify a violinist's motor performance (to an approximation); in the same way, the representations in a knowledge base specify an expert's cognitive performance (to an approximation). In the case of both the musician and the domain expert, symbols provide an opportunity to write down models of behaviors that otherwise could be only experienced. The behaviors and the symbols, however, exist at two different levels.

The concept of the knowledge level allows us to distinguish our goals for an intelligent system from the language that we use at the symbol level to represent those goals. Thus, *knowledge-level analysis* of an application task specifies the behaviors that are required to solve a problem in the world; analysis of a knowledge base at the *symbol level* specifies the computational mechanisms needed to model the requisite behaviors. The two kinds of specification are very different. Knowledge-level specifications are semantic; symbol-level specifications are largely syntactic. To create a knowledge base, we must pay attention to both knowledge-level and symbol-level design. Building systems using the rapid-prototyping, incremental-reformulation approach can obscure the distinction.

Researchers in AI increasingly agree that it is important to understand a domain task in terms of its knowledge-level specification before proceeding to a symbol-level implementation. There is little consensus, however, about how to go about describing tasks at the

---

[1] Bylander and Chandrasekaran (1987) refer to Newell's observation that knowledge representations are dependent on the processes that interpret them as "the interaction problem."

Figure 3.1: Symbol-Level Notations

> The notations in this figure are symbol-level entities. They represent a melody that exists only at the musical equivalent of the knowledge level. The symbols can generate the music only when a process is applied to them, just as the representations in a knowledge base require application of some inference mechanism to generate intelligent behavior.

knowledge level. Some notation must be chosen to write down an approximation for the knowledge, even though the knowledge itself may never be had *in hand*. Newell (1982) and Nilsson (1981) advocate the use of predicate logic. Other workers contend that, in practice, natural language is sufficient (for example, Prerau, 1987). Clancey (1985) notes that the particular language a system builder chooses for knowledge-level analysis is not nearly as important as are the specific terms and relations that are used to describe the appropriate problem-solving behavior. The goal becomes to understand a system's behavior in terms of an abstract *model*, rather than by means of a specific set of notations.

3.1.2 Method-Based Knowledge-Level Analysis

Clancey (1985) suggests that a useful way to analyze an application at the knowledge level is to relate the task to a general method of problem solving. Specifically, his model of *heuristic classification* provides a precise set of terms and relations by which certain diagnostic tasks can be characterized. Knowledge-level analysis for these tasks can be

44

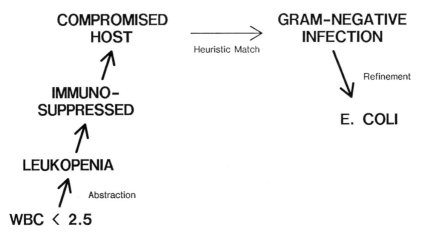

Figure 3.2: Heuristic Classification in MYCIN

Heuristic classification involves derivation of abstractions from primary data, making associations between abstract concepts and solution categories, and refinement of solution categories to include one or more members of a pre-enumerated set. Formalization of the method of heuristic classification has provided a set of terms and relations by which the behavior of programs such as MYCIN can be characterized at the knowledge level. (Source: Adapted from Clancey, 1985, p. 295)

viewed as a matter of identifying (1) the particular elements in the application area from which the solution is selected (in the case of MYCIN, for example, organisms that may be causing the infection), (2) the data that bear on the selection process, (3) the abstraction hierarchies (taxonomies) in the domain, and (4) the heuristics that link elements from one abstraction hierarchy to those in another (for example, attributes of the patient that raise the likelihood of particular classes of pathogens being present). By defining a heuristic classification task in terms of Clancey's model, it is possible to achieve complete specification of a reasoning system's behavior, independent of any implementation (Figure 3.2).[2]

Few problem-solving methods are as well formalized as is the method of heuristic classification. The area of solving problems by *constructing a solution* appears to be much

---

[2]It is important to be aware of a potential confusion in terminology. *Problem-solving method* must not be confused with *inference mechanism*. A problem-solving method is a behavior at the knowledge level. An inference mechanism, on the other hand, is a process that has relevance at only the symbol level. For example, many of MYCIN's actions can be described at the knowledge level in terms of the *heuristic classification method*. The program has been implemented to perform heuristic classification by invoking symbol-level rules via the inference mechanism called *backward chaining*.

more complex, and is not nearly as well worked out as is classification. Constructive methods such as *skeletal-plan refinement* (Friedland and Iwasaki, 1985) and *abductive assembly* (Smith, 1985) have been identified in the literature. Characterization of most constructive methods, however, has not yet been sufficiently precise to serve as the basis for analysis of tasks at the knowledge level, because we do not have the necessary terms and relations. Many applications consequently will have to await development of more complete models of their problem-solving behavior before Clancey's form of method-oriented, knowledge-level analysis can be applied. Nevertheless, when such models do exist, they can be used effectively both by knowledge engineers (Clancey, 1984) and by computer-based knowledge-acquisition tools to define a system's behavior. I shall discuss such computer-based tools in Section 3.3.2.

By framing the problem of knowledge-level analysis in terms of a presupposed problem-solving method, Clancey's approach does not address directly how knowledge engineers should identify the essential elements of the application task in the first place. For example, the heuristic classification method itself provides no guidance for determining what the components of the abstraction hierarchies *are;* the method establishes only the the role that these components play in problem solving.

3.1.3 Task-Based Knowledge-Level Analysis

Both because of the need to understand the structure of a domain task before a problem-solving method can be optimally applied, and because existing models of many problem-solving strategies are grossly incomplete, a number of workers have chosen to concentrate more on the application *task* than on its required method of solution. Researchers at Tektronix Laboratories, for example, have advocated a task-oriented approach called *ontological analysis* (Alexander et al., 1986). Knowledge engineers use ontological analysis to describe systems at the knowledge level in terms of the entities, relationships, and transformations among entities that occur when a person performs a task. Ontological analysis involves describing the structure of domain knowledge within three broad categories: (1) *the static ontology,* consisting of the objects, attributes, and relationships in the domain; (2) *the dynamic ontology,* defining the states that may occur as a result of problem solving and the possible transformations from one state to another; and (3) *the epistemic ontology,* consisting of the knowledge that bears on the state transformations within the dynamic ontology. The Tektronix group records an ontological analysis using a language that they have designed called SUPE-SPOONS, the notations of which are based on the domain equations of *denotational semantics.*[3]

Although ontological analysis assumes that a task can be viewed at some level as a search problem, the structures generated by the technique are derived by asking the knowledge engineer to focus on the application domain, not on the method of search. Thus, an inference strategy for the reasoning system cannot accrue directly from the analysis, because the knowledge-level description is incomplete. Current work at Tektronix concentrates on addressing this limitation (Freiling and Jacobson, 1988). Proponents of the technique believe that the greatest strength of ontological analysis lies in its ability to conceptualize knowledge-engineering problems at meaningful levels of abstraction.

Like the Tektronix group, Breuker and Wielinga (1987) at the University of Amsterdam have emphasized knowledge-level analysis from the perspective of the application task. The Knowledge Acquisition and Documentation Structuring (KADS) system that these authors have designed comprises a comprehensive approach to the development of new knowledge bases. With the KADS system, users construct knowledge-level models of the application task in three stages: First, knowledge engineers perform a functional analysis of the task, work environment, and potential users of the expert system. Second, the static ("textbook") knowledge in the domain is analyzed. The knowledge-engineering team develops a systematic domain (referred to as a *domain lexicon*) and structures the terms hierarchically. Third, knowledge engineers observe application specialists solving actual problems, which allows them (1) to refine the taxonomies of static terms, (2) to identify knowledge sources (that is, elements that bear on the experts' behavior), and (3) to determine the corresponding responses that the experts make (Breuker and Wielinga, 1987; de Greef and Breuker, 1985). The KADS system supports a number of text editors and representation tools that facilitate this analysis. These tools facilitate both the identifi-

---

[3]Denotational semantics represents formally the meaning of computer programs by mapping the syntactic elements of the program code to a set of abstract functions. Stoy (1977) has written a useful textbook on the subject.

cation of fundamental task concepts and the organization of these concepts into useful abstraction hierarchies and other structures.

As with ontological analysis, the task description produced using the KADS methodology is not associated with any particular problem-solving method. Recently, however, the developers of the KADS system have started to build a library of *interpretation models* that define the terms and relationships of a number of well-understood problem-solving methods (such as heuristic classification). Workers in Amsterdam and elsewhere (Karbach et al., 1988) have used these interpretation models to transform a knowledge engineer's structuring of an application task into a complete knowledge-level analysis that includes an applicable solution strategy in addition to the task definition.

3.1.4 The Modeling Problem Revisited

I reemphasize that knowledge specification is a problem in modeling. The goal in building an expert system is to develop a computational model of some useful problem-solving behavior in the world. Yet, if knowledge engineers are all building models, why is there no standard knowledge-engineering methodology? Why is there still much controversy regarding the role of rapid prototyping? Among those people who advocate deferred implementation, why is there no unanimity regarding techniques for knowledge-level specification?

The lack of consensus is largely a result of fundamental disagreements regarding the optimal *modeling language* with which to represent a task during the conceptualization stage of knowledge acquisition. Whereas all knowledge engineers seem to recognize that formulating an initial model of an application is a major stumbling block, the rapid-prototypers tend to advocate developing that model using the language of the expert system itself; the presumption is that any lack of perspicuousness in the language will be offset by avoidance of the need to reimplement the model in a new representation once the task is finally understood. The availability of a preliminary system the behavior of which can be observed and commented on by domain specialists also may be invaluable (Buchanan et al., 1983). On the other hand, those people who prefer to delay the initial implementation believe that other modeling languages are more appropriate for conceptualization of an application. For example, logic clearly offers a precise and well-understood semantics. As

48

embodied in programming languages such as PROLOG, logic even can be used for rapid prototyping (Komorowski and Maluszynski, 1986). At the same time, languages such as SUPE-SPOONS seem to offer a convenient syntax that allows the developer to concentrate on task structure rather than on programming details. There are other workers, however, who advocate the use of natural language to develop an initial specification, believing this alternative approach is most "natural." Unfortunately, what often has been missing from these debates is discussion of the *criteria* by which we should chose a modeling language in the first place. The participants also have made the assumption that there is a single choice at issue.

In this book, I suggest that the language used to model an abstract task during the conceptualization stage need not be the same language as that used to define particular, task-specific details. Moreover, neither modeling language need reflect the representations used at the symbol level. The PROTÉGÉ knowledge editor incorporates a modeling language the semantics of which are based on a predefined problem-solving method. This abstract language allows users to enter general models of relevant application domains. PROTÉGÉ then uses the general domain models to generate *custom-tailored* languages with which individual tasks within the application areas can themselves be modeled. The modeling languages generated by PROTÉGÉ are tailored to particular applications, making the languages almost self-explanatory to domain experts. The advantage is that application specialists can learn to enter new knowledge autonomously, without the need for knowledge engineers to interpret the developing models.

Workers in AI have long hoped that domain specialists might someday be able to enter their knowledge directly into expert systems, thus greatly accelerating the process of knowledge acquisition (Davis, 1976; Buchanan et al., 1983). Section 10.2.4 discusses the degree to which PROTÉGÉ—and the knowledge-editing programs generated by PROTÉGÉ—may be successful in that regard. Before discussing the current research, however, I shall review existing approaches for the acquisition of knowledge from experts, both interview-based and computer-based. Without an appreciation for the varied techniques that knowledge engineers currently put into practice, it will be difficult to place PROTÉGÉ in perspective.

3.2   Interviewing Techniques

Most of the model building that takes place during traditional knowledge engineering is under the direction of the knowledge engineer. Although creating a knowledge base is necessarily a collaborative process, the domain expert typically remains illiterate in the language being used to build the model. The expert consequently assumes a more passive posture, responding to the knowledge engineer's questions as a model of the former's expertise is filled out.

Techniques used to interview domain experts have received increasing attention in the AI literature. Many interviewing strategies have been borrowed from original work in psychology and cognitive anthropology, disciplines in which the methods that people use to categorize their world and to solve problems have been focal points of investigation. Although this book concentrates on computer-based tools to facilitate knowledge acquisition, we can best understand these automated approaches in the context of the interviewing strategies frequently used during more traditional interactions with experts.

3.2.1   Direct Questioning

The simplest way to elicit information from experts is to ask them questions. Unfortunately, direct questioning has a number of major limitations. An expert's response to a question may depend in subtle ways on how the question is asked. The reply may assume implicit background information that is not directly articulated.

The words used to phrase a question can have an enormous effect on an expert's response. For example, La France (1987) cites work by Loftus (1979) demonstrating that eyewitnesses to an automobile accident, when asked "How fast was the car going when it *crashed* into the wall?" reported significantly higher velocities than did witnesses asked "How fast was the car going when it *ran* into wall?" Similarly, more headaches were revealed when survey respondents were asked "Do you get headaches *frequently,* and if so how often?" than when asked "Do you get headaches *occasionally,* and if so, how often?" To ensure the accuracy of reported information, La France advocates posing large numbers of questions using different formats to elicit the same knowledge. Many of the strategies that she describes are reminiscent of the interviewing techniques employed by successful ethnographers (for example, Spradley, 1979).

A knowledge engineer may ask myriad well-formed questions and still elicit misinformation. As described in Section 2.2.1, much of skilled knowledge is tacit and is thus unavailable to consciousness. When asked direct questions about tacit processes, experts volunteer plausible answers that may not reflect their true behavior (Nisbett and Wilson, 1977; Cleaves, 1987). Johnson (1983) refers to these believable, although sometimes inaccurate, responses as *reconstructed* reasoning methods. Reconstructed methods typically are acknowledged and endorsed by entire problem-solving communities. They form the basis of most major textbooks. However, "the disadvantage of these methods of reasoning is that they do not always work, sometimes not even in the hands of those who devise them" (Johnson, 1983, p. 82).

Slovic and Lichtenstein (1971), for example, asked stock brokers to weight the importance of various factors that influenced these brokers' investment decisions. A regression analysis of actual decisions made by the stock brokers revealed computed weights for these factors that were poorly correlated with the brokers' subjective ratings. More important, there was a *negative* correlation between the accuracy of introspection and the stock brokers' years of experience. More recently, Michalski and Chilausky (1980) found that decision rules elicited from plant pathologists for the diagnosis of soybean diseases performed less accurately than did a rule set that was automatically induced by the computer from a library of test cases. (The experts' actual diagnoses were used as the gold standard against which the two sets of rules were judged.)

Johnson (1983), among other authors, has argued for the elicitation of *authentic* (as opposed to reconstructed) methods of reasoning. The goal is determination of the behaviors actually used by experts in performing relevant tasks. Acquisition of authentic knowledge, not surprisingly, requires more than just asking direct questions.

3.2.2   Protocol Analysis

The most extensively studied methods designed to elicit authentic knowledge all involve *protocol analysis,* a technique developed by cognitive psychologists (Ericsson and Simon,

1984). Protocol analysis requires subjects to be studied while they are in the process of solving problems. The subjects are encouraged to "think aloud" while working on either real or simulated cases. They are asked to report their problem-solving goals and the data that they are considering at each point in time, but are asked not to rationalize or to justify their actions. The result is a *verbal protocol* that traces execution of the particular task.

Knowledge engineers then can use the recorded protocols to create a model of problem solving. Substantial anecdotal evidence suggests that this method of knowledge acquisition can be quite effective (Buchanan and Shortliffe, 1984; Fox et al., 1985). Nevertheless, some authors remain concerned that asking experts to speak out loud during their problem solving may still cause distortion of these experts' behavior, resulting in less-than-authentic protocols. Recently, Belkin and others (1987) have suggested using detailed analyses of transcripts of actual interactions involving experts and their clients (*discourse analysis*) as a means of eliminating the verbalization artifact. However, because workers have to be present at and record these expert–client interactions, discourse analysis is much less convenient and far more labor-intensive than is protocol analysis. It is unlikely that discourse analysis will achieve widespread use until there are more data to substantiate the possible advantages of this technique.

3.2.3 Psychometric Techniques

Researchers interested in psychological testing frequently are concerned with how people classify elements in the world and solve problems. Just as protocol analysis has been adopted from the methods of cognitive psychologists, formal psychometric techniques also have worked their way into the knowledge engineer's tool box.

Perhaps the most important contribution has been George Kelly's (1955) *personal construct theory.* Kelly was a clinical psychologist who developed special interviewing techniques to elicit the idiosyncratic characterizations (*personal constructs*) that patients may have used to classify people and other entities in the world. Kelly's structured interviews began by selecting a set of entities—called *elements*—from the patient's personal experience (for example, psychologically important people such as the patient's parents, friends, and teachers). The interviewer identified a patient's personal constructs by asking the patient to volunteer distinguishing features of the various elements. For example, a patient might report that one of his friends is "easy to talk to" whereas his parents are "not understanding"; this distinction would represent one of the patient's personal constructs. Ultimately, the interviewer asked the patient how *each* construct applied to *each* element. The result was a matrix of personal constructs and elements, which Kelly called a *repertory grid* (Figure 3.3). Analysis of the grid revealed associations and dependencies among the patient's constructs—interactions that Kelly found valuable in targeting his psychotherapy.

Personal construct theory soon became an important focus for work in psychometry, particularly because Kelly's interviewing strategy and repertory-grid analysis lent themselves so well to automation (Shaw, 1981). Cognitive anthropologists saw the technique as a useful way to learn how people in other cultures form distinctions among entities in the world and then act on those distinctions (Frake, 1972). More recently, knowledge engineers have begun to use Kelley's methods to learn how domain experts make and act on distinctions (Hall and Bandler, 1985). Furthermore, personal construct psychology has formed the basis for a number of important computer-based knowledge-acquisition tools, which I shall discuss in Section 3.3.2.

Other psychometric techniques have been used for knowledge acquisition, primarily in experimental settings. Cooke and McDonald (1987), for example, advocate the use of multidimensional scaling techniques such as cluster analysis. The authors argue that formal statistical approaches offer considerable precision in knowledge elicitation without the biases that are introduced when experts are asked to introspect.

3.2.4   Combining Methodologies

Direct questioning, protocol analysis, and psychometric techniques are seldom used in isolation. The various approaches generally are alloyed by knowledge engineers to create heterogeneous strategies for knowledge elicitation. Each method has a particular advantage with respect to the convenience with which it can be applied and to the likely authenticity of the knowledge that is derived. Unfortunately, the techniques that provide the most authentic knowledge also tend to be the ones most difficult to put into practice. It is therefore not surprising that a number of researchers have begun to explore the use of

ELEMENTS							CONSTRUCTS
E1	E2	E3	E4	E5	E6	E7	
						X	Don't believe in God/Very religious
		X	X				Same sort of education/Different education
X		X	X	X	X		Not athletic/Athletic
	X			X	X		Both girls/A boy
X	X	X		X	X		Parents/Ideas different
			X				Understand me better/Don't understand me
	X	X	X				Teach the right thing/Teach the wrong thing
	X		X				Achieved a lot/Hasn't achieved a lot
		X	X				Higher education/No education
			X		X		Don't like other people/Like other people
X	X	X		X	X		More religious/Less religious
X	X	X	X		X	X	Believe in higher education/Don't believe in
	X		X				More sociable/Not sociable

Figure 3.3: A Repertory Grid

The structured interview developed by Kelly (1955) that is used to elicit a patient's personal construct system allows construction of a *repertory grid*. The repertory grid is a matrix in which each *element* in the world discussed during the interview is rated according to each of the patient's *personal constructs*. In this example, each element (labeled *E1, E2,* and so on) is a specific member of the patient's family or an important role model for the patient; the two extreme poles of each personal construct (for example, "Don't believe in God" and "Very religious") are taken verbatim from Kelly's structured interview and define a spectrum according to which each element (E1, E2, and so on) can be classified. In the figure, the patient has stated that the person who corresponds to element E7 is "very religious," whereas those who correspond to the other elements "don't believe in God." Although the correlation may well be spurious, all the people whom the patient has classified as "not atheletic" also are classified as not believing in God. Analysis of such associations in the repertory grid can reveal important relationships and dependencies in the patient's personal-construct system. (Source: Adapted from Kelly, 1955, Figure 1; unnumbered page) computer-based tools to augment and compliment these manual approaches.

3.3 Computer-Based Tools for Knowledge Acquisition

In this section, I review the use of computer-based tools for knowledge acquisition. My emphasis is on programs that can be used by knowledge engineers and application specialists to create, to review, and to refine the contents of expert-system knowledge bases. Although substantial progress has been made on the problem of autonomous machine-based learning techniques, I shall focus primarily on *knowledge editors*—interactive programs that sometimes are referred to as "intelligent interviewing systems."

A fundamental attribute of every knowledge-editing program is the manner in which the contents of the knowledge base are displayed for the user. I refer to this notion as *knowledge presentation*. For the purposes of understanding prior work on computer-based tools for knowledge acquisition, perhaps the most important aspect of knowledge presentation is the *conceptual model* of the knowledge projected by the program to the user. The conceptual model provides a set of terms and relations that define the semantics of the knowledge-base elements that the program displays, and that ascribe meaning to the data entered by the user (Musen, 1988).

Every computer program, regardless of its purpose, is written with particular semantic assumptions about the data on which it operates. These semantic assumptions, which are shared between the program's users and the program's developers, permit the program and its end users to communicate. The resulting semantic framework forms the conceptual model of the data entered by the user. For example, simple text editors generally employ a conceptual model in which the data represent characters in a document; such programs accept commands the semantics of which relate to modifying characters or lines of text. In spreadsheet programs, on the other hand, data are viewed as rows and columns of interdependent numbers.

Similarly, knowledge-editing programs must adopt conceptual models that frame their presentation of the contents of a knowledge base. Whereas most knowledge-acquisition tools have modeled the knowledge in terms of the symbol-level representations required by the advice system (for example, production rules in EMYCIN), several recently-described programs have used a more abstract kind of model—that of the problem-solving method in which the knowledge is ultimately brought to bear. Alternatively, some knowledge editors adopt a conceptual model based on the semantics of the application task itself. I shall consider these three major paradigms in detail.

3.3.1   Representation-Based Conceptual Models

John McCarthy (1968) first suggested the idea of a computer program for knowledge acquisition, the Advice Taker, into which a user could enter knowledge about the world using predicate logic. The program then would be able to perform deduction with the user's logical statements to generate advice. The Advice Taker, although never intended to be implemented as a working system, motivated McCarthy's argument for the declarative representation of knowledge. The concept was seminal for subsequent work in knowledge-based systems, and it provided a foundation for future work on knowledge-editing tools.

TEIRESIAS (Davis, 1976) was designed as a knowledge-acquisition system for the MYCIN program; it was intended to allow expert physicians to identify and to correct errors in the MYCIN infectious-disease knowledge base (Figure 3.4). TEIRESIAS was the first well-described knowledge editor intended for direct use by application specialists, although no physician ever actually ran the system after it was developed. Davis' program used both the context in which an error occurred during a MYCIN consultation and *metalevel* knowledge[4] of the MYCIN rule base to help the user to construct new rules or to modify faulty ones. For example, the program's observation that rules conditional on an organism's morphology frequently also were conditional on the organism's Gram stain allowed TEIRESIAS to screen new rules for potentially missing clauses. Thus, if a user entered a new rule predicated on morphology *alone,* the program would indicate that the rule was inconsistent with its model of the existing rules and thus was possibly incorrect (that is, too general because of failure to mention Gram stain). TEIRESIAS' metalevel

---

[4] *Metalevel knowledge* is knowledge *about* knowledge.

The following rules were used in deducing that the identity of ORGANISM-1 is pseudomonas-aeruginosa.

RULE184
Since   [1.1] the category of ORGANISM-1 is not known
             [1.2] the gram stain of ORGANISM-1 is gramneg
             [1.3] the morphology of ORGANISM-1 rod
             [1.4] the aerobicity of ORGANISM-1 is facultative
There is weakly suggestive evidence (.3) that the identity of
             ORGANISM-1 is pseudomonas-aeruginosa

Is this rule correct?
++**Y
Should its premise have failed for this case?
++**Y
Which clause of the premise should have been false? [give #]
++**1
No conclusions were reached concerning the category of ORGANISM-1. Should it have been possible to
conclude a category?
++**Y
Which one?
++**ENTEROBACTERIACEAE
There were no rules successfully invoked in the attempt to deduce that the category of ORGANISM-1 is
enterobacteriaceae. The following (potentially applicable) rules were not executed because the
starred [**] clause failed:

RULE116
IF: 1) the identity of ORGANISM-1 is not known
        **   2) the gram stain of ORGANISM-1 is not known **
             3) the morphology of ORGANISM-1 is not known
             4) the site of CULTURE-1 is csf
             5) the infection is meningitis
             6) the age (in years) of the patient is less than or
                  equal to .17
THEN: There is weakly suggestive evidence (.3) that the category
             of ORGANISM-1 is enterobacteriaceae
Are all these rules correct?
++**Y
Should any of them have been successfully invoked?
++**N
Is there a rule missing?
++**Y
OK, then I need a rule that would allow me to deduce that the category of ORGANISM-1 is
enterobacteriaceae. Would you like to give me such a rule now?
++

Figure 3.4: Sample Interaction with TEIRESIAS

TEIRESIAS allowed users to repair faulty rules and to enter new ones to refine
the MYCIN knowledge base. The conceptual model of the knowledge was one of
independent production rules. The interactive dialog was conducted in a subset of
natural language. (Source: Davis, 1976, pp. 77–78)

knowledge was derived automatically from the syntax of the rules that already had been entered into the knowledge base. Because the program made no assumptions about the *meaning* of any of the knowledge-base components, TEIRESIAS could, in theory, be used to refine knowledge bases in any application area.

The conceptual model of the knowledge base adopted by TEIRESIAS was the same as that used by the MYCIN inference engine. To interact with TEIRESIAS, the user had to view the knowledge base as a collection of individual rules. Although TEIRESIAS did take great pains to attempt translation between MYCIN rules and a subset of natural language, the user still had to think about the knowledge in terms of rule clauses and of the parameter values that the rules concluded. Whereas the various rules in the knowledge base collectively defined a problem-solving strategy (heuristic classification in the infectious-disease domain), TEIRESIAS could not address the knowledge from that perspective; instead, the system was designed to focus on the individual rules in a single chain of reasoning. The user therefore concentrated on the "notes," not on the "music."

Other knowledge editors also have adopted conceptual models that directly reflect the symbol-level representations used by their associated inference engines. The rule editor in EMYCIN—which was derived from parts of TEIRESIAS—fell into this category. A knowledge engineer using EMYCIN saw the knowledge base as a collection of rules, parameters, and context definitions. In recent commercial adaptations of EMYCIN—in fact, in every known expert-system shell that is marketed currently—the same representation-based conceptual model is used for knowledge entry; users are asked to view their knowledge bases directly in terms of symbol-level entities.

Investigators have studied the representation-based approach in a large number of knowledge editors since the time of TEIRESIAS. Prospector, for example, was an expert system for mineral exploration. The program's knowledge base was represented not as rules, but rather as a semantic network[5] of nodes corresponding to various field observations, linked to other nodes corresponding to particular hypotheses. A special knowledge-acquisition tool, KAS (Reboh, 1981), was used to build and to maintain the knowledge

---

[5] A semantic network is a form of knowledge representation that incorporates labeled, associational links between nodes that correspond to the particular entities in the world being modeled.

58

base of ore-deposit models.

KAS had two principal components. RENE (REsident Network Editor) was used to build and refine the Prospector semantic network. An important feature of RENE was an automatic bookkeeping function that could prompt the knowledge engineer for missing nodes and links in the emerging knowledge base. RENE's suggestions about the knowledge-base elements that might be missing, unlike those of TEIRESIAS, were derived not from assumptions made by the program itself, but rather from information the knowledge engineer had already given the system regarding the intended structure of the knowledge base. The second component of KAS, the Semantic Network Matcher, could show the relationship between new facts and knowledge that already was encoded in the semantic network. The Matcher thus helped the knowledge engineer to expand and to refine the knowledge base. KAS was an important system that helped the developers of Prospector to build several large knowledge bases. Yet the conceptual model of the knowledge that KAS presented to its user was that of Prospector's complex semantic network; if a person did not understand the nuances of the network representation, he could not use KAS.

HYDRA (Miller et al., 1987), a tool that encodes potential treatment plans for expert critiquing systems of the ATTENDING family (Miller, 1983), also requires its user to think in terms of the underlying knowledge representation formalism—in this case, an augmented transition network (ATN).[6] Similarly, understanding the concept of an ATN is a prerequisite to using Peritus (Bonollo and Georgeff, 1983), a knowledge-acquisition program for a proposed expert-system architecture in which ATNs are used to control the order in which inferences are made (Georgeff and Bonollo, 1983). It would be impossible for domain experts to use these tools independently without first learning something about computer programming.

Knowledge-acquisition tools that present the contents of a knowledge base in terms of symbol-level entities inherently ignore the knowledge level. Because the programs display

---

[6]An ATN contains a set of nodes, each one representing a unique state in the world, with pathways between the nodes that determine when it is permissible to go from one state to another. A pathway between two nodes can be *augmented* to include some predefined action that must be performed each time there is a transition between the corresponding states. In the case of ATTENDING, each node in the ATN represents a state in a plan for administering anesthesia; the transitions between the states indicate when it is appropriate to follow one element of an anesthetic plan by another.

only the symbols, knowledge-level analysis of the application is left entirely to the user. For the user to perceive the knowledge base at the knowledge level requires that he have an understanding not only of the knowledge-representation language, but also of the inference mechanism that will be applied to the representation. Knowledge-editing tools in this class consequently require the user to appreciate in large measure how the expert system is implemented.

3.3.2 Method-Based Conceptual Models

Although symbol-level editors are by far the tools most commonly used for construction of expert systems, a number of workers have begun to experiment with programs that view an expert-system knowledge base from the knowledge level. Rather than discussing the knowledge in terms of symbol-level representations, users of such tools attempt to communicate knowledge specifications in terms of the *behaviors* that are to be achieved by the target expert system. These knowledge-level behaviors are described for the computer using special-purpose languages that, like all languages, are necessarily composed of symbols.

At first glance, the reliance on symbols for entry of knowledge-level specifications would seem to run contrary to Newell's description of knowledge as an abstraction that can never be written down completely. Yet it is still possible to use symbols to express the results of a knowledge-level analysis when the *meanings* of those symbols can be derived from a predefined model. The use of the underlying model to establish the semantics of the symbols contrasts with the approach taken in traditional knowledge engineering, where the semantics of a user's specifications are defined only operationally by the inference engine of the target expert system.

Models of problem solving such as that of heuristic classification can be used effectively as the conceptual models for interactive knowledge-acquisition tools. In the use of such tools, the human–computer dialog does not center on the rules, frames, or other symbol structures in the knowledge base; instead, the interaction concentrates on the methods by which task-specific knowledge is used to arrive at a problem's solution.

Such a method-oriented conceptual model may be based on some *explicit* set of terms

60

and relationships, such as those of the heuristic-classification model. To enter knowledge into tools of this class, the user must apply the terms and relationships of the model to the features of the application task at hand. In the case of heuristic classification, for example, the user would be asked to identify the elements of the *solution set,* the *data-abstraction hierarchies,* the *solution-refinement hierarchies,* and the *heuristics* that associate one hierarchy with another (see Figure 3.2). A second approach is to shield the user from specific details of the problem-solving method, even though a model of that method drives the behavior of the knowledge-acquisition tool internally; the model of problem solving thus becomes *implicit* from the conceptual perspective of the user. When the problem-solving model is made implicit, the user's interaction with the knowledge editor does not need to refer to all the specific terms and relationships in that model. This alternative technique requires that the knowledge-acquisition tool make significant assumptions about the knowledge that a user enters.

Explicit Models of Problem-Solving

The first knowledge-acquisition tool to adopt a method-oriented conceptual model was ROGET (Bennett, 1985), a program designed to assist knowledge engineers and domain experts in developing EMYCIN-based expert systems. Using an explicit model of diagnostic problem solving that can be viewed as a specialized form of heuristic classification, ROGET conducted a dialog with its user, asking what kinds of evidence might be gathered during a consultation and how that evidence might suggest or discriminate among possible problems and their causes.

The dialog was driven by the terms and relations in ROGET's model of problem solving (Figure 3.5). For example, ROGET knew that hypothetical "problems" might be concluded on the basis of classes of evidence, such as "directly observed signs," "predisposing factors," "reported symptoms," and "laboratory tests." The program prompted the developer for information regarding the evidence that end users would enter into an advice system by asking the developer which of the various categories best described the anticipated data. Based on the developer's responses, the program could solicit additional knowledge. Thus, if ROGET's user indicated that "laboratory tests" are required to support a particular

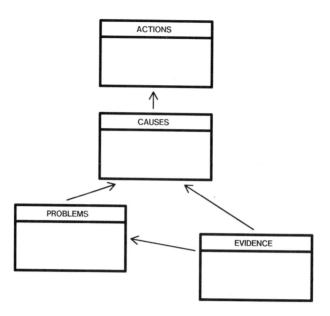

Figure 3.5: Conceptual Structures in ROGET

ROGET adopted a conceptual model in which the contents of a knowledge base were viewed in terms of a predefined model of classification problem solving. ROGET assumed that *evidence* from the environment would be used to generate abstractions and heuristic conclusions about *problems* that might be present, as well as various *causes* of the problems. At the same time, the *problems* might be refined into *causes,* and the *causes* further refined into *actions* to be recommended to the users of the expert systems that ROGET would ultimately generate. (Source: Adapted from Bennett, 1985, p. 59)

hypothesis, the program would ask for the *names* of the tests and their possible *values*, as well as how the values bore on the hypotheses under consideration. Once the conceptual knowledge had been entered through ROGET, the program generated the corresponding EMYCIN rule base (Figure 3.6).

ROGET used its domain-independent model of classification problem solving to anticipate the strategies that knowledge engineers would want to apply to relevant application tasks when building diagnostic expert systems. Bennett's approach thus had an advantage over that used by TEIRESIAS, in which metalevel knowledge provided guidance for the user only on the basis of the symbols already entered into the knowledge base. (Consequently, TEIRESIAS could offer no assistance in the development of knowledge bases

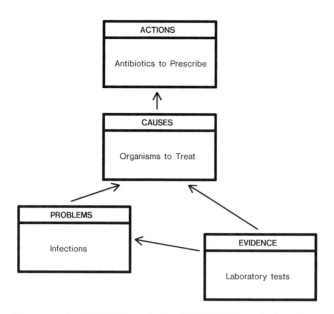

Figure 3.6: ROGET and the MYCIN Knowledge Base

ROGET acquires knowledge by asking the user to elaborate the conceptual categories that constitute the program's model of classification problem solving. In this example, the nature of some of the categories in the original MYCIN knowledge base has been entered. (Source: Adapted from Bennett, 1985, p. 53)

de novo.) ROGET, in theory, could assist the user in the construction of any expert system that conformed with Bennett's particular model of classification problem solving. Although Bennett tested ROGET by recreating a subset of the MYCIN knowledge base, the program was never put to significant use. He consequently never had an opportunity to explore the limits of ROGET's model.

ROGET's model of classification provided a mechanism by which a knowledge engineer could describe an expert system's behavior at the knowledge level. ROGET asked how primary data were abstracted into "problems" and how "problems" were associated with "causes" of the disorder under consideration; particular symbols that might be used to *encode* such relationships never entered into the human–computer discussion. A dialog with ROGET thus resulted in a knowledge-level specification of the application, much like the method-oriented knowledge-level analyses that Clancey (1984) has advocated. However, unlike pencil-and-paper specifications, the knowledge-level analyses produced by ROGET were in machine-readable form. Bennett wrote complex LISP programs to translate these knowledge-level descriptions into EMYCIN symbols that could form the basis of working consultation programs.

There are now numerous computer-based tools that have conceptual models for expert-system knowledge based on explicit models of problem-solving. Unlike ROGET, some of these systems have been put to practical use.

A tool called MORE (Kahn, G., et al., 1985), for example, adopted a model of classification problem solving not unlike that of ROGET. MORE asked its user to specify knowledge in terms of *symptoms, hypotheses,* and *conditions* that might modulate the strength of associations between symptoms and hypotheses. Unlike ROGET, MORE did not take its user's knowledge-level description of an application at face value; instead, MORE used a number of knowledge-acquisition heuristics to probe the knowledge engineer for possible deficiencies in the entered knowledge. For example, MORE would point out instances in which given symptoms would not permit competing hypotheses to be distinguished adequately. The program would then suggest locations where the user could augment the knowledge by entering additional symptoms that might better discriminate among possible hypotheses. MORE was difficult to use, however, because the program would typically ask for an overwhelming number of potential enhancements to the knowledge base.[7] Recently, a system called MOLE has been developed as a successor to MORE (Eshelman et al., 1987). The MOLE program incorporates a more detailed model of classification problem solving and consequently can use more refined heuristics in suggesting changes to the knowledge. Furthermore, MOLE adopts an important strategy first used by Davis in TEIRESIAS: Questions regarding possible refinements to the knowledge-base are asked only in the context of errors encountered when a consultation is run. As a result, MOLE can conduct an extremely focused dialog with its user once the initial knowledge base has been laid out.

Unlike ROGET, MORE, and MOLE, which model classification problem solving, a system called SALT (Marcus et al., 1985; Marcus, 1988) models a strategy for *constructing*

---

[7]L. Eshelman, personal communication, 1986.

solutions. SALT[8] assumes that a task can be mapped onto a "propose and revise" method of problem solving, in which a partial plan is incrementally extended while the program constantly verifies that the extensions are consistent with known constraints. SALT requires a structured language for entry of specific concepts, such as methods for determining values, constraints on values, and corrections for constraint violations. The program then converts the resulting knowledge-level description of the application into rules in OPS5. SALT has been used by engineering experts to specify knowledge for configuring electromechanical elevators in new buildings, and has been applied in a number of other domains, such as constraint-based scheduling. Like other method-oriented knowledge-acquisition tools, SALT presumes that the user will be able to conceptualize the solution to the problem in terms of the method provided by the system.

To a great degree, the usefulness of programs such as SALT and ROGET is limited by the ability of intended users to recognize correctly whether the method of problem solving embraced by the particular tool pertains to the task at hand. For example, classification problem solving probably is of no value in configuring elevators, because a solution set cannot be preenumerated. On the other hand, the strategy of "propose and revise" might be satisfactory (albeit inefficient) for choosing antibiotics. A knowledge engineer might be able to use SALT to describe a portion of MYCIN's task, but would be hard pressed to specify how to design an elevator using ROGET or MOLE. Each of these programs presumes that the user somehow knows *a priori* that its model of problem solving is applicable. Moreover, these programs also presuppose that the user will be able to apply the relevant terms and relationships of the problem-solving model to an application task correctly and consistently. ROGET, for example, requires that the user appreciate the difference between a "cause" and a "problem," a distinction that is not necessarily obvious at first blush. Because the program described in this book in large part adopts an explicit, method-oriented conceptual model for the knowledge being entered, the same caveats pertain to PROTÉGÉ.

---

[8]kNowledge ACquisition Language (NaCl)

Implicit Models of Problem Solving

Not all method-oriented knowledge-acquisition programs require the user to understand explicitly the terms and relationships of some model. In particular, a growing number of knowledge-acquisition programs based on personal construct psychology (Kelly, 1955) solicit knowledge in a manner that largely conceals the problem-solving model from the user.

ETS, for example, is a system that acquires knowledge directly from application specialists during the early stages of expert-system development (Boose, 1985). Building on earlier work by Gaines and Shaw (1980), Boose's program automates the structured interview and repertory-grid analysis originally developed by Kelly (1955) to elucidate an individual's system of personal constructs (see Section 3.2.3). After ETS conducts an initial dialog to elicit the constructs used by an application specialist to classify elements in the selected domain (Figure 3.7), the program presents the knowledge it acquires visually as a repertory grid (see Figure 3.3). Analysis of the grid allows the program to determine the implied hierarchical relationships among the expert's constructs and to display these relationships graphically (Figure 3.8). ETS then can use the manner in which particular constructs seem to entail the presence of other constructs to generate knowledge bases for prototype expert systems using a variety of shells such as KS-300 (a commercial version of EMYCIN) or OPS5.

ETS assumes a model of classification problem solving in which solutions are selected from a preenumerated set by the abstraction of primary data. The method is one of hierarchical (that is, decision-tree) classification. Consequently, heuristic associations that could link different abstraction hierarchies are not modeled. The entailment graph in Figure 3.8 is a visual representation for the decision tree that ETS generates from the repertory grid. Whereas the conceptual model behind the entailment graph is one of hierarchical classification, the domain specialist using ETS is insulated from the model's specific terms and relationships. Unlike a user of programs such as ROGET, the user of ETS does not need to understand the problem-solving model, because the classification hierarchies in ETS are generated *indirectly*. The user merely has to answer the simple questions generated during the structured interview (see Figure 3.7), indicating what the possible diagnostic

66

What is the name of the kind of thing you wish to classify (ie, DATABASE, DISEASE, etc.)?
ETS** **BUS-GRAPHICS-TOOL**

Do you already have a list of things which you wish to classify?
ETS** **YES**

Please enter a list of bus-graphic-tool types, one to a line. When you're done, enter STOP
or a RETURN.
ETS** **TELL-A-GRAF**
ETS** **BIGS**
ETS** **DISSPLA**
ETS** **GRAFMAKER**
ETS** **DI-3000**
ETS** **CLUECHART**
ETS**

Think of an important attribute that two of TELL-A-GRAF, BIGS, and DISSPLA share, but
that the other one does not. What is that attribute?
ETS** **MULTI-FONTS**

What is that attribute's opposite as it applies in this case?
ETS** **SINGULAR FONTS**

Think of an important attribute that two of BIGS, DISSPLA, and GRAFMAKER share, but
that the other one does not. What is that attribute?
ETS** **NO MENU GENERATION**

What is that attribute's opposite as it applies in this case?
ETS** **MENU GENERATION**

Figure 3.7: Knowledge Entry in ETS

ETS acquires knowledge by conducting a structured interview, eliciting the personal
constructs by which an expert classifies objects in a domain. In this example, an
expert wishes to develop a knowledge-based system to recommend business graphics
tools that are best suited for particular needs. After the expert lists the possible
elements to be considered (for example, "Tell-a-Graf" and "BIGS"), ETS conducts
a dialog that helps to establish the constructs that can classify the various graphics tools. Ultimately, the elicited constructs (for example, "MULTI-FONTS" and
"MENU GENERATION") and the manner in which they apply to the specific elements are used to generate a prototypical knowledge base. (Source: Adapted from
Boose, 1985, pp. 500–501)

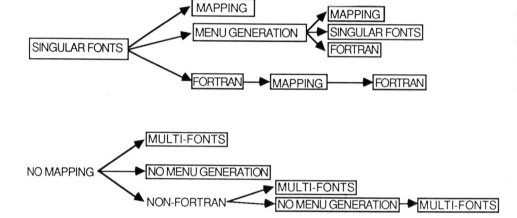

Figure 3.8: ETS Entailment Graph

Analysis of the repertory grid (Figure 3.3) allows ETS to determine how each of the constructs may entail other constructs entered by the application specialist. These relationships are displayed graphically for the user. (Source: Adapted from Boose, 1985, p. 504)

solutions are and how well the various constructs (features of the diagnostic possibilities) pertain to each member of the solution set. The user then views the knowledge as a simple table of diagnostic solutions and the features of those solutions (that is, as a repertory grid). The *program*—not the user—attempts to fit the answers to the questions into the problem-solving model. The advantage is that ETS can be used almost immediately by computer-naive application specialists after only very little training. The major limitation is that it is impossible for the program itself to generate a robust model of the application based on the often spurious and incomplete relationships implied by the repertory grid. An imperfect model, however, is better than no model at all.

ETS becomes particularly useful during the early stages of expert-system construction. The names of the elicited constructs and elements of the solution set form the initial systematic domain of discourse required to develop the expert system (Section 2.2.2). The entailment graph provides a preliminary set of associations that knowledge engineers can explore further during interviews with the application specialist. Although ETS has been used in the construction of several hundred expert systems, its major role has been in rapidly laying a groundwork so that system builders then can apply traditional knowledge-engineering techniques.

More recently, Boose and Bradshaw (1987) have begun work on a successor to ETS, called AQUINAS, that allows users to define multiple abstraction hierarchies with heuristic links between one hierarchy and another. Specifying these hierarchies and links in AQUINAS, however, requires the user to have explicit appreciation for the heuristic classification model of problem solving. AQUINAS is much more comprehensive than ETS is with respect to the knowledge that can be entered, but, at the same time, AQUINAS is much more difficult to use without special training (Kitto, 1988).

A number of other computer-based knowledge-acquisition tools have been based on repertory-grid analysis. At the University of Calgary, for example, Shaw and Gaines (1987) have developed a series of tools that serve as workbenches for accessing a variety of integrated programs that use personal construct psychology. Most recently, the KSS0 system for Apple Macintosh computers has provided the foundation for a number of knowledge-acquisition projects. A commercial version of KSS0, called NEXTRA (Rappaport and Gaines, 1988), has been announced by Neuron Data, Inc. Other knowledge-acquisition tools that use repertory-grid analysis, such as a program called Auto-Intelligence (IntelligenceWare, Inc.; Los Angeles, California), also are entering the marketplace (Parsaye, 1988).

Like the knowledge-acquisition tools based on *explicit* models of problem solving, those using personal construct psychology assume that the user knows *a priori* that his task can be solved via a form of classification. More important, these programs presuppose that the model of classification provided will be sufficient for representing the task. Like all knowledge-editing programs that adopt method-based conceptual models, knowledge that falls outside of the problem-solving model generally cannot be entered by the user.

3.3.3 Task-Based Conceptual Models

Unlike the knowledge-acquisition tools that ask their users to define an application in terms of some predefined problem-solving method, some programs have instead concentrated on the domain task. Rather than presenting the user with the terms and relations of some model of problem solving (such as heuristic classification), this last group of knowledge-editing programs presents the terms and relations of predefined models of general *tasks* to be performed. Defining a particular application then requires applying the terms and relations of a general task model to a specific problem. Thus, in the case of OPAL (see Chapter 6), a general model of cancer-treatment plans is used by the program to elicit the details of specific cancer-treatment plans from physicians. The specific plans entered into OPAL then form the basis of the treatment advice offered by the ONCOCIN expert system.

Several other knowledge-acquisition programs based on task models have been described recently. A prototype system called Student (Gale, 1987), for example, adopts a general model of how to organize and to submit data for processing and analysis by a statistical program such as SPSS or SAS. The terms and relations of the model are used to enter the specific knowledge needed to advise researchers on particular statistical questions (for example, how to perform a regression analysis and then to plot the results).

A program called KNACK (Klinker et al., 1987a; Klinker, 1988) adopts a predominantly task-based approach for the construction of advice systems that generate descriptive reports. Because KNACK has evolved over the years, the degree to which the program can be classified as "task-based" depends on which version of the system one considers. The first-reported version of KNACK (Klinker et al., 1987b) was used to create expert systems that assessed the design of electromechanical devices and that generated printed reports describing the expert systems' assessments. Experts and knowledge engineers entered into KNACK how the report should be formatted, how application-specific text items should be incorporated within "boilerplate" prose, and how those text items should be derived from an end user's description of a particular device. As in OPAL and Student, much of a user's interaction with this early version of KNACK involved filling in blanks that corresponded with terms in a predefined model of the target expert system's task—namely, that of analyzing properties of an electromechanical device and of generating an appropriate report. The questions that KNACK asked the user thus dealt with the organization of the printed reports and the structure of the particular devices that needed to be evaluated.

In subsequent versions of KNACK, facilities have been added that allow users to enter different task models. Although the the expert systems that KNACK creates still make assessments and generate corresponding reports, the subjects of those assessments no longer are restricted to pieces of electromechanical hardware. The most recent version of KNACK has created report-writing expert systems for topics ranging from evaluations of project planning to assessments of marketing plans for new products (Klinker et al., 1988). With the current program, after the knowledge engineer has defined an initial task model, KNACK uses that task model to generate questions for the user to answer; consequently, interaction with KNACK may concern notions such as the resources allocated to a project (in the case of the project-planning task), marketing strategies (in the case of the product-marketing task), and so on. The program's developers had hoped that, in addition to answering such questions, application specialists would be able to use KNACK independently to develop new task models. Experience has shown, however, that this creative aspect of knowledge acquisition currently can be accomplished only with the aid of knowledge engineers who are already experienced in using KNACK. Answering the specific questions that KNACK derives from an existing task model, however, can be done expeditiously by domain experts working alone (Kitto, 1988).

KNACK has similarities to PROTÉGÉ, in that there is a preliminary phase of knowledge acquisition during which a conceptual model for the task is elaborated, followed by a second phase during which the model is used to elicit knowledge regarding specific applications. Unlike the PROTÉGÉ approach, however, KNACK does not clearly separate the process of creating a task model *de novo* from that of extending the model with application-specific content knowledge; at various stages in the knowledge-entry process, KNACK may request its users to refine the current task model. When such a request occurs, it becomes difficult for application specialists to work alone with KNACK (Kitto, 1988).

In purely task-oriented programs, the *methods* required to solve the tasks are predetermined. For example, OPAL contains no explicit model of the planning steps needed to produce a cancer-therapy recommendation; in Student, the strategies needed to set up a data-analysis job stream are transparent. Moreover, users of the programs are insulated from the mapping between the task models and the problem-solving methods used by the underlying expert systems. Users need only supply the *content knowledge* required to distinguish one task instance from another (see Section 2.2.1). The *process knowledge* already is assumed by the knowledge-editing tool. Thus, both the structure of the tasks and the methods by which individual tasks are solved are already built into the system and need not be of direct concern.

Knowledge-acquisition tools that adopt a task-oriented conceptual model necessarily come with a predefined mapping between the task description and some computational problem-solving method. Knowledge-level analysis of the general application therefore must be done *in advance,* by the system designers. The knowledge-level description originates from the ontology of the task (Alexander et al., 1986) and incorporates the problem-solving methods available within the expert-system shell that will ultimatley generate the advice. I shall discuss in detail the knowledge-level analysis that was required for the development of OPAL in Chapter 6.

3.3.4 Summary

A large number of computer-based knowledge-acquisition tools have been developed in the past few years. It is helpful to classify these programs on the basis of the conceptual knowledge-base model that they present for their users. Most knowledge-editing programs have adopted a conceptual model based on symbol-level representations. Others, such as ROGET, couch their presentation of the knowledge being edited in terms of a predefined model of problem solving at the knowledge level. The third class of programs allow users to edit knowledge in terms of a predefined model of the domain task. The choice of conceptual model has a direct bearing on who is responsible for the knowledge-level analysis required to define new applications (Table 3.1).

Some knowledge-editing tools may not fit precisely into this taxonomy. It is possible for example, that both method-oriented programs and task-oriented programs may permit users to enter as symbol-level data structures those concepts that are not expressible in terms of the tools' knowledge-level models. Similarly, some method-oriented tools may incorporate considerable domain-specific knowledge. The conceptual models of such tool consequently have similarities to those of task-oriented tools; the difference is that the

72

Table 3.1: Conceptual Models for Knowledge-Editing Programs

Conceptual Model of Knowledge Base	Responsibility for Knowledge-Level Analysis	Example Systems
Symbol-level representation	User	TEIRESIAS, EMYCIN, KAS, Expert-system "shells"
Problem-solving method	Knowledge-editing system	ROGET, SALT, MORE, MOLE, PROTÉGÉ
Domain task	System designers	OPAL, Student, Tools generated by PROTÉGÉ

method-oriented programs require their users to perform additional domain modeling (that is, knowledge-level analysis).

3.4 Knowledge Acquisition for Knowledge Acquisition

Many AI researchers consider the term *knowledge acquisition* to encompass both the problems of deriving knowledge from experts (which a few authors have called *knowledge elicitation*) and the autonomous discovery of new knowledge by computers (*machine learning*). I do not use such a broad definition of *knowledge acquisition* in this book because I believe that the interactive extraction of knowledge from human experts generally entails a different set of research questions than does the extraction of knowledge from data structures. For example, the cognitive barriers to knowledge elicitation that I outlined in Chapter 2 are not the limiting factors in current machine-learning systems; at the same time, issues such as the computational tractability of performing a generalization do not matter when there are experts whom we can ask.

Consequently, I have not discussed in this chapter the considerable work that AI researchers have done on the *automated* development and refinement of knowledge bases.[9]

---

[9]Two excellent anthologies of current work on machine learning are the volumes edited by Michalski, Carbonell, and Mitchell (1983, 1986).

Yet knowledge engineers and theorists in machine learning ultimately share the same goal—that of procuring new knowledge in machine-usable form. Although the two groups may use dissimilar methods and face different obstacles, they frequently build on each other's results. In particular, members of the machine-learning community have proposed a model for learning systems that provides an important perspective on the knowledge-acquisition research presented in this book.

The *performance learning model* of Buchanan, Mitchell, Smith, and Johnson (1977) defines machine learning as the process whereby computer systems use information obtained during interaction with their environment to improve their performance during future interactions. Improved performance may accrue from the incorporation of additional knowledge (*knowledge-level learning*) or may occur because existing knowledge is used more efficiently (*symbol-level learning*) (Deitterich, 1986). The performance learning model allows PROTÉGÉ and the editors that it generates to be viewed as knowledge-level learning systems.

According to the model, learning systems comprise four principal components (Figure 3.9):

- The **performance element** is the program the behavior of which is to be improved as a result of the learning. In the case of a knowledge editor such as OPAL, the performance element is the target expert system (that is, ONCOCIN).

- The **critic** is the component responsible for detecting weaknesses in the performance element for which learning ought to take place. Interactive knowledge-editing tools tend to give this responsibility to the user, who will ultimately decide where knowledge-base deficiencies lie. In programs such as MORE (Kahn, G., et al., 1985) and MOLE (Eshelman et al., 1987), however, the knowledge editor itself also may point out situations in which additional knowledge may be needed.

- The **instance selector** is the part of the system that determines the elements in the environment from which the system will learn. Some autonomous learning system can generate their own training instances. In the case of an interactive knowledge editor, however, the instance selector is always the user; only the user can select the

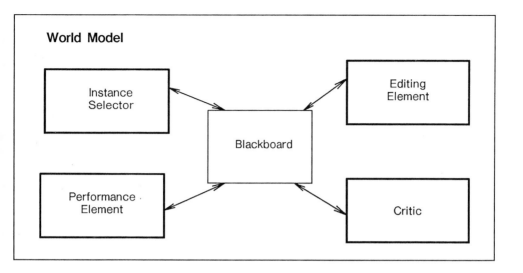

Figure 3.9: Components of a Learning System

A learning system attempts to improve the behavior of the *performance element*. An *instance selector* determines elements from the environment from which the system will learn. The *critic* identifies weaknesses in the performance element that the training instances might address. The *editing element* makes necessary changes in the performance element to effect learning. The four modules communicate via a *blackboard* within the constraints of a world model. (Source: Adapted from Buchanan et al., 1977, p. 35)

knowledge that will be incorporated into the knowledge base.

- The **editing element** is the component that incorporates the results of what is learned into the performance element. In OPAL, for example, this editing task represents the work done by the routines that translate the knowledge entered graphically by the user into the representations required by the ONCOCIN knowledge base.

The four components of the learning system communicate with one another via a structure called the *blackboard*. In PROTÉGÉ and the editors that it generates, the blackboard function is performed by a relational database system.

Interactive knowledge-editing systems must rely on human beings to serve in the roles of both *instance selector* and *critic*. Although some workers in the machine-learning community question whether the performance learning model can pertain to systems that are not fully automated, the model, in fact, does not require that *any* of its components be computer-based. When applied to the work in this book, the model provides a useful perspective from which the relationship between PROTÉGÉ and the editors that PROTÉGÉ generates can be better understood.

According to the model, all learning systems operate within the fixed conceptual framework of a *world model* that includes (1) the definitions of the objects and relations in the application area, (2) the syntax and semantics of the elements to be learned, and (3) the methods to be used for learning (see Figure 3.9). (The first two of these components are part of what Winograd and Flores (1986) refer to as a *systematic domain*.) All the assumptions used during learning are derived from the world model. Thus, whereas the learning process can alter knowledge stored in the blackboard, the knowledge contained in the world model is invariant; the assumptions of the world model can be modified only from "outside" the system. Because the knowledge in the world model defines much of the appearance and behavior of the learning system, there are obvious advantages to representing this knowledge in a format that can be easily viewed and manipulated. More often than not, however, learning programs have concealed world-model assumptions in program code.

The conceptual model that defines how users interact with a knowledge-acquisition tool is derived from the program's world model. For example, in the original OPAL system, the program's world model includes the terms and relations of the oncology *task model* (see Chapter 6). The OPAL world model thus influences how the system presents and acquires knowledge from the user. If physicians using OPAL are dissatisfied with the manner in which oncology knowledge is represented in a particular form, the original OPAL program itself cannot incorporate any necessary changes. However, a programmer can readily alter OPAL's *world model* to revise the graphical representation. When making these kinds of modifications, the programmer views OPAL as a program the performance of which needs to be improved; the programmer selects instances of possible modifications, tries them out, criticizes their performance, and finally edits the OPAL program accordingly. Thus, the human programmer in a sense acts as part of a *learning system* for which the *performance element* is OPAL itself.

76

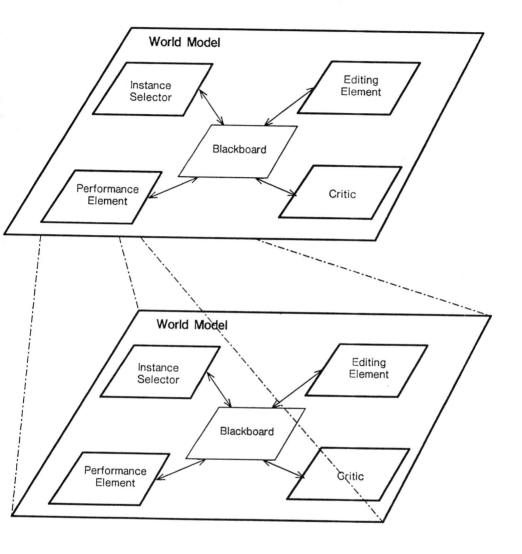

Figure 3.10: Hierarchical Learning Systems

The performance element of a learning system may itself be a learning system. Actions by the higher-level learning system represent the only mechanisms by which the world model of the lower-level system can be altered. (Source: Adapted from Buchanan et al., 1977, p. 39)

Learning systems can thus be layered (Figure 3.10; Buchanan et al., 1977). A given learning system may constitute the performance element of some higher-level (metalevel) learning system, where the metalevel system has its own instance selector, critic, editing element, and world model. A learning system's world model may be adjusted by only a metalevel learning system, the performance element of which is the lower-level learning system to be changed; in theory, the world model of the metalevel system can be altered by a learning system at a still higher level. Ultimately, all learning systems have a human designer as their final critic and editor.

In this book, I shall describe a two-tiered approach to knowledge acquisition for clinical-trial consultation programs. At one level are the knowledge editors used by clinical researchers to develop knowledge bases for new treatment protocols. At the metalevel is PROTÉGÉ, a knowledge editor that creates and modifies the world models of the lower-level knowledge-acquisition tools. Although a number of AI researchers have speculated on the advantages of making one learning system the performance element of another (see, for example, Dietterich and Bennett, 1986; Wilkins, 1986), few hierarchical learning systems have been implemented. Those that have been are mostly in the area of pattern analysis.

Uhr and Vossler (1963), for example, described a pattern-recognition program that identified printed images encoded as a 20 x 20 matrix of binary digits. The program first generated at random a set of matrix operators that, when applied to an input pattern, resulted in a list of *characteristics* that could be used to classify the input. As new test cases were evaluated by the system, unsuccessful characteristics were removed from further consideration. At the same time, the program optimized numeric coefficients that were applied to these matrix operators to classify the various patterns. Although the two learning processes were embodied in a single program, one portion of the system learned new coefficients for the operators in its particular world view, while the other adjusted those operators. As a result, the latter component changed the performance of the first learning component.

Similarly, one of the programs developed by Samuel to play checkers (Samuel, 1967) evaluated a linear polynomial function to calculate a player's board strength. The terms of the polynomial were based on the presence of various binary parameters that were determined from measurable board features, such as control of the king row and the center of the board. At one level, the program learned to adjust the coefficients of the polynomial function to improve its performance in future games. At another level, the program learned to select the best board features for use in the polynomial to optimize the evaluation function.

In both these programs, the learning that took place resulted in the refinement of an arithmetical scoring process. The knowledge that improved system performance was represented either as a mathematical function or as a numeric coefficient. If an expert system is to acquire knowledge, however, the learning system must contain a process that incorporates knowledge that conforms to a qualitative model of some task in the world. Just as Samuel's program learned to optimize the terms in a polynomial scoring function, a PROTÉGÉ user learns to optimize the terms and relationships in a *task model*. Just as the checkers program could acquire better coefficients when it first learned more germane polynomials, a PROTÉGÉ-generated knowledge editor can acquire more relevant knowledge from experts when its task model (and thus its *conceptual model*) is more refined. A primary motivation behind PROTÉGÉ is to improve the performance of task-oriented knowledge editors by improving the conceptual models on which those editors are based. Previous workers have blurred the distinction between (1) creating a task model and (2) extending such a model to define new applications. PROTÉGÉ clarifies these two phases of knowledge-acquisition activity, allowing knowledge engineers to produce diverse knowledge-editing tools that are tailored to novel skeletal-planning applications.

4 The Application Domain: Clinical Trials

PROTÉGÉ can be used to generate knowledge-editing tools for a variety of application areas. The program makes strong assumptions regarding how applicable tasks are structured and what problem-solving methods are required to produce a recommendation. Nevertheless, it should be possible to model a diverse set of planning problems using PROTÉGÉ (see Section 9.5).

In this book, I demonstrate my ideas in the general area of controlled clinical trials. Understanding this application domain helps to clarify many practical aspects of the use of PROTÉGÉ and provides a basis for judging PROTÉGÉ's success in addressing a significant knowledge-acquisition problem. At the same time, the use of knowledge-based systems to advise physicians in the care of patients treated according to formal medical protocols constitutes a valuable, appropriate use of AI technology. Knowledge-editing programs such as those generated by PROTÉGÉ also can provide important opportunities for improved design, dissemination, and administration of clinical protocols. In this chapter, I review controlled trials in medicine and discuss previous work by other investigators to provide computer-based support for clinical research.

4.1 Controlled Clinical Trials

The adoption of the scientific method in clinical medicine is a relatively recent phenomenon. Lewis Thomas relates:

For century after century, all the way into the remote millennia of its origins, medicine got along by sheer guesswork and the crudest sort of empiricism. It is hard to conceive of a less scientific enterprise among human endeavors. Virtually anything that could be thought up for the treatment of disease was tried out at one time or another, and, once tried, lasted decades or even centuries before being given up. It was, in retrospect, the most frivolous and irresponsible kind of human experimentation, based on nothing but trial and error, usually resulting in precisely that sequence. (Thomas, 1979, p. 159)

The first rumblings of change were heard in the nineteenth century; physicians began to realize that "almost all of the complicated treatments then available for disease did not really work, and ... that most of them actually did more harm than good" (Thomas, 1979, p. 160). "Modern" medicine is commonly said to have begun in the 1930s, with the introduction of penicillin and the sulfonamides. The widespread embracement of controlled medical experimentation, however, did not take place until the following decade, when controlled clinical trials were first used to study the relative efficacy of antibiotics for tuberculosis.

4.1.1 Background and Terminology

Clinical trials now represent the standard by which physicians attempt to prove the utility of new treatments. The results of clinical trials form the basis by which all physicians make therapeutic decisions. Whereas anecdotal and epidemiological evidence often can contribute substantial support for the use of certain interventions (Feinstein, 1983), physicians now require that new therapies be proven safe and effective in controlled experiments. Prompted by the thalidomide tragedy in Europe,[1] the Food and Drug Administration (FDA) has monitored the scientific evidence substantiating the efficacy and safety of all new drugs marketed in the United States since 1962.

The Harris-Kefauver amendment to the Federal Pure Food and Drug Act mandates that extensive pharmacological and toxicological research be performed before the FDA

---

[1]Thalidomide is a sedative that caused an epidemic of crippling birth defects in the early 1960s. The drug was never marketed in the United States.

can approve a drug company's application for use of an investigational new drug in human subjects. Three rigorous phases of clinical testing must then be carried out before a New Drug Application (NDA), and subsequent conditional release of the new drug, can be granted.

- *Phase I* testing involves administration of the new drug to a limited number of volunteers. The biological actions and metabolism of the drug are studied in an attempt to determine the amount of drug that might result in toxicity.

- *Phase II* testing is performed on selected patients who have the disease that the drug is intended to control. The goal is to refine the basic pharmacologic data obtained during Phase I studies and to establish the therapeutic dosage range in humans.

- *Phase III* testing involves study of the drug in a large group of patients. Patients typically are selected at random to receive either the new drug or an alternative— usually an established—therapy. Relative efficacy and toxicity of the new drug can then be assessed.

By assigning patients at random to receive one of the alternative treatments in Phase III studies, clinical researchers can control for both known and unknown covariables that could affect patient outcome. For example, some subjects may have more serious disease than others do. Some may be more compliant with the medication-administration schedule. Some may be genetically predisposed to a better or worse prognosis. The randomization procedure is designed to create homogeneous treatment and control groups, so that any observed differences in outcome should be ascribable to the *intervention* and not to possible confounding variables. A study with this form of internal control is called a *randomized clinical trial* (RCT). The particular treatments to which patients are randomly assigned are referred to as *arms* of the study.

In other clinical experiments, referred to as *crossover trials*, patients serve as their own controls. After being tested on one intervention, the patients are given another, and may not be aware when the crossover actually has taken place. This methodology is particularly useful when accrual of sufficient numbers of patients for a statistically significant randomized study is impractical.

In both traditional RCTs and crossover studies, it is important to prevent human biases from affecting the recording of experimental results. Because subjects often have preconceived ideas about what to expect from a given intervention, a frequent condition for participation in a clinical trial is that subjects not be told which treatment they are being given. Such a study is said to be *blinded*. Because researchers likewise may be biased by their own expectations concerning the alternative interventions and because those biases can affect their perceptions of patient outcomes, the clinical investigators also may not be told which treatments the individual patients are receiving. Such a study is said to be *double-blinded*.

The guidelines by which clinical investigators care for patients enrolled in clinical trials form what is called a *protocol*. Protocols, which are described in detailed documents (Schmidt, 1985), are designed to define the therapy and diagnostic studies to be administered to study patients. Among the controls built into clinical trials is an attempt to provide uniform care for patients assigned to individual treatment arms. Such standardization of treatment is possible only if the protocol author is able to anticipate the various conditions that might dictate therapy modifications and if the protocol document provides clear specifications for what providers should do in these circumstances. Protocol documents for well-controlled studies are therefore quite detailed. Complex clinical trials, such as those in medical oncology, may require protocol documents that exceed 50 pages. Physicians are accustomed to following protocols for clinical trials. Because physicians often are unfamiliar with novel modalities of treatment and because they recognize the importance of providing standardized care for the purposes of medical experimentation, they will readily consult protocol documents to determine what to do in specific circumstances.

4.1.2 Problems of Clinical Trials

Because the relative advantages of one proposed treatment plan over another often are subtle, clinical trials typically require large sample sizes in order to show statistically significant differences among groups of patients. Thus, a major problem for many clinical studies involves accrual of sufficient numbers of patients. Due to the finite patient base at academic medical centers, many workers recently have considered the idea of enrolling the private patients of community physicians in clinical trials (Begg et al., 1982; Koretz et al., 1983). Some investigators have proposed computer-based advice systems as a means to allow physicians who are remote from academic centers to coordinate care for patients assigned to experimental protocols (Wirtschafter et al., 1979; Hickam et al., 1985).

The large sample sizes required for many trials make this form of clinical investigation among the most expensive of scientific enterprises. Total expenditures for clinical research in the United States have been estimated at more than $6 billion annually (Davis, 1985). Much of the cost of clinical trials involves expenditures for direct patient care at large academic centers. The accrual of study subjects from community hospitals, where patient care generally is less expensive, has been discussed as one mechanism to reduce the cost of clinical research.

The huge price tag for controlled trials has brought the process of clinical research under increasing scrutiny (Feinstein, 1983; Schechter and Sheps, 1984). Because many problems in patient selection, experimental methodology, and data collection may not become apparent until long after a study has been completed and the data are analyzed, many large studies have been severely criticized for providing results that are of uncertain clinical significance (Mosteller et al., 1983); because of the great expense of controlled trials, however, few clinical investigations can be redone.

One problem results from the vast numbers of patient data that physicians must record. For example, Eastern Cooperative Oncology Group trials typically demand between 300 and 1000 data items per patient (Begg et al., 1982). A variety of procedures are customarily adopted in clinical trials to help ensure data integrity, including the use of research datasheets that are kept separate from patients' general medical records, and reliance on special nonclinical personnel whose primary responsibility is to ensure that the datasheets are kept up to date (Knatterud, 1981). Recently, a number of computer-based tools have been described that assist physicians in the process of data collection (Wirtschafter et al., 1981; Friedman ct al., 1983; Pollak, 1983; Kent et al., 1985). Marked improvements in data capture have been attributed to the direct use of the computer by physicians caring for study patients (Kent et al., 1985).

Another set of problems in clinical research is caused by health-care providers' varying adherence to protocol guidelines. The primary purpose of research protocols is to ensure uniform care for patients assigned to each treatment arm; a study cannot be considered controlled if therapy is given in a nonstandardized manner. Thus, a primary concern of protocol administrators is to maintain the validity of their clinical experiments by requiring that individual providers abide by protocol specifications (Sylvester et al., 1981; Begg et al., 1982; Koretz et al., 1983). When health-care providers deviate from certain protocols even slightly, patient outcome can be affected. For example, failure of oncologists to administer certain drugs either in recommended dosage or on recommended schedule has been cited as a principal cause of relapse from complete remission in Hodgkin's disease (Armitage and Corder, 1982).

Yet health-care providers do not necessarily follow protocols as written. Frequently, protocol violations occur because experienced clinicians disagree with certain aspects of the prescribed treatment plan. For example, the Northern California Oncology Group reported that, in a 1-year period, patients were given treatment in accordance with protocol guidelines in only 60 percent of their visits to academic centers (Koretz et al., 1983). Almost always, the departures from the protocols involved either "inappropriately" delaying treatment or administering drug doses that were lower than those recommended. At Stanford University, when three senior oncologists retrospectively reviewed possible therapy for a cohort of lymphoma patients, the treatment that would have been dictated by a strict reading of the protocol document was deemed "acceptable" in only 58 percent of 105 clinic visits.[2] The faculty experts consistently stated that unmodified adherence to the protocols would have resulted in failure to delay treatment or to attenuate drug doses adequately. Although not conforming precisely to the protocol document, the experts believed their own preferred therapy would have been closer to the "intentions" of the protocol study designers (Hickam et al., 1984). Thus, even when a protocol explicitly designates a specific treatment, health-care providers may sometimes second guess the directives written in the document and take actions closer to what they *assume* the person who wrote the protocol would have wanted in certain situations (Musen et al., 1986).

---

[2]The treatment actually given by Stanford oncology fellows was considered "acceptable" 67 percent of the time.

Other protocol violations have been attributed to simple lack of familiarity on the part of clinical investigators with particular protocols. When the European Organization for Research on Treatment of Cancer (EORTC) studied the quality of institutional participation in a clinical trial for treatment of soft-tissue sarcoma (Sylvester et al., 1981), 81 percent of patients enrolled at "major" participating centers (those having more than 12 patients entered into the study) both met the protocol eligibility criteria and received appropriate treatment. In "minor" centers (those with fewer than 12 study patients), only 39 percent of the enrolled subjects were considered "valid" patients. Furthermore, 22 percent of the patients studied by the minor participants could not be evaluated because of missing data, an issue for only 1 percent of the patients treated at major centers. To address such problems, researchers have proposed that expert systems be used to assist physicians in the management of patients on research protocols, particularly when the providers are not familiar with the details of particular clinical studies (Hickam et al., 1985).

Frequently, nonuniformity of care is the result of neither physician judgment nor physician error. Often, protocol documents are simply ambiguous and inadequately specify what providers should do in certain circumstances. Review of a large number of oncology protocols, for example, has shown significant areas of deliberate underspecification of the treatment plan by protocol designers, errors of omission, and wording that has varying interpretations (Musen et al., 1986). Many of these errors did not become obvious to physicians until the protocols had to be encoded for the knowledge base of an expert system. Computer-based protocol-authoring environments could allow researchers to design clinical protocols that are free of such ambiguities.

4.2 Computer-Based Decision Support for Clinical Trials

Many automated tools have been developed to assist physicians in the care of patients enrolled in clinical studies. In this section, I review the best-documented of these systems, with an emphasis on how the systems might address problems of clinical research. All these programs share an important goal: improving the quality of both data collection and physician decision making in clinical trials. Researchers have met this goal using a wide range of computational techniques, including database technology, computer-stored algorithms, and expert systems.

4.2.1 Clinical Database Systems

A large number of database systems have been developed expressly to support clinical trials (Wiederhold, 1981; King et al., 1984). Most systems, such as CLINFO (Whitehead and Bilofsky, 1980) and MEDLOG (Layhad and McShane, 1983), are designed for the long-term storage and analysis of generic patient data. Although they maintain the data in the time-oriented fashion required by research protocols, such systems are not intended to provide advice to clinical investigators. One exception is the Oncology Center Information System (OCIS) developed at Johns Hopkins Hospital (Lenhard et al., 1984); OCIS is a comprehensive database-management utility designed specifically for clinical trials in cancer therapy. The system not only maintains the time-oriented data for patients actively undergoing chemotherapy, but also provides a tumor registry of all cancer patients seen at Johns Hopkins. Physicians can use the system to display textual synopses of current research protocols on terminals located in the Johns Hopkins oncology clinic. Furthermore, portions of protocols for bone-marrow transplantation and cancer chemotherapy have been represented in a relational database. Queries to the database are used to generate patient care plans that provide written reminders of expected laboratory tests and treatments (Blum, 1983).

Like OCIS, PDQ (Hubbard et al., 1987) is a large database that can assist physicians directly in their decision making. Unlike the previous systems, PDQ contains no patient data; instead, PDQ is a database of *protocols*. Developed by the National Cancer Institute, PDQ allows physicians to obtain detailed information concerning clinical trials in which they may want to enroll their cancer patients. Each research protocol is stored in a textual format. Using a special query language similar to those used for bibliographic retrieval, PDQ permits any physician with access to a terminal to search for those protocols for treatment of patients with particular tumors that are in use within specific geographic regions or at specific medical centers. PDQ allows physicians to view the full text of protocol documents online. Thus, although PDQ was designed to help practitioners locate relevant clinical trials in which to enroll their cancer patients, the system does not prevent physicians from administering protocol treatments to their own patients without formally enrolling these patients in the corresponding research studies. In such circumstances, it is the physician's responsibility to interpret the text of the protocol and to administer therapy appropriately.

Although database systems play an important role in conducting medical research, they are limited in their ability to assist physicians in the ongoing care of individual patients enrolled in clinical trials. In general, database systems cannot provide detailed protocol advice that is tailored for specific patients. Several decision-support systems have been designed to include this additional capability, however. Almost all have been in the area of oncology, probably reflecting the great prevalence of clinical trials for cancer therapy[3] as well as physicians' need for assistance in managing patients enrolled in these especially complex studies.

4.2.2   Computer-Encoded Clinical Algorithms

The earliest work in providing computer-based decision support for clinical trials involved the use of clinical algorithms. The Consultant-Extender system developed by the Clinical Information Systems Group at the University of Alabama (Wirtschafter et al., 1979) enabled community physicians with no special training in oncology to administer adjuvant chemotherapy to their patients who had breast cancer. Starting in 1975, a computer-encoded algorithm was used to print custom-tailored forms with visit-specific advice rules for the administration of either melphalan or CMF chemotherapy.[4] Each report listed the recommended treatment to be given at a particular patient's next visit, all required laboratory tests, and contingency plans in case any of the tests were abnormal. The university medical center mailed the form to the community physician in advance of the patient's

---

[3]Sixty-five percent of the clinical trials supported by the National Institutes of Health in 1979 were funded by the National Cancer Institute (Meinert, 1982).

[4]CMF represents combined administration of the drugs cyclophosphamide, methotrexate, and 5-fluorouracil. In a cancer protocol, a group of drugs administered conjointly is referred to as a *chemotherapy*. The name given to a chemotherapy usually is an acronym derived from the names of the individual drugs.

next scheduled visit to the local doctor. At the time of the patient's visit, the necessary laboratory-test results were written on the form. The community physician administered the indicated treatment and kept one copy of the original form as a progress note. A carbon copy of the form, indicating the current laboratory data and the physician's actual therapy, was mailed back to the academic center so that a new form could be generated for the next patient visit.

A similar approach was used to assist oncologists in the management of patients enrolled in a protocol for treatment of Hodgkin's disease (Wirtschafter et al., 1981). Although the protocol was more complex than either of the two breast-cancer regimens,[5] analogous patient-specific, visit-specific forms were used. Turnaround time between the university and the participating physicians was decreased by the use of facsimile transmission of the forms over telephone lines.

The Alabama system represented an important experiment in the use of computers to provide assistance for medical decision making. Community physicians were shown to follow the protocol algorithms reliably (Wirtschafter et al., 1979), although the algorithms themselves were not formally validated. A randomized study demonstrated almost perfect data capture when physicians were prompted with the computer-generated forms (Wirtschafter et al., 1981). As a result, researchers at the University of Alabama were able to accrue large numbers of valid patients from remote rural areas for their clinical trials—patients who were quite grateful that they did not have to commute long distances to the university medical center to receive treatment. Yet the paper-oriented approach of the Consultant-Extender reflects the limitations of the technology that was available in the 1970s; such a system, requiring bulk transcription of patient records by nonclinical personnel, would be clumsy at best for protocols that require frequent patient visits.

The protocol knowledge in the Alabama system was represented directly as procedures in the PL/I programming language. There are no published data indicating the amount of time required to develop and maintain the encoded algorithms. The need for revision was reportedly "minor" (Wirtschafter et al., 1979). Despite the apparent success of the

---

[5]The protocol specified the administration of alternating DTIC and ABVD chemotherapy *versus* ABVD alone.

system, the algorithms were never expanded beyond a small number of protocols.

A more recent algorithmic program is the Cancer Data Management System (CDMS) at Boston University Medical Center (Friedman and Frank, 1983). The CDMS generates paper forms used by physicians in caring for a variety of cancer patients. Although patient data may be reviewed interactively by physicians using display terminals, data management is performed mainly by clerical personnel who must transcribe the physician's written notations from the computer-generated medical-record forms. Visit-specific forms are designed to notify the provider of necessary tests and anticipated treatment. A formal evaluation of the system's therapy advice has not yet been published.

Knowledge in the CDMS is encoded algorithmically using what Friedman and Frank (1983) refer to as *deterministic rules.* Libraries of text phrases, written in a structured subset of English, are used to denote the conditions and actions of the rules. Oncology protocols are represented as a fixed list of *conditions* that must be considered and evaluated. If present, the conditions cause execution of specific *actions.* Thus, the conditions and actions of rules act as *subroutines* in a high-level programming language.[6] The developers claim that "knowledge or rule acquisition in the CDMS can be accomplished by direct interaction between a non-programmer user and the computer system. This is accomplished without the user being aware of how the rules are stored in the computer or how they are applied in practice" (Friedman and Frank, 1983, p. 386). Although no data have been published that address this assertion, separating out the steps of the protocol algorithm from the rest of the program code certainly would aid in the development and maintenance of the CDMS. The approach is analogous to the separation of the knowledge base from the inference engine in typical expert systems.

4.2.3 Knowledge-Based Systems for Clinical Trials

Another well known decision-support aid for clinical trials is ONCOCIN (Shortliffe et al., 1981). Like the algorithmic systems just described, ONCOCIN has been developed for research protocols in oncology. However, the system abandons the use of paper reports

---

[6]The CDMS itself is written in MUMPS.

and data transcription by nonclinical personnel in favor of an interactive approach that involves physicians directly.

ONCOCIN has been designed so that, each time a patient is seen in the Stanford oncology clinic, physicians can use the computer to record pertinent patient findings and laboratory tests. Clinicians enter the data directly into the ONCOCIN system; there is no paper flowsheet that must be filled out and later transcribed. Once the data have been entered, ONCOCIN offers the physician recommendations for the current therapy, based on the patient's clinical status and the program's knowledge of the treatment protocol (Figure 4.1). The physician can either accept the computer's suggested therapy or specify a different course of action. In a study of the program's advice, expert oncologists deemed that the therapy recommendations made by ONCOCIN were as satisfactory, in general, as the treatment actually administered by oncology fellows at Stanford who did not have access to the system (Hickam et al., 1985). More important, the experts were likely to prefer ONCOCIN's recommendation to the therapy that would have been dictated by a strict reading of the protocol documents (Hickam et al., 1984). ONCOCIN's knowledge base can thus be used to standardize the *judgmental* knowledge with which physicians may varyingly interpret written protocol guidelines (Musen et al., 1986).

Originally designed as a time-shared program on a large, central computer (Shortliffe et al., 1981), ONCOCIN recently has been reimplemented for use on workstations (Xerox 1100 series computers). The new system incorporates a completely revised scheme for protocol knowledge representation (Musen et al., 1985), as well as a database component that services time-oriented queries from the ONCOCIN inference engine (Kahn, M. G., et al., 1985). I shall describe the details of the current ONCOCIN implementation in Chapter 5.

Knowledge acquisition for the mainframe version of ONCOCIN was accomplished using traditional methods. Two computer scientists, who served as both programmers and knowledge engineers, worked with a Stanford oncology fellow for 2 years encoding the original knowledge base of 23 similar protocols for lymphoma. Although the computer scientists spent a great deal of this time refining the ONCOCIN inference engine, the later addition of three protocols for the adjuvant chemotherapy of breast cancer still required

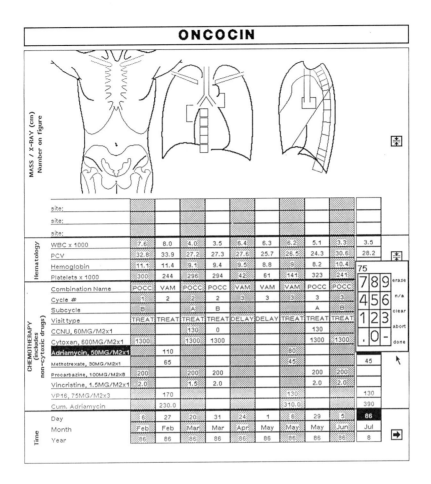

Figure 4.1: The ONCOCIN User Interface

Physicians enter patient-specific data collected during each clinic visit directly into the computer via a graphical form that resembles the traditional paper flowsheet used for data collection. The form is divided into a number of sections—for laboratory data, toxicity data, and so on. ONCOCIN reasons with the data entered for the current visit, the past patient data, and its knowledge of the protocol to arrive at a recommendation for therapy. The system prints its recommendation in the section of the flowsheet where the physician would ordinarily record the treatment administered for each visit. In the figure, the physician is choosing to modify ONCOCIN's recommended dose of Adriamycin; he is thus entering an alternate dose using a software input device known as a *register*.

several more months of tedious work. In part, the enormous expense of knowledge engineering for the original ONCOCIN prototype made one critic suggest that the system might be trying to do "too much" (Pollak, 1983).

In the workstation version of ONCOCIN, protocols are added to the knowledge base largely using the OPAL knowledge-editing tool (see Chapter 6). OPAL allows physicians to work independently of knowledge engineers, updating ONCOCIN's content knowledge of oncology protocols. The knowledge editors generated by PROTÉGÉ have much of OPAL's functionality, but are tailored for a variety of clinical-trial applications and are not limited to oncology.

4.3   Computer-Aided Design of Clinical Trials

Just as computers can play an important role in the execution and analysis of clinical studies, they may one day be helpful in the initial design of research protocols. Although no computer systems have yet been used by medical researchers to lay out the specifications for new clinical trials, computer-based tools have proven themselves invaluable in a large number of analogous design problems.

In the past 20 years, engineers have done considerable work in the application of computers to assist in the fabrication of physical objects and devices. Computer-aided design and manufacturing systems (CAD/CAM) have revolutionized the production of many kinds of products, from automobiles to printed circuits. CAD/CAM systems anticipate the design problems inherent in some particular creative process, and provide application-specific mechanisms to help the user to refine the design plans. These systems best offset their large development costs when the design process being automated is (1) labor-intensive, (2) intolerant of errors, and (3) repetitively applied to similar tasks.

The development of research protocols for clinical trials possesses the same three features that make computer-aided design of physical objects so attractive. First, a large amount of human labor clearly is required to design current protocols. Clinical investigators must anticipate all the contingencies that will necessitate modifications in the treatment, make sure that adequate data will be collected to identify when patients enter

94

one of these contingent states, and specify the modifications to the protocol that should be made in each case. Second, whereas protocols must be free of errors and ambiguities to be internally valid, many clinical studies nevertheless have significant design flaws. Some of these weaknesses reflect overt, pragmatic decisions made by the developers of the protocol; others, unfortunately, are unintentional (Mosteller et al., 1983). Third, new clinical studies constantly are being developed on the basis of previous experimental findings. The specification of clinical trials is thus an inherently repetitive process. Computer programs can exploit the consistency of structure from protocol to protocol when assisting in the design process.

Masand (1982) was among the first to suggest that sufficient structure existed in cancer protocols for computers to aid oncologists in the development of new treatment plans. He developed a prototype program, called the *Protocol Writer's Assistant,* that solicited partial specifications for new treatment plans for lung cancer. The system prompted the user for potential stratification criteria (patient variables recorded on entry into the study that are required for later statistical analysis) and the names of the different treatment arms. A single chemotherapy could be assigned to each treatment arm, with provisions made for modification of the therapy based on changes in the extent of a patient's tumor. Masand's program contained additional domain knowledge concerning drug toxicities. For each drug in a chemotherapy, the system would note potential toxicities and would ask the user for appropriate actions should a toxic effect occur. The program also would verify that appropriate laboratory tests had been incorporated into the protocol to monitor for the adverse conditions.

Masand's work demonstrated that large portions of oncology protocols could be regarded as instances of a generic protocol model. Thus, the Protocol Writer's Assistant could prompt the user for the values needed to instantiate[7] the model, defining a new clinical study. The same model-driven approach is used by OPAL and by the knowledge editors generated by PROTÉGÉ. Although Masand's model of lung-cancer protocols was limited, his program did show how certain AI techniques such as frame instantiation and constraint satisfaction could be helpful to physicians in the design of clinical trials. The

---

[7]The process of creating an instance of an abstract concept is called *instantiation.*

output of Masand's program was not intended to serve as the knowledge base for an advice system.

Goldberger and Schwenn (1983) also have examined the design of clinical protocols, and have proposed a system of hand-held microcomputers to assist rural health workers in developing countries with diagnosis and treatment. A program called MEdit allows physicians to construct graphical flowcharts of clinical algorithms on the display screen of a professional workstation using a boxes-and-arrows notation.[8] The boxes in the diagram contain the text of the directions to be given to the patient or the questions to be asked; the arrows point to boxes for further questions depending on the patient's responses. MEdit converts the flowchart representation into an internal format that can be interpreted by a program called MEDIC, which runs on a portable microprocessor. The developers intend to use MEdit-defined algorithms to assist village health workers in the third world, just as clinical algorithms direct paramedical personnel in industrial countries.

Like Masand's program, OPAL allows a user to define oncology protocols for ONCOCIN in terms of a predefined model. The model is presented as a series of graphical forms on a computer display. Instantiation takes place as the user fills in the blanks in the forms. For the more arbitrary *procedural* aspects of the protocol (that is, the sequence of chemotherapies and radiation treatments over time), a graphical flowchart language like that in MEdit is used to draw a diagram of the protocol's top-level algorithm. OPAL was originally developed as a knowledge-acquisition tool, not specifically as a protocol-design aid. As emphasized in Chapter 2, however, knowledge acquisition is fundamentally a problem in design. A language that is good for designing protocol knowledge bases also should be good for designing protocols themselves. At the knowledge level, the two design tasks are equivalent.

Similarly, protocol developers can view PROTÉGÉ as a tool for generating not only programs to acquire the knowledge of existing protocols, but also programs to assist researchers in the authoring of new clinical studies. In the computer-aided design of physical objects such as printed circuits, the design specifications developed with the computer often can be used automatically in the manufacturing process. Analogously, in the design

---

[8]H. Goldberger, personal communication, 1986.

of new protocols using programs created by PROTÉGÉ, the design specifications can be incorporated automatically into the knowledge bases of expert systems. The methodology described in this book fosters the design of both clinical trials and clinical-trial advice systems. Thus, futurists can imagine the dissemination of research protocols in the form of *expert systems* with precise knowledge bases, rather than as text documents that individual physicians might subsequently interpret in varying ways. Formalizing protocol knowledge using tools such as those created by PROTÉGÉ could thus have benefits for clinical research in many areas of medicine.

5 The Inference Engine: ONCOCIN

The concepts in PROTÉGÉ sometimes are difficult to appreciate intuitively when they are described without reference to the previous work that served as a foundation for this book. A discussion that starts at the ground level and then works its way up is much easier to understand, particularly because it is possible to keep concrete examples in mind. PROTÉGÉ generates knowledge editors that have much of the functionality of OPAL, the knowledge-acquisition program developed for ONCOCIN. Understanding ONCOCIN makes it possible to apprehend the ideas in OPAL. Knowledge of OPAL makes it easy to understand PROTÉGÉ. Accordingly, I start at the ground level in this chapter by reviewing the implementation of ONCOCIN. In the following chapter, I discuss OPAL. I describe PROTÉGÉ itself in Chapter 7.

Because ONCOCIN represents the results of nearly one decade of work, I can provide only a brief overview here. My intention is to summarize those aspects of ONCOCIN that are important for understanding how PROTÉGÉ generates advice systems based on the ONCOCIN architecture.[1] I shall therefore tend to simplify certain aspects that are not relevant to the current research. More complete information about ONCOCIN can be found in the references cited.

The ONCOCIN system is composed of four parts: (1) A knowledge base of oncology protocols, (2) an inference engine called the *Reasoner*, (3) a database of time-ordered patient data, and (4) a graphical user interface called the *Interviewer*. Figure 5.1 shows the relationships among these components, each of which I shall discuss.

---

[1] As I described in Chapter 1, PROTÉGÉ is used in conjunction with a domain-independent version of ONCOCIN called *e-ONCOCIN*. Because the inference engine and user interface in e-ONCOCIN are nearly identical to those in ONCOCIN, the discussion in this chapter applies to both systems.

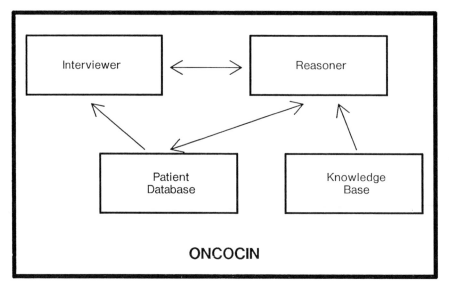

Figure 5.1: ONCOCIN System Architecture

ONCOCIN contains four separate modules. The *knowledge base* consists of symbolic representations for the oncology protocols known to the system. The *Reasoner* is the inference engine that generates recommendations for therapy. The *Interviewer* is a graphical interface that (1) displays past patient data for review by the physician, (2) solicits current patient data, and (3) presents the Reasoner's treatment recommendation to the physician at the conclusion of the session. Both the Reasoner and the Interviewer require access to a patient's past data. This information is stored in a separate time-oriented *patient database.*

5.1   The ONCOCIN Knowledge Base

Three different kinds of representation are used to encode protocol knowledge for ONCO-CIN: (1) frames,[2] (2) production rules, and (3) augmented transition networks (ATNs) called *generators.* The particular representation employed depends on the kind of knowledge being encoded.

---

[2] *Frames* are a common form of knowledge representation in AI, popularized by Minsky (1975). A frame is a data structure that denotes some concept. A frame has *slots,* where each slot denotes some attribute of the concept represented by the frame. A prototypical concept is represented by a frame and its associated slots. (For example, a frame for the abstract concept *automobile* might have slots such as *year* and *model.*) If a computer program assigns *values* to the slots, the frame then denotes a particular *instance* of the concept (for example, a 1978 Cutlass). The value of a slot can be any kind of symbol including a pointer to another frame instance. The process of assigning values to the slots of a frame is called *instantiation.*

5.1.1 Frames

The *structure* of a protocol is captured by creating a hierarchy of frames using an object-oriented language called OZONE (Lane, 1986).[3] The knowledge base thus contains instances of a *protocol* frame for each oncology protocol in the knowledge base. Each chemotherapy (drug combination) is similarly represented by a unique frame of the *chemotherapy* class. Each frame of a given class has the same types of attributes, although the *values* for many of the attributes vary from instance to instance. There are additional classes of frames that represent drugs and radiation treatments. Links among the individual frames are used to denote the compositional relationships among the parts of a particular treatment plan (Figure 5.2). (The compositional relationships also are called *part-of links*.) Thus, each protocol frame points to chemotherapy and radiotherapy frames, because protocols are made up of specific chemotherapies and radiotherapies. Each chemotherapy frame in turn points to a number of drug frames. Apart from this compositional hierarchy is an additional frame that contains general knowledge about the action of visiting the oncology clinic. This *visit* frame is common to all protocols in the system.

5.1.2 Parameters

Each frame in the knowledge base has a number of attributes that describe the treatment modality represented by the frame. These attributes are referred to as *parameters*.[4] For example, all chemotherapies have a certain *duration* and all drugs have a certain *dose*. At the start of an interactive session with ONCOCIN, many of these parameters do not have values, and it thus becomes the goal of the ONCOCIN Reasoner to arrive at values for them.

---

[3] *Object-oriented programming languages* (see Cox, 1986; Stefik and Bobrow, 1986) often are used to implement frame systems. Note that the word *frame* refers to a functional description (the notion of prototype classes, slots, and values), whereas the word *object* denotes a particular kind of data structure in which data, organized as slots and values, are stored with the program code that pertains to those data. In practice, the two words often are used interchangeably. Because ONCOCIN also encodes rules and generators using objects, I will consistently use the word *frame* when discussing the structural portion of the knowledge base.

[4] This terminology is a vestige of the prototype implementation of ONCOCIN (Shortliffe et al., 1981), which was based largely on EMYCIN-like production rules that concluded values for special variables called *parameters*. In the current system, the parameter data structures are still present, but each is linked to a slot in one or more of the frames.

101

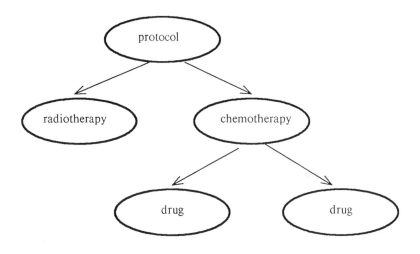

Figure 5.2: Hierarchy of Frames in ONCOCIN

The ONCOCIN knowledge base contains a hierarchy of frames that reflect the components of oncology treatment plans. A protocol comprises specific radiation treatments
and chemotherapies. The chemotherapies are made up of various drugs.

By concluding parameter values, ONCOCIN ultimately arrives at its treatment recommen-

dation. (For example, if ONCOCIN concluded that the parameter DRUG.DOSE.TO.GIVE

associated with the drug Adriamycin had the value 50, the program ultimately would

recommend that the physician administer 50 mg of that drug.)

ONCOCIN can ascertain values for its parameters because each parameter is associated

with a list of *methods*—a means by which the Reasoner can establish that parameter's

value. One method in ONCOCIN is simply to ask the user for the value. In the case of

the laboratory data that are entered into the system by the physician, ONCOCIN can

always ask for the value. The principal method for such parameters is therefore "ASK."

Other parameters have their values computed internally by ONCOCIN using one of two

additional types of methods: (1) production rules or (2) generators.

5.1.3 Production Rules

The production rules in ONCOCIN (Figure 5.3) contain a premise and a conclusion. The

premise may have two parts, a *precondition* and a *condition*. Both parts of the premise

ONCOCIN Rule:

PRECONDITION:

CONDITION: (NCOMPARE > CREATININE.VAL 1.5)

CONCLUSION: (DRUG.DOSE.TO.GIVE
                       (PERCENT.OF
                       (VALUE.OF DRUG.DOSE.TO.GIVE
                           PREVIOUS
                           (DRUG (DRUG.NAME)))
             50))

English Translation:

"If the serum creatinine is greater than 1.5 mg/dl, then the drug dose to give is 50 percent of the previous dose."

Figure 5.3: Sample ONCOCIN Production Rule

This rule is used as a method to conclude the value of a parameter called DRUG.DOSE.TO.GIVE. This parameter is associated with the frames for all drugs in ONCOCIN, although the rule shown here applies to only the frame for the drug *methotrexate* within a particular protocol. The rule has a condition that queries whether CREATININE.VAL (a parameter associated with the *visit* frame) currently has a value greater than 1.5 mg/dl. If the condition of the rule is satisfied, the value of DRUG.DOSE.TO.GIVE is reset to 50 percent of the value that this parameter had the last time the drug was administered. This rule lacks a *precondition,* and thus will always reach its conclusion whenever the *condition* is true.

check to see whether statements about indicated parameters are true (for example, whether a certain parameter has a certain value). In the case of the *condition* part of the premise, if ONCOCIN does not know whether the statements about the given parameters are true, the system will use backward chaining to see whether other rules in the knowledge base can establish the missing parameter values. In the case of the optional *precondition,* however, no backward chaining is initiated if the truth of the statement is unknown; the rule simply fails to reach a conclusion.

A production rule's conclusion assigns values to ONCOCIN parameters. The conclusion also may have an *action* component that invokes LISP functions directly, if necessary, to achieve certain desired side effects. The conclusion is executed only if both the *precondition* and the *condition* of the rule are true.

Although rules in ONCOCIN are in many ways similar to rules in EMYCIN, ONCO-CIN's rule language does not include a mechanism for representing uncertainty expressly in the concluded values of parameters. Because the data entered by the physician are presumed to be correct, and because oncology protocols are categorical in their guidelines, there is no need for the system to be concerned with probabilistic values.

5.1.4   Generators

The generators are used to encode sequences of operations over time (for example, the ordering of chemotherapy and radiotherapy treatments for a given protocol). They are encoded as a table of the possible states that might be encountered during these sequences of operations. Each entry in the table contains a unique name, followed by a list of possible transitions to other states (Figure 5.4). Each transition has an associated *condition*, written in the same language as are the conditions in ONCOCIN's production rules. If the condition for a particular transition evaluates to *true,* the transition will be executed; otherwise, the next transition in the list will be considered. A transition may be *augmented* in that it may indicate new actions for ONCOCIN to take, such as the administration of a specific chemotherapy treatment. (The need to commence such an action causes ON-COCIN to suspend traversal of the state table.) Each time ONCOCIN is run, it resumes executing transitions in the generator starting from where it left off during the previous session. Accordingly, a designated ONCOCIN parameter serves as the *state variable* for each generator, allowing the system to keep track of the current generator state for each patient.

In summary, the ONCOCIN knowledge base for a given protocol can be viewed as a hierarchy of frames of different classes. Each frame has several *parameters,* the values of which must be concluded. Linked with each parameter is an ordered list of methods that the Reasoner can use to conclude the parameter's value. The methods include production rules, generators, and queries to the user. Defining a protocol knowledge base thus requires (1) creating the frame hierarchy and (2) specifying the required rules and generators.

104

NAME: GENERATOR
STATE VARIABLE: PROTOCOL.STATE
STATES:

START/1	CONDITION: *true* NEXT STATE: **CHEMO/2** ACTIONS: *none* TRANSITION TYPE: NON-RETURN
CHEMO/2	CONDITION: *true* NEXT STATE: **CHEMO/3** ACTIONS: *VAM Chemotherapy* TRANSITION TYPE: RETURN
CHEMO/3	CONDITION: *true* NEXT STATE: **DECIDE/4** ACTIONS: *POCC Chemotherapy* TRANSITION TYPE: RETURN
DECIDE/4	CONDITION: *If* CR *is false* NEXT STATE: **CHEMO/3** ACTIONS: *none* TRANSITION TYPE: NON-RETURN
	CONDITION: *If* CR *is true* NEXT STATE: **STOP/5** ACTIONS: *none* TRANSITION TYPE: NON-RETURN
STOP/5	CONDITION: *true* NEXT STATE: *none* ACTIONS: *STOP* TRANSITION TYPE: RETURN

Figure 5.4: Stylized ONCOCIN Generator

A generator contains the name of a *state variable* (here the parameter PROTOCOL.STATE) and a *transition table.* Each state in the table has a unique name followed by a list of possible transitions. If the *condition* associated with a transition evaluates as *true*, the transition is executed, and any associated actions are applied. When a transition of type RETURN is encountered, execution of the generator is suspended; when the same patient returns for a subsequent consultation, execution of the generator resumes from where it left off. The simplified generator shown here specifies that patients receive a single cycle of VAM chemotherapy followed by repeated cycles of POCC chemotherapy until the value of the parameter *CR* (complete response) is concluded to be *true.*

5.2 The Reasoner

The goal of the ONCOCIN Reasoner is to construct a plan for treatment whenever a patient visits the oncology clinic. Whereas the protocol itself predefines a broad plan for the therapy to be given over time, ONCOCIN must develop the detailed plan needed for treatment at any particular instant. These two kinds of plans must not be confused. The general, longitudinal plan of the protocol is predetermined and thus is stored in the ONCOCIN knowledge base. The specific treatment for particular visits, on the other hand, must be *computed* by the ONCOCIN Reasoner, which refines what is initially a *skeletal* treatment plan. The process of entering patient data and receiving a recommendation from the system regarding specific treatment is called a *consultation*.

The structure of the ONCOCIN knowledge base plays an important function in controlling the system's inference during each consultation. The implicit links between the frames that define the compositional relationships among elements in the protocol serve as a road map for the Reasoner (Figure 5.5). The program starts at the top of the hierarchy of frames and successively attempts to instantiate each frame by invoking the methods that apply to the frame's parameters. (If it is impossible to conclude the value of some parameter because ONCOCIN is missing certain information, the Reasoner will make a note of this fact and will attempt to determine the value later.) One of the parameters associated with each frame in the knowledge base is used to redirect the Reasoner's attention. Concluding a value for this parameter establishes the relevant links to the frames that lie *beneath* the current frame in the planning hierarchy (given the current situation). For a *protocol* frame, this parameter may designate instances of *chemotherapy* and *radiotherapy* frames; for a *chemotherapy* frame, this parameter may point to specific *drugs*. ONCOCIN then examines these other frames and attempts to find values for each component's parameters. Eventually, there are no more frames in the hierarchy that require instantiation, and the reasoning process terminates. The program's recommendation to the physician is embedded in the values of certain parameters that were concluded as the treatment plan was instantiated. Accordingly, the values of these parameters are displayed on the workstation screen for the physician's review.

106

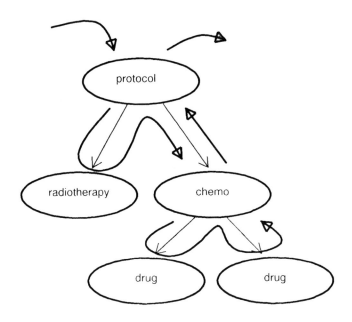

Figure 5.5: Control of the Consultation in ONCOCIN

ONCOCIN arrives at a recommendation by successively instantiating the components of a treatment plan, by concluding values for certain attributes of each frame in the knowledge base (*parameters*). ONCOCIN attends to each component in the treatment plan by traversing the frame hierarchy in a depth-first manner.

At the symbol level, the ONCOCIN Reasoner selects a path through a network of frames, concludes values for attributes of those frames, and displays the values of a subset of those attributes to the user. At the *knowledge level,* however, ONCOCIN is constructing a solution to a problem. The system is generating a plan.

ONCOCIN's problem-solving method is a form of *skeletal-plan refinement* (Friedland and Iwasaki, 1985). Starting with an abstract, incompletely specified plan (such as "Give treatment according to protocol"), ONCOCIN attempts to refine the plan by filling in gaps based on available data (for example, "The protocol should be Number 20-83-1"). Even when these gaps are filled in, the plan still may be underspecified—in which case ONCOCIN establishes whether the plan can be decomposed into constituent parts *appropriate for the current situation* (for example, "Give treatment according to protocol" might be decomposed into (1) "Terminate VAM chemotherapy" and (2) "Administer PCI radiotherapy"). The component plans themselves may be underspecified and thus may require refinement based on available data, possibly involving decomposition into *their own* components. The refinement process continues until there are no more plans to be decomposed.

This skeletal-planning method has served as the basis for a number of important AI systems, including Silverman's (1975) Digitalis Therapy Advisor and the Friedland's (1979) MOLGEN program for designing experiments in molecular genetics. In these applications, as in ONCOCIN, the method assumes that a basic plan outline already exists and that the system will concentrate on filling in the details. Unlike other problem-solving methods for constructing solutions, skeletal-plan refinement does not require that one generate complete plans from scratch. Because the skeletal-plan components are instantiated in a strictly sequential fashion, the method can easily fail if the individual planning steps interact significantly (see Stefik, 1981). ONCOCIN, for example, requires a special backtracking mechanism that allows it to recover should the constraints that govern a previously instantiated part of the plan later become violated as new component plans are refined (Tu et al., 1989).

5.3 The Patient Database

ONCOCIN's planning task is to determine the proper therapy for a given patient at a particular instant in time. Precisely what such therapy should entail is a function of the protocol, the patient's current condition (as reflected in data entered by the physician), and the patient's past responses to treatment. The Reasoner must therefore have access to data from previous patient visits when formulating its recommendation. In addition, all the data entered into ONCOCIN have to be saved for statistical analysis by clinical researchers at the conclusion of the protocol.

Accordingly, ONCOCIN maintains a database of information on each patient (Kahn. M. G., et al., 1985). ONCOCIN stores the values of all parameters in the database each time it finishes a consultation. These parameters include the clinical data entered by the physician and details of the treatment administered to the patient, as well as all the

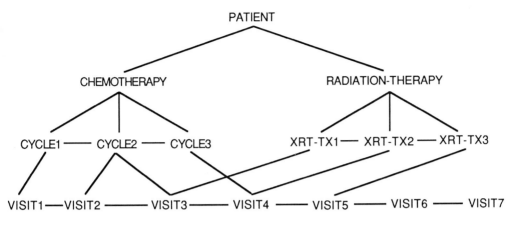

Figure 5.6: ONCOCIN Patient Database

Time-ordered data on each patient are stored in a database that is accessed by both the Reasoner and the Interviewer modules in ONCOCIN. The treatment modalities that were in effect during each visit are represented explicitly in the database. The system maintains connections among the data for each visit and a network of nodes that denote the temporal sequence of administered treatments. This *temporal network* serves as an index into the data that expedites many of the Reasoner's queries. (Source: Kahn, M. G., et al., 1985, p. 174)

other concluded values that are used internally by ONCOCIN. These data are saved separately for each patient in the system, and are organized chronologically according to visit date. Imposed on this linear sequence of patient data is a structure that improves ONCOCIN's efficiency in searching the database (Figure 5.6). Because the individual treatment modalities (chemotherapies, radiotherapies, and so on) that were being given during each patient visit are represented explicitly, certain queries from the Reasoner are greatly facilitated. For example, the rule in Figure 5.3 requires that ONCOCIN retrieve the value for the parameter DRUG.DOSE.TO.GIVE at the last time that a particular drug was given. Rather than searching through the database visit by visit to find this information, ONCOCIN can access the necessary data directly.

5.4   The Interviewer

ONCOCIN incorporates a separate module that is responsible for the graphical user interface (Lane et al., 1986). This *Interviewer* component reads in past data from the patient database and displays them in a time-oriented spreadsheet format that mimics the paper flowsheets typically maintained for cancer patients (see Figure 4.1, page 93). The Interviewer is responsible for soliciting the current patient data from the physician and sending the data to the Reasoner for processing. When the Reasoner arrives at its recommendation, the Interviewer displays the results in the "therapy" section of the graphical flowsheet (Gerring et al., 1982).

Each datum entered into the Interviewer represents the value of some ONCOCIN parameter. The data may be entered using customized graphical menus or special software input devices called *registers* (Lane et al., 1986). ONCOCIN maintains data structures in its knowledge base that define certain attributes of its parameters. The Interviewer examines these data structures to determine the mechanics of how users should enter parameter values into the computer. The parameter specifications also tell the Interviewer what ranges of values it should question as possibly erroneous and how it should label the parameter on the flowsheet.

5.5   Summary

The ONCOCIN inference engine, called the *Reasoner,* communicates with a separate module that manages the user interface, called the *Interviewer.* The Interviewer solicits the values for certain parameters related to the current patient visit and passes those values to the Reasoner for processing. The Reasoner constructs a treatment plan by successively instantiating frames in its knowledge base, using rules and generators to conclude the values of those parameters not supplied by the Interviewer. The rules and generators often need to know the values of certain parameters during *previous* patient visits. The Reasoner accesses a custom-tailored time-oriented database for this purpose. The same database also is used by the Interviewer to display past patient data on the workstation screen. A

110

the end of an ONCOCIN consultation, the Reasoner sends to the Interviewer the values of those parameters that establish the concluded treatment plan. The program's recommendation is shown to the physician, who may either accept ONCOCIN's proposed treatment or enter an alternate plan.

I emphasize that ONCOCIN has been tailored for the domain of clinical trials in oncology. The appearance of the Interviewer's graphical flowsheet, the classes of frames in the knowledge base, and the specifications for ONCOCIN's *parameters* all have been inscribed into the system by knowledge engineers. These items are common to all cancer protocols and are considered invariant in the way that ONCOCIN abstracts the oncology domain. As a result, to adapt the version of ONCOCIN now running in the Stanford oncology clinic for protocols in other application areas, we would have to reprogram the system.

An important goal of the research described in this book is to provide a general mechanism by which ONCOCIN can be applied outside of the oncology domain. Just as it was possible to abstract the task-specific MYCIN program into EMYCIN, it has been possible to take ONCOCIN and removed its cancer-therapy knowledge base to create the program called e-ONCOCIN. Development of e-ONCOCIN required changing a small number of LISP functions in the ONCOCIN Reasoner and Interviewer so that all oncology-specific assumptions were replaced by references to the explicit data structures that PROTÉGÉ generates (see Section 8.4).[5] In e-ONCOCIN, the appearance of the Interviewer flowsheet, the knowledge base, and all parameters are defined via declarative representations that can be modified easily. In future chapters, I shall use the term *e-ONCOCIN* when referring to this more generic system. The name *ONCOCIN* applies to only the oncology-specific consultation program that predates my research.

---

[5] These revisions to ONCOCIN were performed by Samson Tu and Cliff Wulfman in less than one week.

6 OPAL: A Knowledge Editor for Clinical Trials in Oncology

Each protocol in the ONCOCIN knowledge base has roughly the same format. The same classes of frames are used in different protocols. There are similar types of rules and generators. The protocols in ONCOCIN are similar at the *knowledge level* as well. They are made up of analogous chemotherapies and radiotherapies. Whereas individual protocols may be very complex, collectively the protocols are all variations on a theme. The protocols in ONCOCIN are *congeners*.

This consistency at the knowledge level has been exploited in the development of OPAL, a knowledge editor that adopts a model of treatment planning in oncology as its conceptual model for the knowledge in ONCOCIN. In this chapter, I shall discuss the motivation that lead to the development of OPAL, and shall describe the program's task-oriented knowledge presentation.

6.1 The Task Model in OPAL

Oncology protocols are sufficiently alike that it has been possible to develop a model of the concepts typically present in cancer-treatment plans (Musen et al., 1987). The model is a set of terms and relationships by which a person can specify the *task* of planning cancer treatment for a given patient visit. For example, the terms of the model allow definition of what chemotherapies are to be given and what treatment modifications should be considered. However, the model says nothing about the steps by which an oncologist actually arrives at a treatment recommendation, as there is no explicit notion of the *problem-solving methods* that are required. The model merely addresses the structure of the task itself.

A task model can play an important role in defining systems at the knowledge level. As I discussed in Section 3.1.1, knowledge-level analysis requires that a system builder describe (1) the task to be done, (2) the problem-solving methods to be used, and (3) the mapping that applies the methods to the task. Suppose the system builder starts with an abstract model of some class of tasks (in our case, a model of oncology protocols *in general*). If the developer knows in advance what specific problem-solving method might be applicable (for example, skeletal-plan refinement) and can define a mapping between the general task model and the method, then completing the knowledge-level description for a particular application is straightforward: The task model needs to be *instantiated*. The utility of being able to instantiate a task model is the motivation behind OPAL—and behind the knowledge editors generated by PROTÉGÉ as well. In all these programs, users define knowledge by filling out a model of the application task to be done. The mapping between the task description and the problem-solving method can be handled transparently by the system, because the *process knowledge* required for the application has been predefined. Instantiating the task model requires that the user specify knowledge about only *content*.

In the remainder of this chapter, I describe OPAL's use of the task model in acquiring knowledge of new cancer protocols. As my goal is to lay the groundwork required for understanding PROTÉGÉ, my emphasis will be on the *model*, not on the OPAL system itself. Details concerning OPAL's implementation have been described previously (Musen et al., 1988a; Musen et al., 1988b; Walton et al., 1987).

6.2   Components of the Model

As I discussed in Section 3.1.3, *ontological analysis* (Alexander et al., 1986) has been proposed recently as a technique for developing models of application tasks. The notions of static ontology, dynamic ontology, and epistemic ontology suggested by Alexander and colleagues are useful when describing the task model in OPAL. Although I have not performed a formal analysis using these authors' techniques, I shall attempt to highlight the corre-

114

spondences between OPAL's task model and what an ontological analysis of ONCOCIN might reveal.

6.2.1 Planning Entities and Their Relationships

The first component of the task model consists of an identification of the possible entities in the application area and of the relationships among them (the *static ontology*). In the ONCOCIN domain, the entities are the therapeutic elements that make up the planning problem (see Figure 5.2). The "relationships" are defined in part by the composition hierarchy that specifies how each element may be defined in terms of more specific components. Each of the entities in the model has predefined attributes (for example, drugs have *dosages* and *routes of administration*). Part of OPAL's job is to establish the treatment entities required in the particular protocol being entered and to determine values for each entity's attributes.

The OPAL user interface consists primarily of a number of graphical "forms" that facilitate instantiation of the task model. For example, the OPAL form in Figure 6.1 allows the user to specify the names of the individual drugs that make up a particular chemotherapy. The program presumes that chemotherapies and drugs are entities in the domain and that they are related compositionally. When a user interacts with OPAL, he enters the names of the drugs into the blanks of the graphical form by selecting appropriate choices from a predefined menu. If a required drug does not appear in the list, the user can type in the drug name from the keyboard. (It will then be added to the menu.)

OPAL uses an *intermediate knowledge representation* to store the task model as it is instantiated via the graphical forms (Figure 6.2). Thus, when the user enters new knowledge into OPAL or revises existing specifications, the intermediate representation (not the ONCOCIN knowledge base) is updated. The intermediate representation consists of a system of frames that, unlike the knowledge base, *directly represents the terms and relationships of the task model in OPAL*. OPAL ultimately uses the intermediate representation to produce the frames, production rules, and generators that constitute the knowledge base. It is more efficient for OPAL to build and edit this frame-based representation of its task model than for it to use the heterogeneous symbol-level structures in ONCOCIN.

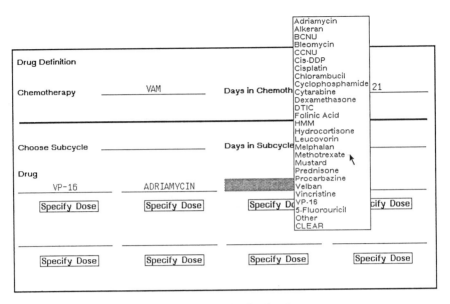

Figure 6.1: Sample OPAL Form

This table, which has been reproduced directly from the computer screen, displays information concerning the drug combination "VAM," which consists of VP-16, Adriamycin, and methotrexate. The drug methotrexate is about to be selected from a menu of all drugs known to the system. For each entered drug, OPAL creates a separate frame in the intermediate representation of the ONCOCIN knowledge base. These drug frames are linked to the frame for VAM chemotherapy, thus defining their context.

Of course, it would be possible to use the intermediate representation *directly* as the knowledge base for a consultation program. Such an approach would require a highly customized, *task-specific* inference mechanism (as in Gale, 1987). Encoding knowledge of the task domain procedurally within the inference mechanism would have the disadvantage of limiting the system's use to a single application area. The knowledge representation used in ONCOCIN, on the other hand, supports an inference mechanism that can be applied to a variety of tasks. Without this task independence, it would have been impossible to develop PROTÉGÉ.

Whenever the user fills in a blank requesting a drug ·name, knowledge stored in the definition of the graphical form causes OPAL to create a new drug frame in the intermediate representation and to link it to the frame for the related chemotherapy. Additional

```
(OBJECT  (SYSTEM
              (NAME DRUG13)
              (LINKS (DRUG))
              (CREATED  "8-Oct-85 10:17:01" by dmc)
              (EDITED   "2-May-86 08:36:09" by mm))
          (VARIABLE
              (IDS.TYPE DRUG)
              (DRUG.NAME METHOTREXATE)
              (ABBREV MTX)
              (DOSAGE ((DOSEREC (30 MG/M2)
                                NIL
                                (NIL NIL)
                                1 1 IVPUSH (5 MG)
                                NIL NIL NIL)))
              (DELAY  (DELAY NIL 50 STD NIL 75 MINIMUM))
              (CLINACTIONLIST  ((CLINACT EFFUSIONS
                                           ((GIVEACTION 0 STD 1 MINIMUM)
                                            (DISPLAYACTION
                                                "Hold methotrexate because of
                                                  effusions")))
                                (CLINACT (BONE.MARROW.INVOLVED FIRSTVISIT)
                                           ((GIVEACTION 100 STD 1 OVERRIDE)))))
              (LABACTIONLIST  (SPARSETABLE 2 NIL NIL
                                  ((CREAT.SERUM.VAL
                                      (1 (LABACT CREAT.SERUM.VAL GT NIL 1.5
                                          ((GIVEACTION 50 PREV 1 MINIMUM)))))))))))
```

Figure 6.2: Portion of OPAL Intermediate Knowledge Representation

The graphical forms in OPAL store data in a frame-based intermediate knowledge representation. This figure shows part of this representation for the drug methotrexate as used in a protocol for the treatment of lung cancer. Programs that incorporate knowledge of both the structure of this oncology-specific representation and the structure of the ONCOCIN knowledge base translate frames such as this into ONCOCIN frames and rules. For example, the slot labeled LABACTIONLIST is translated into the ONCOCIN rule shown in Figure 5.3 (page 103). The contents of the slot are derived from the OPAL form in Figure 6.7. The slot labeled DOSAGE, on the other hand, gets its values from the OPAL form in Figure 6.3.

forms in OPAL contain blanks that can define values for the slots in the generated frames. For instance, selecting the box labeled *"Specify Dose"* beneath one of the drug names in Figure 6.1 causes another form to be displayed in which certain properties of the designated drug can be entered (Figure 6.3). By noting the pathway used to access the form in Figure 6.3 (that is, which box in Figure 6.1 was selected), OPAL can store the knowledge specified via the second form in the appropriate drug frame. Thus, the user's path through the various forms in the system determines the particular entities to which entered knowledge is related at each step. Furthermore, whenever knowledge is specified graphically using the OPAL forms, it is simultaneously translated internally to the intermediate representation.

The graphical forms in OPAL provide an efficient means for physicians to instantiate the entities in the therapy plan. In general, each blank corresponds to a particular attribute of some entity in OPAL's task model. Whenever the user fills in a blank, the system can establish the value of the corresponding attribute. However, the "fill in the blanks approach" works for only those attributes the values of which can be easily typed at the keyboard, selected from menus, or entered using the special software input devices called *registers*. In particular, the forms-based approach breaks down when the value of an attribute represents a *procedure* (Combs et al., 1986).

6.2.2 Procedural Knowledge

OPAL's task model assumes that each *protocol* entity includes an attribute that represents the sequence of chemotherapy and radiation treatments to be administered over time. This series of steps constitutes the broad, longitudinal plan of the protocol. It is a predefined, protocol-specific procedure that ONCOCIN must follow. (As I discussed in Section 5.2, each step in this time-ordered procedure serves as the basis of a *skeletal plan* that must be refined during an ONCOCIN consultation.) Whereas the forms-based approach to knowledge entry is sufficient throughout most of OPAL, a special graphical language must be used for specification of this procedural knowledge (Musen et al., 1988b).

When the user first approaches OPAL, the workstation display is devoted to a large rectangular region within which the user will create a visual program that represents the

118

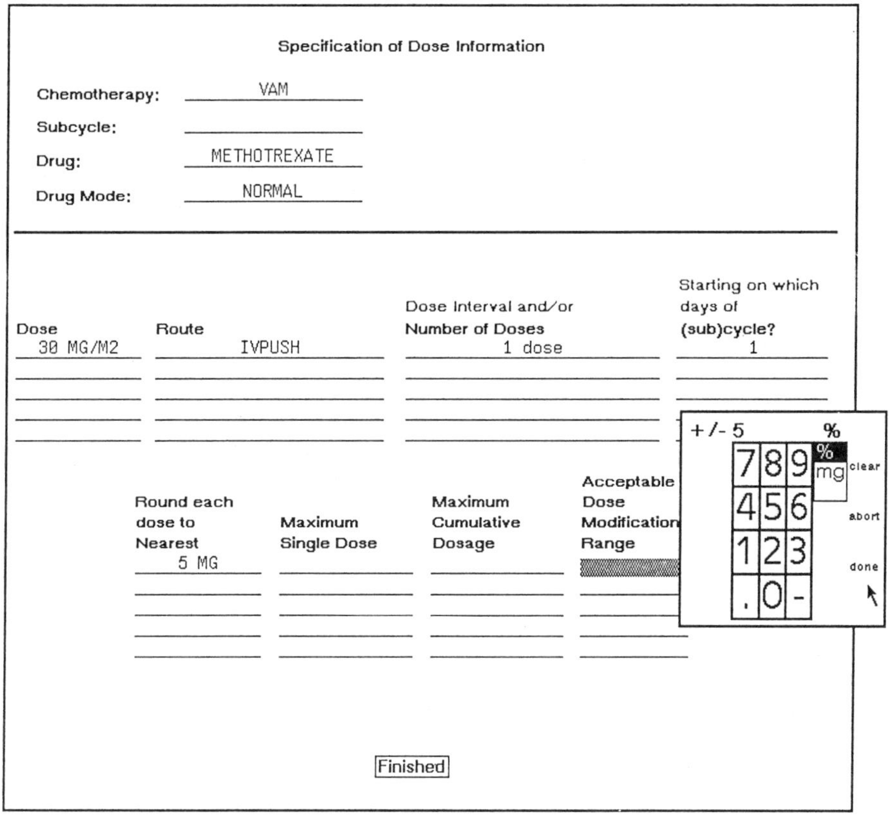

Specification of Dose Information

Chemotherapy: _____VAM_____

Subcycle: _____

Drug: ___METHOTREXATE___

Drug Mode: _____NORMAL_____

Dose	Route	Dose Interval and/or Number of Doses	Starting on which days of (sub)cycle?
30 MG/M2	IVPUSH	1 dose	1

Round each dose to Nearest	Maximum Single Dose	Maximum Cumulative Dosage	Acceptable Dose Modification Range
5 MG			

+/- 5   %

7 8 9 | %/mg | clear
4 5 6 | abort
1 2 3 | done
. 0 -

Finished

Figure 6.3: Attributes of the "Drug" Entity

This form was invoked from the one shown in Figure 6.1 when the user selected the region labeled *"Specify Dose"* beneath the blank for the drug methotrexate. The blanks in this figure allow physicians to enter knowledge about the administration of a drug in the context of a particular chemotherapy, in this case a drug combination called VAM. Using a software input device known as a *register*, the OPAL user is entering the percentage by which two individual doses of methotrexate must vary before ONCOCIN considers them to be significantly different.

sequence of chemotherapies and radiotherapies in the selected protocol.[1] Beneath this area is a palette of *icons,* graphical symbols that correspond to certain basic syntactic elements of the visual language (Figure 6.4). These icons will be used to enter the procedural knowledge, and include control operators such as START (begin execution), STOP (end execution), and DECIDE (binary branch). The basic treatment modalities CHEMOTHERAPY

---

[1]Oncologists refer to this general algorithm as the protocol's *schema.*

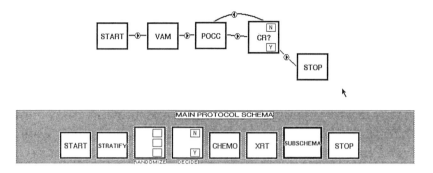

Figure 6.4: Entry of Procedural Knowledge in OPAL

The user creates a visual program corresponding to the procedural specification of chemotherapies and radiotherapies in the given protocol. Below the region where the visual program is entered is a palette of reference icons, used to add new nodes to the graph. The icons include basic control elements such as START, STOP, and DE-CIDE, as well as domain-specific processes such as cycles of chemotherapy (CHEMO) and radiation treatments (XRT, for *X-Ray Therapy*). The specification that has been constructed in this figure calls for a single cycle of VAM chemotherapy to be administered, followed by cycles of POCC chemotherapy until the parameter CR (complete response) becomes *true*. The visual program corresponds to the ONCOCIN generator shown in Figure 5.4 (page 105).

and RADIOTHERAPY also are represented.

Each time a physician selects one of the icons from the palette with the mouse pointing device, a copy of the icon appears in the main graph region. The user can position the new icon anywhere in the graph by moving the mouse. If the user adds a CHEMOTHERAPY or RADIOTHERAPY icon to the graph, the name of the particular *instance* of the treatment is selected from a menu that pops up once the icon is moved into place. The name chosen from the menu then appears as a label for the icon. In a similar manner, if the user creates a DECIDE node in the graph, a menu of ONCOCIN *parameters* is displayed. The user is asked to supply the name of the parameter the Boolean value of which, during the ONCOCIN consultation, will determine the flow of control at the branch point.

The user creates a flowchart by adding icons to the graph, positioning the icons appropriately, and drawing links between pairs of them. When the user selects with the mouse icons previously added to the graph, a menu appears to allow her to move the icon elsewhere, to erase it from the graph, or to link it to another icon. She then uses the mouse to carry out the desired operation. The user can specify concepts associated with traditional programming languages, such as sequential control, conditionality, iteration, exception handling, and concurrency, using a graphical syntax. The features of this iconic language have been described in detail previously (Musen et al., 1988b). The language also is used in a modified version in the knowledge-editing programs that are created by PROTÉGÉ (see Section 8.3 for a complete description). OPAL automatically translates the visual programs into one or more *generators* (see Figure 5.4, page 105) associated with the relevant *protocol* frame in the ONCOCIN knowledge base.

The OPAL interface allows the user to pass easily between this iconic environment for entering procedural knowledge and the forms-based part of the system. By selecting one of the CHEMOTHERAPY or RADIOTHERAPY icons in the visual-program graph using the mouse, the user can invoke all the appropriate forms needed to specify the attributes of the chosen treatment modality. Then, when using the forms-based part of the system, the user can redisplay the original procedural graph with another simple mouse operation. The flowchart thus has the additional function of serving as a menu by which a user can gain access to the appropriate forms in OPAL.

6.2.3   Task Actions

Much of ONCOCIN's skeletal planning task is predefined by the hierarchical relations among entities in the domain (see Figure 5.2). For example, initiating a plan for a new chemotherapy always requires invoking plans to administer the component drugs. Because the planning hierarchy is built into OPAL's model of the domain, the user does not have to specify such actions explicitly when she enters new protocol knowledge. These refinement operations are assumed to be constant from protocol to protocol.

On the other hand, there are several ways in which the simple instantiation of the skeletal plans defined by the domain entities can be modified. Fortunately, the list of these possible actions is small. At the knowledge level, oncologists can identify such behaviors as altering the customary dose of a drug, substituting one drug for another, or aborting or delaying chemotherapy. These actions, which form the next major component of OPAL's

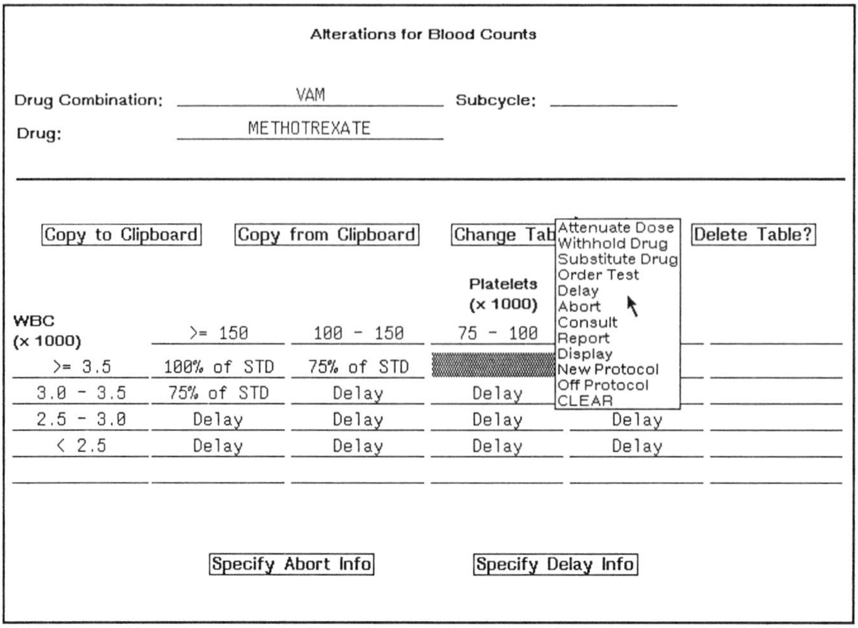

Figure 6.5: Task Actions in OPAL

Users of OPAL specify operations that modify the plan of the protocol by selecting task actions from menus, such as the one toward the right side of this figure. These actions are translated into expressions involving ONCOCIN parameters when the knowledge base is generated from the intermediate representation. The OPAL form shown here displays actions to take with the drug methotrexate in a chemotherapy called VAM. The user is about to specify that, when a patient's white-blood-cell (WBC) count is greater than or equal to 3500 and the platelet count is between 75,000 and 100,000, treatment should be delayed.

task model, would be classified by Alexander and colleagues (1986) as part of the *dynamic ontology* of the domain.

In OPAL, physicians can select the actions that form the dynamic ontology directly from menus when they enter descriptions of new protocols (Figure 6.5). They then can enter attributes of the particular action, such as how much to alter a dose or how long to delay treatment, using additional graphical forms (Figure 6.6). The subsequent translation of the intermediate knowledge representation into the knowledge base used by ONCOCIN requires conversion of these OPAL task specifications into expressions that operate on internal ONCOCIN parameters. For example, when a physician uses OPAL to specify that

122

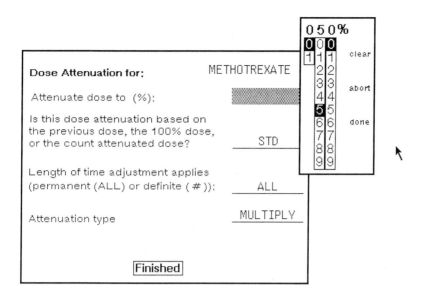

Figure 6.6: Attributes of Task Actions in OPAL

Many of the task actions entered with OPAL have attributes that must be defined by the user. As in the specification of the attributes of the treatment entities (see Figure 6.3), custom-tailored graphical forms allow the OPAL user to enter these details. The form in the figure solicits information on how ONCOCIN should attenuate the dose of a given drug.

chemotherapy should be delayed in a particular clinical context, the corresponding DELAY frame in the intermediate knowledge representation causes a number of production rules to be added to the ONCOCIN knowledge base. The right sides of these rules conclude values for ONCOCIN parameters, such as VISIT.TYPE, VISIT.NEXT.DAYS, and DRUGS.TO.GIVE. The user of OPAL, however, needs to be concerned with only those actions that are at the knowledge level.

6.2.4   Variables Predicating Actions

Just as there is a limited set of task actions, there are limited classes of *conditions* that can cause modification of the basic treatment plan. The results of laboratory tests, certain patient symptoms, and manifestations of treatment-induced toxicity (side effects) are the principal factors that can dictate particular actions in OPAL's domain.

Much of the knowledge needed to specify ONCOCIN's planning task consists of a mapping of specific conditions onto corresponding domain actions. This is part of the *epistemic ontology* of Alexander and associates (1986). OPAL simplifies entry of this portion of the knowledge by using a different graphical form for each *class* of conditions. For example, in Figure 6.7, OPAL displays a predefined list of all the relevant laboratory tests known to the system. When the user selects one of the laboratory tests, he can enter rules predicated on the results of the test. In Figure 6.7, the expert has indicated that, when a patient's serum-creatinine level is greater than 1.5 mg/dl, the dose of the drug methotrexate should be reduced by 50 percent. The values entered by the physician using OPAL correspond to a high-level production rule: **If** creatinine is greater than 1.5, **then** attenuate the dose. Because such a task specification cannot be interpreted by the ONCOCIN Reasoner, OPAL uses the intermediate representation of this rule (see Figure 6.2) to create standard ONCOCIN rules such as the one in Figure 5.3 (page 103). The ONCOCIN rule is applicable only within a specific context—in this case, when giving a particular drug (methotrexate) in a particular chemotherapy (VAM) in a particular protocol (the one being entered). As in the specification of the static attributes of domain entities (see Figure 6.3), the context of the knowledge is determined from the sequence of forms by which the user accessed the current form.

Figure 6.8 shows an analogous OPAL form that is used to define the mapping between different grades of drug toxicity (generally recorded on a five-point scale) and corresponding actions. All rules regarding actions to take because of drug toxicity are entered using this graphical form.

The forms in Figure 6.7 and Figure 6.8 are completely independent. OPAL does not at present provide a convenient mechanism to specify rules predicated on the presence of *both* an abnormal laboratory result *and* toxicity. Fortunately, rules based on such conjunctions of predicates are relatively uncommon in OPAL's application area. (Any rules requiring logical conjunctions currently must be entered into the ONCOCIN knowledge base by hand.) Rules based on *disjunctions* of predicates (in which only one premise clause need be true for the rule to succeed) are entered easily as two or more individual rules.

There are additional shortcomings to the present process for entering rules using OPAL.

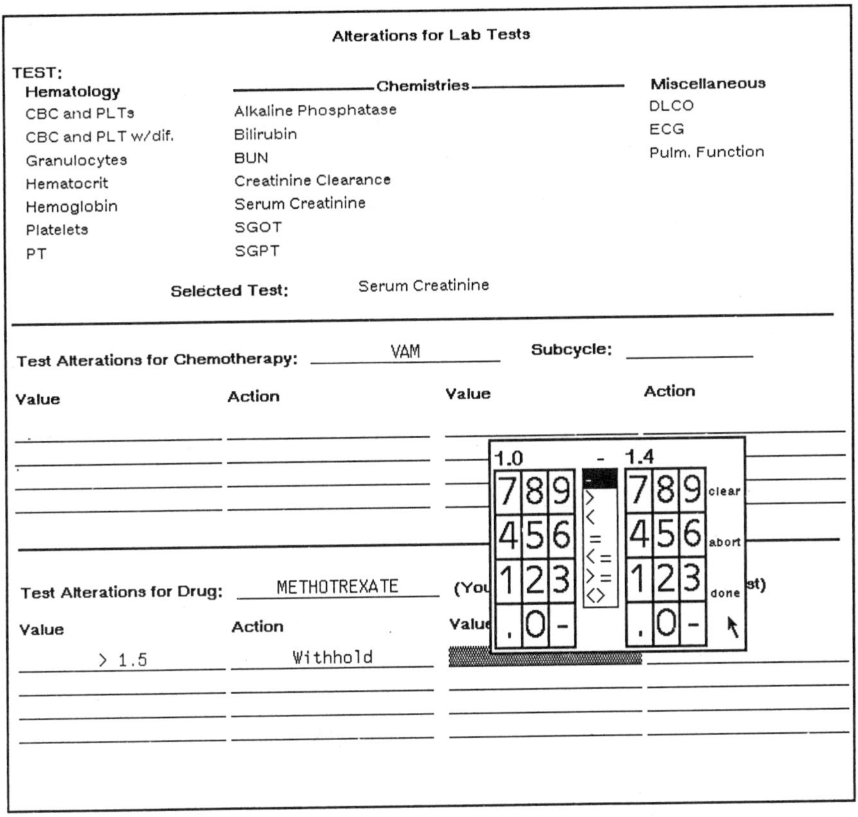

Figure 6.7: Task Rules in OPAL

The blanks in this form allow the expert to specify how the results of laboratory tests should cause modification of the protocol. The knowledge entered is ultimately converted to production rules that can be invoked by the ONCOCIN Reasoner. In this example, the user has specified that when a the patient's serum-creatinine level is greater than 1.5 mg/dl, the the drug methotrexate should be withheld. OPAL uses specialized graphical forms such as this one to allow physicians to indicate the actions that are predicated by different kinds of input data.

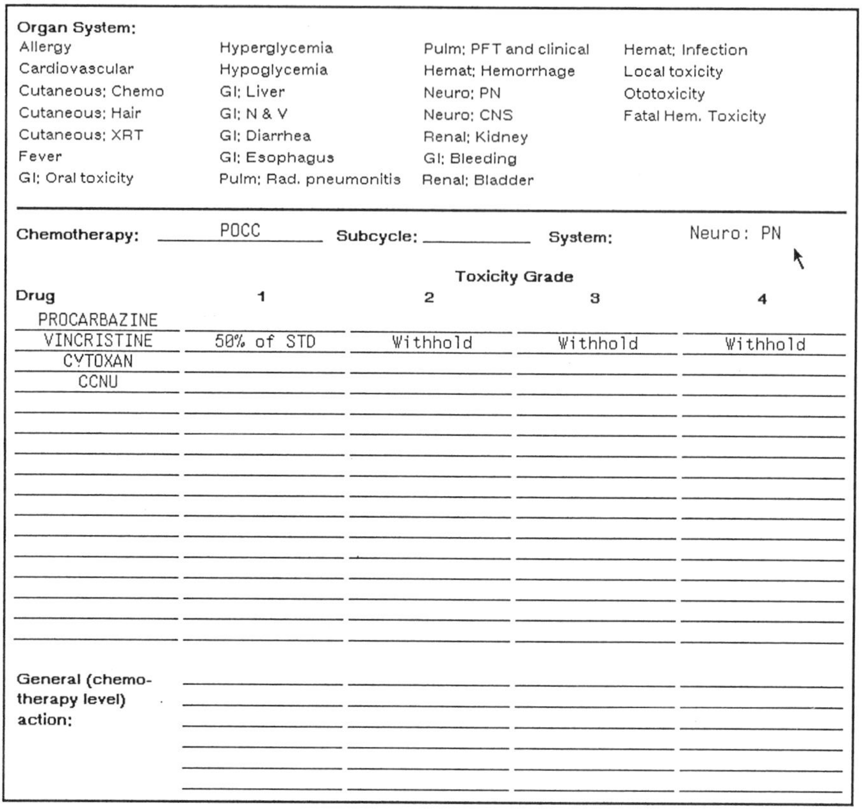

```
┌─────────────────────────────────────────────────────────────────────────────┐
│ Organ System:                                                                 │
│ Allergy            Hyperglycemia         Pulm: PFT and clinical   Hemat: Infection │
│ Cardiovascular     Hypoglycemia          Hemat: Hemorrhage        Local toxicity   │
│ Cutaneous: Chemo   GI: Liver             Neuro: PN                Ototoxicity       │
│ Cutaneous: Hair    GI: N & V             Neuro: CNS               Fatal Hem. Toxicity│
│ Cutaneous: XRT     GI: Diarrhea          Renal: Kidney                              │
│ Fever              GI: Esophagus         GI: Bleeding                               │
│ GI: Oral toxicity  Pulm: Rad. pneumonitis  Renal: Bladder                          │
└─────────────────────────────────────────────────────────────────────────────┘
```

| Chemotherapy: POCC | Subcycle: _____ | System: | Neuro: PN |

Toxicity Grade

Drug	1	2	3	4
PROCARBAZINE				
VINCRISTINE	50% of STD	Withhold	Withhold	Withhold
CYTOXAN				
CCNU				

General (chemo-
therapy level)
action:

Figure 6.8: OPAL Graphical Form for Drug Toxicity

This form is used in OPAL to define the mapping among various clinical grades of drug toxicity and corresponding task actions. Like the form in Figure 6.7, the task specifications ultimately are converted into ONCOCIN production rules.

For example, all input data in the conditions of the rules are assumed to pertain to only the current patient visit. OPAL thus does not make it possible to specify actions that are predicated on past data, even though ONCOCIN's rule language allows programmers to specify complex temporal queries on the patient database. This restriction can be limiting, yet the task model in OPAL is merely being selective in this regard. A degree of *epistemological adequacy* is being sacrificed in exchange for an uncomplicated, easily understandable rule syntax at the OPAL level. Whereas it may not be possible to specify *all* applicable protocol knowledge using OPAL, the simplicity of the program's model seems to facilitate direct entry of a large portion of the required rules by physicians who otherwise have no special experience at programming. System builders could extend the task model in OPAL at the cost of losing some of this simplicity.

6.3 Building the OPAL Task Model

All models are abstractions; they are necessarily selective in what they contain. It is precisely this selectivity that makes models useful. The model of oncology clinical trials in OPAL, for example, makes it easy to define new protocols because it offers a manageable set of terms and relationships. Problems arise, however, when those terms and relationships are insufficient to express critical concepts.

The task model in OPAL makes assumptions regarding everything from the nature of chemotherapy to the kinds of conditions that can mandate task actions. Such assumptions define a *closed world*. There is no way to add new concepts to the model. OPAL allows its user to create novel instantiations of existing concepts (for example, a user can readily define a previously unknown drug or chemotherapy), but the general classes of concepts in the model are predetermined. The task model tends to be sufficient, however, because of the highly stylized nature of clinical trials in oncology. More generally, the stereotypic nature of most clinical trials makes the instantiation of task models a useful approach for the knowledge-editing tools created using PROTÉGÉ.

In 1986, 36 cancer protocols were encoded for ONCOCIN in rapid succession using OPAL. The time required to enter the knowledge for a new protocol, formerly a matter of weeks or months, was with OPAL a matter of days. Any enthusiasm for such results, however, has to be tempered with the understanding that it took approximately 3.5 person-years to build OPAL, before any of these protocols were encoded. The difficult part of developing OPAL, like the difficult part of knowledge engineering in general, was developing the initial task model. A systematic domain of terms and relationships had to be defined; the applicability of the emerging model to large numbers of protocols had to be evaluated carefully. The bottleneck in building OPAL was largely a problem in *modeling*, not in programming. In retrospect, development of the model was greatly facilitated by the availability of the prototype ONCOCIN knowledge base, for which much of the modeling required for OPAL had already been done by ONCOCIN's first knowledge engineers. Similarly, familiarity with the OPAL model makes it much easier to define other tasks using PROTÉGÉ.

Experience with OPAL has shown that, in certain domains, builders of expert systems can gain a great advantage by recasting the work of knowledge acquisition as the instantiation of predefined task models. Even though creating the initial OPAL model was laborious, the availability of the model for reuse has been clearly advantageous. Such a model, however, can be viewed as a collection of terms and relationships. Suppose a knowledge engineer could create a *metalevel* model of the expected classes of terms and relationships in a set of task models. The knowledge engineer then could write a computer program to assist in the instantiation of the metalevel model, defining models for new tasks.

This notion, of course, is the basis for development of PROTÉGÉ. The advantage that expert-system builders gain with programs such as OPAL can be multiplied when they use higher-level tools such as PROTÉGÉ to facilitate the construction of task models. Just as OPAL allows oncologists to generate new ONCOCIN knowledge bases by instantiating a model of cancer protocols, PROTÉGÉ permits knowledge engineers to develop knowledge-editing tools similar to OPAL simply by instantiation. With PROTÉGÉ, workers in AI no longer need to write programs to build systems like OPAL. In the absence of distractions due to programming considerations, the art of knowledge engineering can be seen more clearly for what it is—the creation of models.

128

7 The PROTÉGÉ System

In preceding chapters, I have traced a number of themes. I have discussed knowledge acquisition as the process of modeling the often tacit knowledge of human experts, and have proposed a framework for classifying computer-based knowledge-acquisition tools— one that emphasizes the concepts that individual programs attempt to model. I also have outlined the general task of therapy planning for clinical trials and have discussed how such a task can be modeled within both an advice system (ONCOCIN) and a knowledge-acquisition tool (OPAL). I shall now bring together these ideas and shall show their importance for the primary research of this book: the development of PROTÉGÉ, a tool to generate task-oriented knowledge editors.

In this chapter, I describe PROTÉGÉ in detail. I discuss the model of skeletal-planning systems that PROTÉGÉ presents to its user for instantiation, as well as the computational techniques used to encode that model. The examples I use to illustrate various features of the system are derived from the model of cancer therapy used in OPAL. Consequently, I also shall show how PROTÉGÉ can be used to generate a new knowledge-acquisition tool, called p-OPAL, that has most of the functionality of OPAL. In turn, p-OPAL, like OPAL, can create cancer-protocol knowledge bases for a domain-independent version of ONCOCIN (called e-ONCOCIN). I have chosen to demonstrate the use of PROTÉGÉ to create p-OPAL because, by persisting with the now-familiar application area of cancer therapy, the examples that I use should be most apprehensible. I explore the use of PROTÉGÉ to design knowledge-acquisition programs for clinical-trial domains other than oncology in Chapter 9; readers wishing to assess the generalizability of my techniques may wish to glance ahead to the figures in that chapter while reading this one.

7.1   Implementation

PROTÉGÉ is not simply a single, large program that a computer can execute. Most of PROTÉGÉ consists of data structures (namely, *objects*) that specify a series of graphical forms. These form objects, however, are rich in attached procedural specifications (short segments of LISP code) that collectively define the PROTÉGÉ program. The graphical forms constitute the basis of a visual language used by knowledge engineers to enter task models. Once a task model has been laid out, PROTÉGÉ calls on additional forms to create a knowledge editor that is custom-tailored for the particular task. Like PROTÉGÉ itself, an editor produced by PROTÉGÉ uses forms that also are defined using the object-oriented language.

PROTÉGÉ operates using two large software packages developed by another member of the ONCOCIN project. These modules are (1) a user-interface management system for the creation and display of interactive graphical forms (Combs, 1988) and (2) a relational database system (Combs, 1989) written for the Xerox 1100 series workstation on which PROTÉGÉ runs. Before I discuss PROTÉGÉ itself, I shall describe these basic system components (Figure 7.1).

7.1.1   The Form System

OPAL, PROTÉGÉ, and the editors that PROTÉGÉ generates all use the same software for the definition and execution of graphical forms. The programs present their users with a series of specialized forms that have a number of blanks to be filled in. The forms cluster related data together for presentation to the user, and allow data to be examined and edited using direct manipulation techniques (Shneiderman, 1983). The user can thus indicate to the system that he wants to access a particular blank simply by pointing at that blank with the mouse cursor. After the user enters data into a blank, those data remain in direct view, printed on the form. It it thus always obvious which blanks have been filled in and which blanks do not contain values (and thus may require entries from the user). The form system can be programmed so that some blanks are selectable only under specific conditions; the user can thereby be prevented from filling in these blanks

130

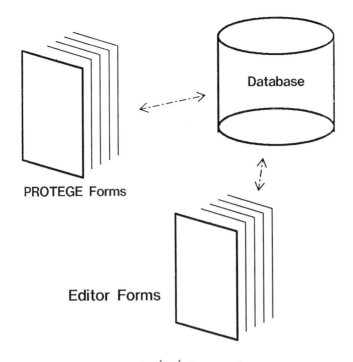

Database

PROTEGE Forms

Editor Forms

Figure 7.1: PROTÉGÉ System Components

PROTÉGÉ is composed of a set of graphical forms that are encoded using objects, which communicate with a relational database system. The knowledge editors that PROTÉGÉ generates also are composed of forms, and share the same database.

inappropriately.

The procedure for interacting with the form system is simple. Passing the mouse cursor over a blank that is waiting to receive input causes the region of the blank on the form to be displayed in reverse video. (The blank is said to *invert*.) Pressing the mouse button when the cursor is positioned over an inverted blank selects that blank. The user then fills in the blank by typing at the keyboard, by making a choice from a pop-up menu, or by entering data via registers.[1] The input method for any given blank is predetermined by the form designer. After the user enters the datum for a given blank, the blank is no longer printed in reverse video and instead displays the appropriate value.

---

[1] *Registers* are menus that allow multiple selections to be pieced together. For example, a register in the form of a 10-key pad allows a user to enter numbers by selecting the appropriate sequence of digits.

Table 7.1: Properties of Form Blanks

BLANKREGION	Region in the form where blank is located
STYLE	Whether blank displays *text* or a *bitmap* image
UNDERLINE	Whether blank is underlined
ACTIVETYPE	Whether blank is *active* or *passive*
INPUTMETHOD	The software input device used to acquire new values
INPUTFLAGS	Options that modify blank's behavior when data are entered
CONDITIONS	Code that controls user's ability to select an active blank
METHODS	Code for SHOW, ADD, CHANGE, and DELETE methods
DEPENDS.ON	Names of form variables used by METHODS
DISPLAYS	Name of form variable, if any, the value of which is SHOWn

Structure of Forms and Blanks

Each form is encoded as an object in the OZONE programming language (Lane, 1986). The blanks that compose a form are represented as *slots* in the corresponding object. The slots for the blanks are themselves complex, as each slot has a number of attributes, the values of which define the appearance and behavior of the blank. Each slot is predefined at the time that the corresponding form object is created, and each has a number of different properties (Table 7.1).

The slot that encodes a blank contains display information, such as where and what size the blank is and whether the blank contains textual data or an arbitrary bitmap image. If the blank displays text, the slot describes the font in which the data should be printed. The blank also can be optionally underlined.

The description of each blank within the form object indicates whether the blank is *active*—that is, the user can select it for input—or whether it is *passive*. In the latter case, form-system routines still can alter the contents of the blank *programmatically,* although the blank will never respond if the user tries to select it with the mouse. The form designer generally uses passive blanks to display information that orients the user about the contents of the form or of other blanks.

Each active blank must have an *input method* by which the user enters new data into it. Typically, the user selects the data from a menu, constructs a value using a specific register or types the input at the keyboard. Some blanks have an input method termed *toggle,* in which case the blanks merely flash their current values when they are selected, without accepting new data. (Such "blanks" usually are programmed to cause a desired side effect to occur when they are selected, such as the display of some other form.) Alternatively, a blank's input method can be *indirect;* selection of the blank causes the form system to evaluate a LISP expression (an attached procedure), the result of which determines how the user should enter the new datum.

Another property of a slot that defines a blank is a set of *conditions* that must be satisfied before the blank can be selectable and active. When the conditions are not met, the blank will not invert when the mouse cursor passes over. Thus, the form system has a mechanism by which it can turn active blanks on and off, preventing the user from making improper entries.

The slots also designate a number of procedural *methods* that are invoked when the user makes changes to a blank's contents. Each blank has separate sequences of LISP statements that are executed (1) when the system displays the contents of the blank (the SHOW method), (2) when the blank is empty and the user enters a value (the ADD method), (3) when the user alters the value of a blank (CHANGE), or (4) when the user specifies that the value stored in the blank should be deleted (DELETE). The form designer must custom-program these statements for each blank. The statements are used to transfer information between the blank and other programs running in the system. In the case of PROTÉGÉ, these procedural methods convert the user's operations on the blank into actions that (1) make changes to the contents and functionality of PROTÉGÉ forms and blanks, and (2) perform operations on the relational database. Because all the information entered into PROTÉGÉ ultimately must be stored in the database, the method statements for the various blanks serve as the link between the forms system and the database system (Figure 7.2).

The form objects have other slots in addition to those that describe the blanks. Some slots specify the labels for the blanks and other predefined text strings that are printed on the form. Other slots designate embellishing lines or bitmap images for the system to draw on the form. A typical form may require several dozen blanks, static text items,

133

```
(FORMBLANKREC (8 600 100 15)
    (STYLE (TEXT) TEXTPOS (CENTER . CENTER) FONT GACHA-10-MRR)
    ((ACTIVETYPE ACTIVE)
    (INPUTFLAGS
        (RANDOMLIST
            (DBFETCH
                (LIST (LIST 'ENTITY 'SYSTEM &SYSTEMNAME) '(ENTITY ROLE PLAN))
                NIL '(ENTITY ENTITY-TYPE)'PROJECT)) (CHOOSEONLY . T))
    (UNDERLINE . T)
    (DISPLAYS &PARENTENTITY1)
    (METHODS (SHOW &PARENTENTITY1)
      (ADD ($BIND &PARENTENTITY1 $VALUE))
      (CHANGE ($BIND &PARENTENTITY1 $VALUE))
      (DELETE ($COND
        (&COMPONENTENTITY1
          (DB2.DELETE 'COMPOSITION 'TABLE
            (DBFETCH
              (LIST
                (LIST 'COMPOSITION 'SYSTEM &SYSTEMNAME)
                (LIST 'COMPOSITION 'ENTITY-TYPE &SYSTEMNAME1)
                (LIST 'COMPOSITION 'COMPONENT &COMPONENTENTITY1))
              NIL T 'SELECT))
          (DB2.DELETE 'ENTITY 'TABLE
            (DBFETCH
              (LIST
                (LIST 'ENTITY 'SYSTEM &SYSTEMNAME)
                '(ENTITY ROLE PLAN)
                (LIST 'ENTITY 'ENTITY-TYPE &COMPONENTENTITY1))
              NIL T 'SELECT)))))
        ($BIND &PARENTENTITY1 NIL)
        ($BIND &COMPONENTENTITY1 NIL))))
```

Figure 7.2: Code for a PROTÉGÉ Blank

This figure shows the properties and attached procedures for one blank from one
of PROTÉGÉ's forms (namely, the uppermost blank in the left column of the form
shown in Figure 7.7). Although the syntax may appear formidable, this is not an
atypically complex blank. This blank displays text in Gacha font, centered in the
region that has been allocated for the blank within the form. The blank is always
active; there are no CONDITIONS that might turn it off. The INPUTFLAGS
indicate that the user should enter values into the blank from a menu constructed
dynamically from the results of a specific database query. The blank displays the
value of a form variable called &PARENTENTITY1. The ADD and CHANGE methods
for the blank both reset this variable to whatever value the user enters from the menu.
The DELETE method clears the value of &PARENTENTITY1 as well as that of a
second variable called &COMPONENTENTITY1. If necessary, the DELETE method
also updates the database to indicate that the entity represented by &COMPONENT-
ENTITY1 no longer exists (that is, the blank deletes the relevant tuples from the
ENTITY and COMPOSITION relations).

134

lines, and bitmaps. As a result, form objects often are composed of a great many slots containing large numbers of data. Although programmers find such large objects almost impossible to inspect and modify using standard editing tools, the form system provides its own what-you-see-is-what-you-get editor that allows a form designer to create forms and to generate many of the required slots automatically. Programmers must enter the attached procedures for the form by hand, however.

Form Variables

The various forms in the system, and the individual blanks within each form, require a mechanism for communicating with one another the results of certain user actions. Thus, if the user selects a blank in one form that opens a second form that describes attributes of a particular drug, the *name* of the drug must be made available to the SHOW method for each blank in the second form. Otherwise, the blanks in the second form have no way of determining which values to display. Similarly, if a form has two blanks that can represent mutually incompatible concepts, the user should not be allowed to select the first blank if the second blank already contains certain values—and vice versa. (For example, it would make no sense to be able to enter the name of a drug to administer into one blank if another blank in the form simultaneously indicated that no therapy at all was to be given.) Although attached procedures can easily bring about the required activation and deactivation of the blanks, the two blanks need a means of informing each other of the data that they contain.

Consequently, in addition to the slots for the different blanks, the form objects also contain slots for special *variables* that serve in this communication role. These form-variable slots are created by the form designer. A PROTÉGÉ form, depending on its complexity, may require from less than a dozen to over a hundred such variables.

A form variable can acquire new values in one of three ways: (1) when the user changes the contents of some blank, the blank's attached procedures can cause prespecified form variables to take on new values based on the user's actions; (2) when an operation involving one form causes a second form to be displayed, the first form may pass to the second form values that are then bound to certain variables in the new form; (3) the form designer can explicitly declare that the value of some variable *depends on* the value of another variable: When the latter variable acquires a new value (by any one of these three mechanisms), a predefined procedure attached to the slot of the dependent variable resets that variable's value.

The procedures attached to active blanks have the ability to examine and to alter the values of form variables. The variables thus provide a mechanism by which the user's actions involving one blank can cause other blanks to change in either their contents or behavior. The form designer's use of these variables to represent dependencies among the blanks allows complex behaviors to be programmed into the user interface.

For example, consider the simple OPAL form that appears in Figure 7.3. When OPAL displays this form, a variable called $CHEMO is set to the name of a chemotherapy previously selected by the user (in this case, a drug combination called VAM). Blank (a) in Figure 7.3 is passive and merely displays the value of $CHEMO. Blank (b), on the other hand, is active and can accept input from the user; its SHOW method causes it to display the first drug (if any) in the list of drugs associated with the chemotherapy indicated by the form variable $CHEMO. The SHOW method also sets the value of another form variable, $DRUG1, to the name of the drug that the blank currently displays. If the user enters a new value for blank (b), the value of variable $DRUG1 will be changed accordingly. Blank (c), like blank (b), requires the value of $CHEMO for its SHOW method to execute, but the method in (c) causes display of the *second* drug listed in the chemotherapy. If the user updates blank (c), a different form variable, $DRUG2, is reset. Analogously, blank (d) resets the form variable $DRUG3.

When the user selects blank (e) in Figure 7.3, the drug-dose form in Figure 6.3 (page 119) is opened. The drug-dose form displays data for a specific drug, methotrexate, because blank (e) in Figure 7.3 explicitly resets a variable called $LOCALDRUG in the new form to the value of $DRUG3 in the old form. All the blanks in Figure 6.3 depend on $LOCALDRUG and consequently use this variable in their procedural methods. Thus, had the user toggled blank (f) in Figure 7.3, the drug-dose form would instead have shown data for the drug Adriamycin, since $LOCALDRUG would then have been set to the value of $DRUG2.

136

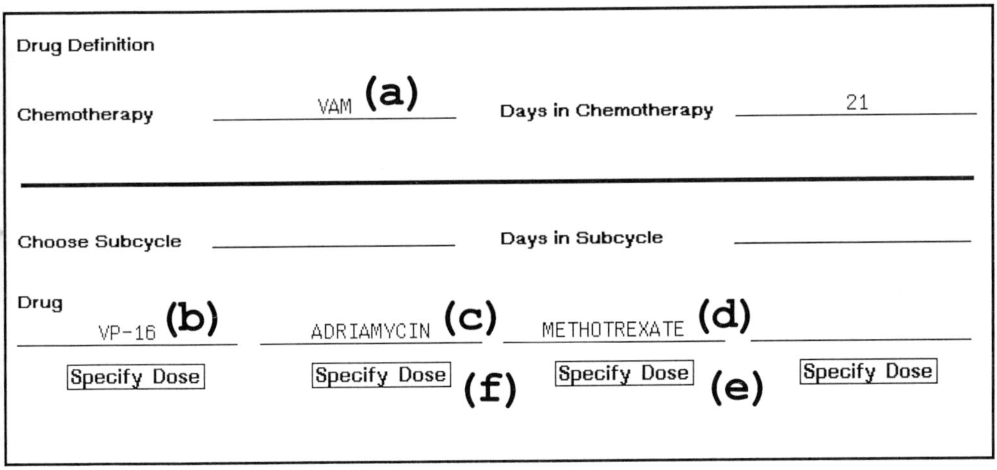

Figure 7.3: OPAL Drug Therapy Form

This form allows users of OPAL to enter the names of the drugs that compose a given chemotherapy. Some of the blanks have been labeled (a-f) to facilitate the discussion in the text of the operations that these blanks perform.

The form variables are used not only to alter the contents of the blanks, but also to modify the blanks' interactions with the user. For example, the *conditions* associated with blank (e) prevent the user from toggling this blank unless the form variable $DRUG3 already has been set to a valid drug name by blank (d). The form designer thus uses the form variables to control the order in which the user is allowed to enter information. The designer can thereby prevent the user from moving from one blank to the next (or from one form to the next) prematurely.

Summary

The form system, with its form objects and special variables, can be viewed as a high-level language with which programmers can create user interfaces capable of complex behaviors. The form system makes no assumptions regarding what the source of the data it displays is or what actions should be taken with a user's input. These application-specific concerns are handled both by the interactions of the form variables and by the procedural methods associated with each blank—methods that must be programmed in LISP by the form

137

designer. In the case of PROTÉGÉ, these methods link the form system to a relational database.

7.1.2   The Database System

The second major component of PROTÉGÉ is a relational database system that stores the information that the user enters into the graphical forms. The PROTÉGÉ database is analogous to the *intermediate knowledge representation* in OPAL. The OPAL intermediate representation, as I discussed in Section 6.2.1, is a hierarchy of frames used to encode the protocol descriptions that physicians enter via the form system. The methods in OPAL's forms (1) retrieve data from this hierarchy, (2) generate new frames whenever novel concepts are encountered, and (3) instantiate the frames according to the user's specifications. Other programs translate OPAL's intermediate frame representation into the various symbol-level entities required by the ONCOCIN inference engine. In PROTÉGÉ, however the corresponding intermediate representation is encoded using a relational database. In the relational approach, all data are stored as tables, such as the one shown in Figure 7.4

The AI community has only recently recognized that problems in the development and maintenance of large knowledge bases have important corollaries that database researchers have been addressing for some time (Brodie and Mylopoulos, 1986). Some justification for PROTÉGÉ's use of a relational approach therefore is in order.[2]

The relational model offers a number of benefits during knowledge editing, the most important of which is simplicity of representation. There is only one conceptual data structure in PROTÉGÉ—the relation. Access to the different relations in the system is obtained easily via query statements that require no knowledge of how or where the individual data items are stored. (PROTÉGÉ does need to know, however, the names of the relations and the fields that each relation contains.)

PROTÉGÉ performs database queries using the well-understood operators of relational algebra: select, project, and join. The *select* operation returns the set of tuples in a relation

---

[2]Although I shall try to provide background material for readers unfamiliar with database concepts additional information may be obtained from any standard textbook on the subject (for example, Wiederhold, 1983; Date, 1986).

138

SYSTEM	DATE-CREATED	DATE-EDITED	DATE-TRANSLATED
p-OPAL	05-May-87	10-Aug-87	10-Aug-87
TRANSPLANT	12-Nov-87	12-Nov-87	
HTN	22-Sep-87	10-Oct-87	08-Oct-87

Figure 7.4: A PROTÉGÉ Database Relation

A relation defines a table of data. This relation, which lists data about knowledge-editing systems that users have created with PROTÉGÉ, has four *fields*. One or more fields of every relation forms a *key* that uniquely identifies every entry in the table. In this example, SYSTEM is a key field; it would thus be impossible to have listed in the table *two* systems called p-OPAL. Each entry in the table is called an n-*tuple* or, more commonly, just a *tuple*.

such that the value stored in one of the fields meets a certain condition. For example, we might want to select only those tuples from the relation in Figure 7.4 in which the DATE-EDITED field contains a particular date or in which the SYSTEM field is equal to "p-OPAL." The *project* operation, on the other hand, returns data from all the tuples in a relation but omits specific fields. A projection on the relation in Figure 7.4 might thus return the values for only the SYSTEM field, ignoring the other fields in each tuple. Finally, the *join* operator generates a set of tuples that selectively merges the tuples from two different relations. In PROTÉGÉ, all join operations combine tuples only when the value of one field in the first tuple is equal to the value of some other field in the second tuple (a procedure called *equi-join*).

These relational operators have the valuable property that the result of every select, project, or join operation is itself a set of tuples (a relation) to which additional relational operators can then be applied. Thus, relational algebra permits the construction of extremely complex queries that can bring together information from many different relations. Unfortunately, such flexibility and power is not available in OPAL; the OPAL intermediate knowledge representation is based on a frame system that tends to lump data together and connects them by only simple *part-of* links. Consequently, OPAL programmers have to encode detailed knowledge of how to locate various data items in the frame hierarchy within the methods of the system's blanks. Although the methods in PROTÉGÉ do require knowledge of the relations in the database and the names of their various fields, the methods never need to determine the physical location of stored values (as they do in OPAL). More important, PROTÉGÉ can perform complex queries on the data using combinations of just three basic functions: select, project, and join.

Each PROTÉGÉ form deals with a single topic. In general, a form must integrate data from several relations in the database to represent any one topic adequately. Consequently, each form may display tuples from a variety of relations—what database designers refer to as a *view* on the database. When the user fills in a form's blanks, the system correspondingly updates several different tuples. Designing such a form requires more than just creating a graphical representation using the form system editor; the form designer also must explicitly specify how to display and how to update the associated database view. Thus, for each blank in the form, the designer must indicate both from where in the database the displayed value comes and what updates to the database are required if the user should change that value. In Figure 7.2, for example, if the user deletes the value displayed by the blank, PROTÉGÉ must delete a specific tuple from both the ENTITY and the COMPOSITION relations.

Updating a *view* is traditionally problematical for relational database systems. Difficulties arise because a view may contain data from more than one relation. When an element of the view is updated, it may not be clear how to update the base relations from which the view was generated originally. For example, in a payroll database, one relation might indicate each employee's job description, whereas a second relation might give the basic hourly wage for each job description. A view on the database could join the two relations to show what the job description of each employee in the company is and how much each earned per hour. If we wanted to increase an employee's hourly wage, we could *either* change the employee's job description to a higher-paying category (updating a tuple in the first relation) or raise the hourly pay rate for all workers with the employee's existing job description (updating a tuple in the other). Without more information, the database system would not know which change we intend. In PROTÉGÉ, there is no such ambiguity, because the blanks' procedural methods explicitly define the relations that are affected and indicate which entries are to be modified or deleted (*cf.* Keller 1986). PROTÉGÉ blanks

140

however, have a requirement that is more subtle than simply that the relations that need to be updated must be identified. The blanks must determine whether such an update seems to *make sense.*

PROTÉGÉ attempts to prevent the user from making semantically inconsistent changes to the database. The relations in the PROTÉGÉ database themselves are *normalized;* the semantic dependencies among the various fields generally have been separated out.[3] When data from different relations are brought together to form a view, however, they are no longer normalized; the way in which the value of one element in the view hinges on the value of another may be no longer obvious. PROTÉGÉ must use the form variables to constrain the user's entries so that semantic dependencies among the blanks are respected. These constraints are similar to those that I discussed previously regarding the OPAL form in Figure 7.3.

In fact, because the form system helps to ensure that the data entered by the knowledge engineer are semantically consistent, it is permissible for some relations in the PROTÉGÉ database to contain semantic dependencies (that is, not to be fully normalized) without suffering from update anomalies. In these cases, the form system prevents the database system from storing any incoherent data. Although there occasionally are good reasons for not completely normalizing a relation (see Section 7.3.2), most relations in the PROTÉGÉ database are in Boyce-Codd normal form.

---

[3]Two fields of a relation are *dependent* when the value of one field is predictive of the value of the other. For example, an employee's job description reveals something about his hourly wage. Our knowledge of common business practices tells us that the two notions are semantically dependent. A database designer would therefore not want to define a unitary relation that included *both* job description *and* hourly wage. Otherwise, it would be possible to update the database so that employees with the same job description could have *different hourly wages.* It would even be possible to enter an hourly wage for an employee with no job description at all. By separating out such dependencies in a process called *normalization,* the database designer attempts to prevent these potential update anomalies. Normal form is achieved when the designer breaks apart relations that have semantic dependencies in their nonkey fields into two or more smaller relations (see Salzberg, 1986). In practice, there are different degrees to which a database can be normalized. *Third normal form* or *Boyce-Codd normal form* is the point at which most database designers stop.

7.2 Interaction with the PROTÉGÉ System

The purpose of PROTÉGÉ is to allow users to define and edit models of classes of application tasks. PROTÉGÉ allows users to create an *intension* of the nature of a class of domain tasks (Addis, 1987). System builders therefore use PROTÉGÉ to specify the structure of application tasks *in general,* but cannot use the system to enter any details about individual tasks within the application area. The latter process—that of creating a task-specific *extension* of the model, is performed exclusively with the custom-tailored knowledge-editing tools that PROTÉGÉ generates. Thus, for example, users may enter into PROTÉGÉ a general description of the task of administering cancer therapy; yet any knowledge of *specific* plans for treating particular tumors cannot be entered at the PROTÉGÉ level. Such application-specific knowledge can be entered into only the oncology-specificn tool that PROTÉGÉ constructs based on the general cancer-treatment model.

Defining a task model in PROTÉGÉ, like instantiating a protocol model in OPAL, is a matter of filling in the blanks of various forms. PROTÉGÉ is composed of 13 different forms containing a total of more than 1000 blanks. The system organizes a user's access to the forms according to the pathways shown in Figure 7.5. The PROTÉGÉ user navigates among these forms much as one traverses a hypertext system (Conklin, 1987). The first form that appears when PROTÉGÉ is activated is the main menu, which simply lists the PROTÉGÉ forms that are available to the user at the next organizational level (Figure 7.6). From the main menu, the knowledge engineer can access the PROTÉGÉ forms that correspond to the three divisions of a task model: (1) the planning entities and their relationships, (2) task actions, and (3) input data that predicate those actions. The user may also select other forms from the menu, such as the *data-types* form that describes the menus and registers used to enter data both into the generated knowledge editor (for example, p-OPAL) and into e-ONCOCIN. PROTÉGÉ also has a *methods* form that allows the knowledge engineer to inspect and edit groups of rules and other methods.

Each item in the PROTÉGÉ main menu is an active form-system blank that has an input method of *toggle.* When the user selects one of these toggles, PROTÉGÉ displays the

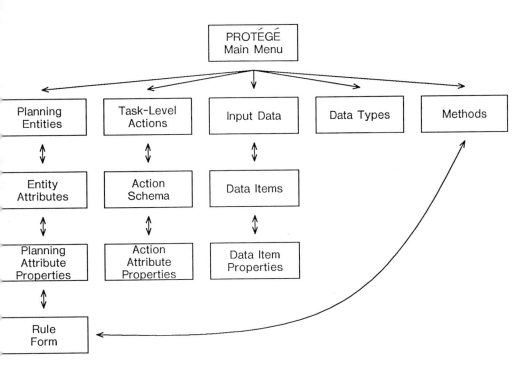

Figure 7.5: Pathways Through the Graphical Forms in PROTÉGÉ

The PROTÉGÉ user is initially presented with the main-menu form. From this starting point, the knowledge engineer can access the other forms in the system by following the pathways shown. Although several forms may be displayed on the workstation screen simultaneously, the user can enter data into only the form that he selected most recently.

designated form on the workstation screen. Once a requested form is displayed, the user can cause additional forms to appear by selecting appropriate blanks. (As in OPAL, the precise *contents* of a form may depend on which blank in the previous form was selected.) Each form in PROTÉGÉ also has a special blank labeled *"Finished."* When the user selects this blank, the indicated form disappears from the workstation screen and the previous form once again becomes active.

Whereas the knowledge engineer is free to move about at will from one form to the next, the organization provided by PROTÉGÉ encourages the user the enter information in an orderly fashion. Although the blanks often can be filled in in any sequence, the *conditions* associated with the blanks ensure that the user cannot select a blank if addi-

143

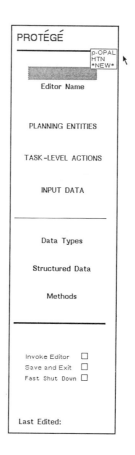

Figure 7.6: PROTÉGÉ Main-Menu Form

The main-menu form asks the user for the name of the knowledge-editing system for which specifications are to be entered or edited using PROTÉGÉ. Once the name of the particular knowledge editor has been entered via a pop-up menu, users can access PROTÉGÉ forms for various topics by toggling the blanks in the main menu. The top three items invoke forms that correspond to the three principle components of PROTÉGÉ's model. The bottom three items relate to other topics: entry of data-type information, specification of structured data types (a feature that has not yet been fully implemented), and entry of rules and other methods. The small squares at the bottom of the form allow the user to exit from PROTÉGÉ, or to start up the selected PROTÉGÉ-generated knowledge editor.

tional information must be entered elsewhere before the contents of that blank would have unambiguous meaning. Thus, the user cannot define an instance of something (for example, the input datum *white-blood-cell count*) before describing the general class of which that instance is a member (for example, *hematology data*). The procedural methods in each blank also prevent the user from entering data that appear to conflict with previously specified information. Thus, if the user has declared that a particular entity is a component of another (for example, that *drugs* are constituents of *chemotherapy*), he cannot also define the component as part of some additional entity (for example, that *drugs* are also a part of *radiotherapy*). Each blank verifies the semantic consistency of the input it receives from the user in an ad hoc manner. Like other interactive programs (for example, that of Masand, 1982), PROTÉGÉ cannot necessarily guarantee the consistency of each datum as it is entered; the program simply has no way of determining *a priori* whether the user will fill in additional blanks and, if so, what those blanks' contents will be. However, the PROTÉGÉ user interface does tend to prevent such errors from occurring in the first place. In addition to activating blanks only when it is appropriate for a knowledge engineer to access them, the interface will, whenever possible, generate menus that restrict the user's entries to values that are consistent with prior data. The interface also makes it easy for knowledge engineers to know when specifications are incomplete; when data are missing, the corresponding blanks are empty.

7.3   The PROTÉGÉ Model

PROTÉGÉ, like many of the knowledge-editing programs discussed in Section 3.3, assumes that the user understands the terms and relationships of a given model. In PROTÉGÉ, that model is primarily one of skeletal-plan refinement—more specifically, skeletal-plan refinement as performed by e-ONCOCIN (see Section 5.2). Knowledge engineers use PRO-TÉGÉ to create task models by extending (instantiating) this built-in model of skeletal-plan refinement. PROTÉGÉ users therefore must learn to represent application tasks using the relationships and terms of this model (words such as *planning entity* and *data class*). The skeletal-planning model provides the basis for a language that can characterize classes

145

of domain tasks that are solvable using e-ONCOCIN.

I describe the terms of the model in words both in this book and in the annotations that I have placed on PROTÉGÉ's graphical forms. Yet the semantics of the PROTÉGÉ model are, in reality, defined *operationally* by the manner in which e-ONCOCIN interprets the particular instantiations that users enter both into PROTÉGÉ and into the editors that PROTÉGÉ creates. Thus, although I may discuss the PROTÉGÉ model as though it had absolute meaning, there is no formal, declarative description for the model's semantics. Given the complexity of the systems produced by PROTÉGÉ, such a description would be impractical. Consequently, data entered into PROTÉGÉ mean whatever e-ONCOCIN ultimately says they mean. Because the knowledge engineers who use PROTÉGÉ understand the correspondance between the terms and relationships of the model and the behaviors exhibited by e-ONCOCIN, the operational nature of the semantics does not, in practice, diminish the model's usefulness. To date, all model-based knowledge-editing tools—for example, ROGET (Bennett, 1985), MOLE (Eshelman et al., 1987), and OPAL—have defined their semantics operationally.

There are three major components in the model: (1) the notion of entities that constitute a skeletal plan, (2) the notion of actions that can modify a skeletal plan, and (3) assumptions about data that bear on the invocation of those actions. Knowledge engineers use PROTÉGÉ to describe specific application areas in terms of this three-part model. For each new domain (such as clinical trials in oncology), knowledge engineers must model the planning entities (for example, chemotherapies and radiotherapies), the task actions (for example, delay chemotherapy or attenuate a drug), and the input data (for example, hematology and chemistry test results). PROTÉGÉ also makes suppositions about the manner in which users will instantiate the model to define specific clinical-trial applications. Thus, the concept of *data types* also becomes important. I shall discuss each of these issues in the following sections.

7.3.1   Planning Entities and Their Relationships

At the core of PROTÉGÉ's model is the plan that e-ONCOCIN must instantiate during a consultation. The plan as a whole is called a *protocol*.[4] The model states that a protocol consists of a hierarchy of skeletal-plan components. Each component in the hierarchy for a particular skeletal plan—including the *protocol* itself—is an instance that belongs to some *class*. For example, the *protocol* class in OPAL is made up of instances from the *chemotherapy* class (for example, VAM and POCC) and from the *radiotherapy* class (for example, *involved field* radiation). Knowledge engineers use PROTÉGÉ to enter the general classes of plan components in the application area. Subsequently, experts in the domain define particular *instances* of these classes using the custom-tailored knowledge editor (for example, p-OPAL) that PROTÉGÉ generates based on the class descriptions.

All the plan instances in a particular class have a set of shared characteristics called *attributes*. Whereas a few attributes denote properties common to all classes of planning entities (thus, all protocols, chemotherapies, radiotherapies, and drugs), other attributes identify features that are unique to particular classes. For example, every entity in OPAL's planning hierarchy has a *name* attribute; only *drugs,* however, have attributes such as *standard dose* and *route of administration.*

A Hierarchy of Processes

PROTÉGÉ's model defines the planning entities as representing *processes* that take place over finite periods of time. Although a process may be modeled as instantaneous in the degenerate case (for example, performing a laboratory test or injecting a drug may be represented as immediate events), more typically, a process will take some discrete amount of time to complete. The duration of a process may be predetermined (as in the case of a cancer chemotherapy administered for 21 days) or may depend on data entered from the environment (for example, a protocol that is discontinued when the patient shows signs of relapse).

Because processes are related hierarchically, the model imposes some additional con-

---

[4]Although some readers might prefer a less domain-dependent term, I have used *protocol* to emphasize that PROTÉGÉ's model has an upper limit to its generality.

straints. A process cannot terminate if any of the subprocesses that it comprises has not terminated. For example, a chemotherapy cannot end if drugs are still being administered. Similarly, a process cannot be active if the more general process of which it is a part is not also active. (It is therefore impossible to give a drug and not also to be administering a chemotherapy; a chemotherapy cannot be started outside of a protocol.) Without these constraints, the top-down hierarchical refinement of skeletal plans by e-ONCOCIN would be impossible.

The problem-solving method of skeletal-plan refinement is based on instantiation (Friedland and Iwasaki, 1985). Instantiation of a skeletal plan requires (1) establishment of instance-specific values for the attributes that are common to all plans of the given class (for example, determining the *duration* of a chemotherapy), followed by (2) selection and instantiation of those component plans that constitute the more general plan (for example, refining plans for the component *drugs*). The terms and relationships of PROTÉGÉ's model allow knowledge engineers to define planning entities that can be instantiated precisely in this manner.

The model recognizes that, during plan instantiation, e-ONCOCIN assigns a value to each attribute in one of three ways. First, a knowledge engineer may have predefined the attribute's value for all possible instances of the class. (For example, a PROTÉGÉ user might have declared that all *drugs* have an attribute called *route of administration* that always has the value *oral*.) In this case, e-ONCOCIN simply uses the value entered into PROTÉGÉ. Alternatively, an application specialist might have used the knowledge editor created by PROTÉGÉ to establish the attribute's value for the specific instance of the class. (Thus, a p-OPAL user might have stated that *methotrexate* always should be given *intravenously*.) In this case, e-ONCOCIN uses the value entered into the editor. Otherwise, e-ONCOCIN computes the attribute's value at the time of the consultation. (For example, e-ONCOCIN might invoke a rule entered with PROTÉGÉ to conclude that the route of administration for the current drug in the current circumstance is *oral*.) For each attribute, the PROTÉGÉ user specifies which of these three mechanisms should be used to establish the attribute's value (Table 7.2).

In PROTÉGÉ's model, the attributes of planning entities have several properties. For

Table 7.2: Mechanisms for Establishing the Values of Attributes

Program Establishing Value	Affected Entity Instances
PROTÉGÉ	All instances of the class
Knowledge editor	Designated instances under all circumstances
e-ONCOCIN	Specific instances under specific circumstances

example, an attribute's value must be of a specific a *data type,* a designation that restricts the potential values that the attribute can acquire (Section 7.3.4). Attributes have either static values or values that change over time; attributes also may be either *single-valued* (mutually exclusive alternatives, such as the *dose* of a drug) or *multivalued* (such as a list of days on which treatment should be given).

Symbol-Level Concerns

Ultimately, PROTÉGÉ translates each attribute that the knowledge engineer defines for a given class of planning entities into a unique ONCOCIN parameter. Thus, planning-entity attributes at the knowledge level (for example, the *name* attribute of the *protocol* entity) map into e-ONCOCIN parameters at the symbol level (for example, PROTOCOL.NAME). This mapping would be irrelevant to the knowledge engineers who use PROTÉGÉ if the PROTÉGÉ model were sufficient to provide a complete knowledge-level description of e-ONCOCIN applications. There are, however, gaps in the model. PROTÉGÉ's model does not provide the terms needed to ascribe *meaning* to individual attributes the same way that meaning can be given to the classes of planning entities. Although the attributes are assumed to play important roles during refinement of skeletal plans, what those roles might *be* is left unsaid. Intuitively, some attributes are used to influence the duration of planning entities. (In the oncology domain, for example, there is an attribute of chemotherapies that puts a limit on the number of times that treatment can be delayed.) At the same time, other attributes bear on the "intensity" of those plans (such as the *drug* attribute that denotes the lowest percentage by which the dosage may be attenuated). It is difficult to say much more than this at present; development of a complete knowledge-level model for

149

all the behaviors needed for tasks that can be represented within e-ONCOCIN will require substantial additional research. In fact, the development of models for constructive (as opposed to classificatory) problem-solving methods is an area of investigation where, in general, few satisfactory results have been achieved to date.

Because PROTÉGÉ's model is incomplete, there are some symbol-level concerns that must enter PROTÉGÉ's knowledge-level description. In particular, knowledge engineers must enter the production rules needed to conclude the values of certain e-ONCOCIN parameters that correspond to planning-entity attributes at the knowledge level. Thus, if the advice system will need a rule to ensure that sufficient dosages of drugs are given, such a rule must be entered by hand. A PROTÉGÉ user simply types in the rule as a symbol-level expression in e-ONCOCIN's rule language (see Figure 5.3, page 103). Such rules are used by *all* protocols within a particular class. The task-oriented knowledge editors that PROTÉGÉ generates for instantiation of specific protocols deal with only knowledge-level concepts.

Specification of Planning Entities

When knowledge engineers use PROTÉGÉ to define the planning entities in the application area, three steps are involved. First, they specify the the hierarchy of planning-entity *classes* (for example, that protocols are comprise chemotherapies and radiotherapies). Second, for each class in the hierarchy, the knowledge engineers enter the names of the *attributes* of entities in that class (for example, that drugs have doses and routes of administration). Third, for each attribute of each class, knowledge engineers declare values for various *properties* of the attribute (for example, that the dose of a drug has a value that varies over time). I shall now describe this process in detail.

Entering the Planning Hierarchy PROTÉGÉ allows knowledge engineers easily to define classes of planning entities, relationships among those entities, and attributes of those entities. When a user selects the item labeled *"Planning Entities"* from the main-menu form (see Figure 7.6), the form in Figure 7.7 opens on the screen. The knowledge engineer uses the right column of the latter form to enumerate the different planning

150

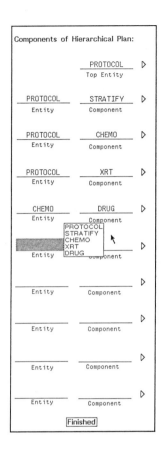

Figure 7.7: Planning-Entities Form

This form is used to enter the planning entities for a particular class of clinical trials and to specify their compositional hierarchy. The knowledge engineer types in the names of the entities using the right column. Before he can type in the name of a new entity, however, the user must identify the "parent" entity of which the new entity is a component. He enters the parent entity into the corresponding blank on the left side of the form by making a selection from a menu that lists all of the plan components typed in previously. Selecting one of the triangular arrows opens the form shown in Figure 7.8, which displays the attributes of the corresponding entity.

151

entities in his model of the task. (The blank containing *protocol,* the topmost entity in every PROTÉGÉ planning hierarchy, already is filled in by the system when the form is first displayed.) Before the knowledge engineer can type in the name of a new entity in one of the right-column blanks, however, the corresponding blank on the left side must specify the "parent" entity of which the new entity is a part. When the user selects a blank from the left column, he is presented with a menu of all the entity classes that have been typed in previously. Thus, Figure 7.7 shows that, in p-OPAL, *protocols* are composed of *chemos* (chemotherapies), *XRTs* (X-ray therapies), and *stratification* steps, and that *chemos* are composed of *drugs.*

The blanks in the form store these data in the relational database. A relation called ENTITY stores all entity classes that knowledge engineers declare using PROTÉGÉ. The form in Figure 7.7 is concerned with only *planning entities.* (The other entity classes in PROTÉGÉ are *data classes* and task *actions.*) Thus, the form causes the following data to be entered into the ENTITY relation:

SYSTEM	ENTITY-TYPE	ROLE
p-OPAL	PROTOCOL	PLAN
p-OPAL	CHEMO	PLAN
p-OPAL	XRT	PLAN
p-OPAL	DRUG	PLAN

The form in Figure 7.7 also captures the hierarchical relationships among the entities. This information is entered into a different relation, called COMPOSITION:

SYSTEM	ENTITY-TYPE	COMPONENT-TYPE
p-OPAL	PROTOCOL	CHEMO
p-OPAL	PROTOCOL	XRT
p-OPAL	CHEMO	DRUG

Entering the Attributes of Planning Entities If the user selects one of the small arrows that appear next to each of the planning entities in Figure 7.7, the form in Figure 7.8 appears on the screen. This new form allows the knowledge engineer to examine

Attributes of	PROTOCOL	Selected Attribute:	ON.PROTOCOL	Finished
NAME ▷	PI.INSTITUTION ▷	_____ ▷	_____ ▷	
STOP.CONDITION. ▷	ON.PROTOCOL ▷	_____ ▷	_____ ▷	
RESUME.CONDITION ▷	CR ▷	_____ ▷	_____ ▷	
POINT.PROCESS ▷	PR ▷	_____ ▷	_____ ▷	
DEFAULT.RULES ▷	_____ ▷	_____ ▷	_____ ▷	
DURATION ▷	_____ ▷	_____ ▷	_____ ▷	
REVISION.DATE ▷	_____ ▷	_____ ▷	_____ ▷	
DISEASE ▷	_____ ▷	_____ ▷	_____ ▷	
HISTOLOGY ▷	_____ ▷	_____ ▷	_____ ▷	
SITE ▷	_____ ▷	_____ ▷	_____ ▷	
PI.NAME ▷	_____ ▷	_____ ▷	_____ ▷	

Figure 7.8: Planning-Entity Attributes Form

This PROTÉGÉ form lists the attributes for a selected entity class, in this case, *PROTOCOL*. PROTÉGÉ enters the first six attributes automatically, as these are common to all classes. The knowledge engineer types in the remainder of the attributes. Selecting one of the arrows causes the form in Figure 7.9 to be displayed.

or to enter the *attributes* of the entity that was listed next to the arrow. Throughout PROTÉGÉ, similar triangular arrows cause additional forms to be displayed, providing additional specifications about the contents of the blank immediately to the left of each arrow. (If the user selects the *blank,* rather than the adjacent arrow, he can change or delete the contents of the blank itself; the new form is not opened.)

The form in Figure 7.8 permits entry and review of the *attributes* associated with particular classes of planning entities (in this example, *protocols*). Six of the attributes that appear on the form are common to all classes of planning entities (Table 7.3). All but one correspond to specific symbol-level parameters that e-ONCOCIN requires of all skeletal-plan components. The other (called DURATION) corresponds to the default number of days that processes that are instances of the class remain active. These six attributes are defined automatically when the knowledge engineer first opens the form.

153

Table 7.3: Entity-Class Attributes Required by e-ONCOCIN

Attribute	Meaning for e-ONCOCIN
NAME	Specifies name of the instance of the class
STOP.CONDITION	Evaluates *true* when active process should terminate
RESUME.CONDITION	Evaluates *true* when suspended process should resume
POINT.PROCESS	*True* if the process is instantaneous
DEFAULT.RULES	Used by e-ONCOCIN to store *frame* rules
DURATION	Default duration of process (measured in days)

When the knowledge engineer types the name of a new attribute into one of the blanks in Figure 7.8, PROTÉGÉ creates a new tuple in a relation called ATTRIBUTE.[5] Selecting the arrow next to the blank causes PROTÉGÉ to display the form in Figure 7.9.

Entering Properties of Attributes of Planning Entities The attribute-detail form in Figure 7.9 allows the user to enter various *properties* of the selected attribute. These properties include how the attribute's value is established (see Table 7.2), what the value's *data type* is (Section 7.3.4), and whether the attribute has singular or multiple values. As the data are entered into the corresponding blanks in the form, fields in the appropriate tuple of the ATTRIBUTE relation are updated (see Appendix A). If the attribute's value is (or values are) predefined at the PROTÉGÉ level, the form provides blanks for this purpose. These blanks display and update tuples from the DEFAULT-VALUES relation.

The menu associated with the blank labeled *"Time Varying?"* has three options: *yes, no,* and *frame.* PROTÉGÉ users generally declare attributes with values computed by e-ONCOCIN to be time-varying, by selecting the value *yes* from the menu. The Reasoner will then attempt to conclude new values for the corresponding parameters each time an e-ONCOCIN consultation is run. If the knowledge engineer states that an attribute is not time-varying, e-ONCOCIN will not attempt to conclude new values for the corresponding parameter. Selecting *frame* for the value of this blank tells PROTÉGÉ that the attribute should be treated as time-varying. Furthermore, if the Reasoner is ever unable to determine

---

[5]Throughout this chapter, I shall provide the names of the database relations that are used to represent particular portions of PROTÉGÉ's model. Interested readers may refer to Appendix A for specific details of each relation.

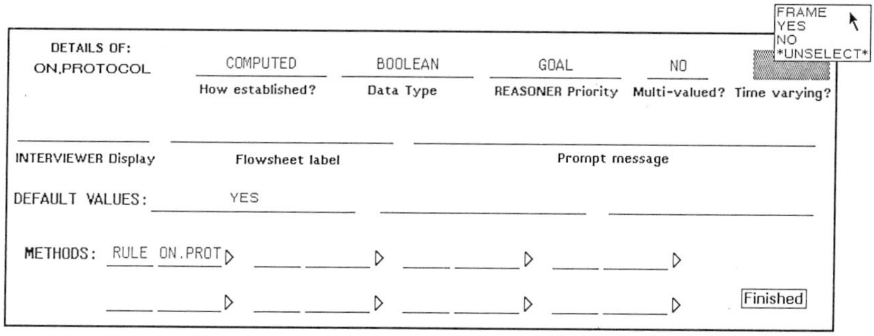

DETAILS OF:
ON.PROTOCOL

COMPUTED	BOOLEAN	GOAL	NO	FRAME / YES / NO / *UNSELECT*
How established?	Data Type	REASONER Priority	Multi-valued?	Time varying?

INTERVIEWER Display   Flowsheet label   Prompt message

DEFAULT VALUES: YES

METHODS: RULE ON.PROT ▷ ____ ____ ▷ ____ ____ ▷ ____ ____ ▷

____ ____ ▷ ____ ____ ▷ ____ ____ ▷ ____ ____ ▷   [Finished]

Figure 7.9: Properties of Plan Attributes

This graphical form allows knowledge engineers to enter properties of a selected attribute—in this case, the ON.PROTOCOL attribute of *PROTOCOL* entities. The knowledge engineer has declared that the Boolean value for this attribute is computed by e-ONCOCIN. He is about to further specify that the value of the ON.PROTOCOL attribute can vary over time, but that, in the absence of rules to the contrary, the value should remain the same from one patient visit to the next.

a value for the corresponding parameter, the *previous* value for that parameter should be used. This third option is needed to address the *frame problem,* a classic dilemma for AI programs that generate plans over time (McCarthy and Hayes, 1969).[6] The *frame* option instructs the system to construct a *frame rule* for this attribute when the e-ONCOCIN knowledge base is generated. The frame rule directs the Reasoner to use the previous value of the attribute in the absence of rules to the contrary. For example, in the oncology domain, the NAME of a chemotherapy would be a *frame* attribute; if there is no new

---

[6] Because it is usually impossible to enumerate *all* the side effects of a planning action, there often is uncertainty as to whether something that was true about the world *before* some action occurs is still true afterwards. A frame rule attempts to clear up some of this ambiguity by explicitly stating things that do and that do not change when particular actions take place. (Incidentally, the frame problem has nothing to do with *frame representations*. The term originates from the difficulty faced by cartoon animators in determining what parts of a scene should change from one frame to the next.)

chemotherapy to start, the name of the "current" chemotherapy is the name of the previous chemotherapy, which is presumably still underway.[7]

If the e-ONCOCIN Interviewer is to present the value of an attribute as part of the consultation recommendation, the knowledge engineer can specify how it should show the value (via the *"INTERVIEWER Display"* blank). He also can enter the label for the attribute that e-ONCOCIN prints on the Interviewer flowsheet (see Figure 4.1, page 93).[8] The PROTÉGÉ user also can specify a description of the attribute that e-ONCOCIN displays in the workstation prompt window when the end user requests a more complete explanation. This text string is entered via the *"Prompt message"* blank.

For those attributes that have values computed by e-ONCOCIN, the knowledge engineer can enter the manner in which e-ONCOCIN processes the corresponding parameter during the consultation via the *"REASONER Priority"* blank. If the PROTÉGÉ user designates that an attribute has a priority of *goal,* the Reasoner will actively attempt to ascertain the parameter's value by means of the inference methods specified at the bottom of the form. The knowledge engineer has the option, however, of setting an attribute's priority to *nongoal.* The values of nongoal parameters will not be explicitly pursued by the Reasoner. Thus, if the knowledge engineer created an attribute the value of which was required only for the purposes of concluding the value of some other attribute, the former could be given a *nongoal* priority. As a result, the reasoning process would be somewhat more efficient and controlled.

Entering Methods for Attributes of Planning Entities When attributes have values computed by e-ONCOCIN, the required methods are specified at the bottom of the entity-attribute form, as shown in Figure 7.10. The form allows up to eight different methods to be entered. The knowledge engineer first selects the type of method (that is, rule, LISP function, generator, or asking the e-ONCOCIN user) from a menu. Except in the

---

[7]The PROTÉGÉ programs that generate the knowledge base do not link the frame rule to the parameter that corresponds to the attribute in question, but rather link it to the parameter that corresponds to the DEFAULT.RULES attribute (see Table 7.3). In this manner, the frame rule will reach its conclusion only if all other rules to determine the current value have been tried and none has been successful.

[8]If application specialists are to enter the value for an attribute at the knowledge-editor level (for example, using p-OPAL), then the string entered into the *"Flowsheet label"* blank also is used by the editor that PROTÉGÉ generates to annotate *its* blanks.

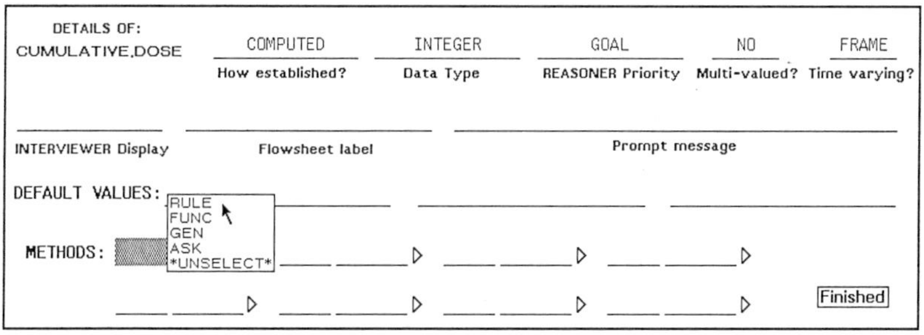

Figure 7.10: Entering Attribute Methods

If an attribute of a planning entity has a value that is computed by *e-ONCOCIN*, the required methods are entered at the bottom of the attribute-detail form. Almost always, the knowledge engineer will designate particular production rules, but LISP functions, generators, and asking the e-ONCOCIN user may also be specified as methods. Selecting one of the triangular arrows next to the name of a rule causes the form in Figure 7.11 to be displayed.

case of the *ASK* method, the knowledge engineer then enters name of the method into the adjacent blank from the keyboard. The names that the user types for these inference methods are arbitrary, but must be unique from one attribute to the next. (The method names are stored in the ATTRIBUTE-METHODS relation.) If the user enters the name of a production rule in Figure 7.10, he can select the arrow to the right of the rule name, causing PROTÉGÉ to open a form that allows him to examine and to edit the given rule (Figure 7.11). The rule form displays and updates data from three relations: RULE-PRECONDITION, RULE-CONDITION, and RULE-CONCLUSION.

At times, it may be useful for the knowledge engineer to view the names of *all* the rules associated with a given entity at one time. He can invoke a special form from the PROTÉGÉ main menu expressly for this purpose. The form displays all the attributes for a selected entity, listing all the rules for each. When the user selects one of the rule names with the mouse, the form in Figure 7.11 appears on the screen, allowing him to examine and update the corresponding production rule.

157

```
RULE CUMDSE                                                          Finished

  Concluded attribute: CUMULATIVE.DOSE   of   DRUG


  Precondition
  _____
  _____
  _____
  _____


  Premise
  (HAS.VALUE (VALUE.OF DRUG.CUMULATIVE.DOSE PREVIOUS (DRUG (DRUG.NAME))))
  _____
  _____
  _____


  Conclusion
  (DRUG.CUMULATIVE.DOSE (SUM.OF
      (VALUE.OF DRUG.CUMULATIVE.DOSE PREVIOUS (DRUG (DRUG.NAME)))
      (PRODUCT.OF DRUG.CURRENT.DOSE DRUG.TOTAL.DOSES)))
  _____
```

Figure 7.11: Rule Form

When the value of a user-defined attribute will need to be computed by e-ONCOCIN, the knowledge engineer can type in the required production rules using this form. In the absence of a sufficient knowledge-level model for the role of plan attributes during e-ONCOCIN consultations, this portion of knowledge entry in PROTÉGÉ currently is done at the symbol level. This form shows the rule that calculates the value of the CUMULATIVE.DOSE attribute of *drug* entities. The rule states that when there is a previous cumulative total known to the system, the current cumulative dose of a drug is the product of the current dose and the total number of doses that will be given, added to the previous total.

Summary of Planning Entities and Attributes

The backbone of PROTÉGÉ's model is a hierarchy of classes of planning entities. The model requires that knowledge engineers (1) define the class hierarchy (for example, state that protocols are composed of radiotherapies and chemotherapies, and that chemotherapies are composed of drugs), (2) declare the attributes common to the entities in each class (for example, state that drugs have *doses*), and (3) enter certain properties of each attribute (for example, state that a drug dose is an integer computed by e-ONCOCIN

158

using specific rules, and that the value varies over time). PROTÉGÉ provides a different graphical form for each of these three operations.

The knowledge engineer must specify how the value for each attribute is established. If the attribute has a predefined value shared by all instances of the class, the value is entered into PROTÉGÉ. If the attribute's value varies from class instance to class instance—but is constant for any particular instance—the user can declare that the value should be solicited by the knowledge editor that PROTÉGÉ will generate for the given application area. Finally, if the attribute's value depends on the circumstances present at the time of an e-ONCOCIN consultation, the knowledge engineer can enter the appropriate e-ONCOCIN rules.

7.3.2 Task Actions

I shall now discuss the second component in PROTÉGÉ's model of skeletal planning, the *actions* that can modify the manner in which the planning entities are carried out. The effects of these actions produce potentially complex changes to the basic plans that e-ONCOCIN would otherwise instantiate. Each action can start and stop different components of the plan, and can change the attributes of multiple plan entities. Experts in the application area, however, tend to regard these *actions* as unitary operations, as single "chunks" of behavior. In the oncology domain, for example, physicians think about actions such as delaying chemotherapy, attenuating the dose of a drug, or ordering a laboratory test as discrete behaviors. ONCOCIN, on the other hand, may invoke dozens of rules to reproduce such actions computationally.

PROTÉGÉ models each task action as an abstract series of operations. These operations typically must be *instantiated* before the action can be applied to the situation at hand. Each action thus has a general script (in the sense of Schank and Abelson, 1977) that defines its execution. The knowledge engineer uses PROTÉGÉ to declare the basic sequence of steps that constitutes the script—a sequence that may intentionally contain some gaps. The particular details needed to make the script operational often must be added later, either by the user of the knowledge editor (for example, an oncologist using p-OPAL) or by e-ONCOCIN itself.[9]

For example, the action script in Figure 7.12 shows how PROTÉGÉ represents the *attenuate* action in oncology. The script consists of two steps that are followed in sequence, allowing the task-dependent *attenuate* action to be specified in a task-independent manner. The knowledge engineer must create such a script for every task action in his model of the application area. The scripts are ultimately used by e-ONCOCIN to bring about desired modifications to the skeletal plans constructed during individual consultations.

A Model for Actions

PROTÉGÉ requires that the knowledge engineer associate each task action with a particular class of planning entity. This association is determined by the semantics of the application area. In p-OPAL, for example, the action to delay treatment is associated with instances of the class *chemotherapy.* The action to attenuate is associated with only *drugs.* The action to administer a new drug is associated with *chemotherapies*—not drugs—because PROTÉGÉ's model of hierarchical planning will not allow a drug to exist outside of a chemotherapy.

The PROTÉGÉ model for a task action has two major components: (1) a procedural script that is followed each time the action is carried out, and (2) a set of *attributes* that are used to particularize the task action for specific circumstances (note the two sections of the form in Figure 7.12). Because knowledge engineers define the script in terms of the attributes, assigning values to the attributes immediately instantiates the script. Just as it does with the values of planning-entity attributes, PROTÉGÉ assumes that the values of action attributes can be (1) predefined by the knowledge engineer, (2) entered by the application specialist using the generated knowledge editor, or (3) computed directly by e-ONCOCIN inference methods.

The PROTÉGÉ model for an action script is based on a set of domain-independent

---

[9]An action script can be viewed as a skeletal plan that is linear in its execution. Unlike the *hierarchical* skeletal plans that e-ONCOCIN refines from the planning entities in the model (for example, instances of chemotherapies and drugs), an action script is composed of sequence of predetermined—although not fully specified—steps. To avoid confusion, I shall use the term *script instantiation* when referring to task actions; *skeletal-plan refinement* will refer to only the instantiation of the *planning entities* themselves.

160

Attributes of __ATTENUATE__   Associated Entity: ____DRUG____   Selected Attribute: __ATTEN-TYPE__   [Finished]

ATTENUATION	▷	NEW.DOSE	▷	_____	▷	_____	▷	_____	▷
DOSE.BASIS	▷	_____	▷	_____	▷	_____	▷	_____	▷
PERMANENT?	▷	_____	▷	_____	▷	_____	▷	_____	▷
ATTEN-TYPE	▷	_____	▷	_____	▷	_____	▷	_____	▷

Action Sequence:	Precondition		Affected Plan Component		Additional Data
1 ALTER ATTR	_____	_____	DRUG	CURRENT.DOSE	NEW.DOSE
2 ALTER ATTR	PERMANENT?	YES	DRUG	STANDARD.DOS	NEW.DOSE
_____	_____	_____	_____	_____	_____
_____	_____	_____	_____	_____	_____
_____	_____	_____	_____	_____	_____
_____	_____	_____	_____	_____	_____
_____	_____	_____	_____	_____	_____
Action Primitive	Action Attribute	Attribute Value	Plan Entity Type	Attribute	Action Attribute

Figure 7.12: Script for Oncology Attenuate Action

This PROTÉGÉ form shows the script for the oncology *attenuate* action, which lowers the dose of a drug and, optionally, changes the "standard" dose for the drug to this new value. The script consists of a sequence of two steps that alter the values of certain planning-entity attributes. In the first step, the script resets the value of a drug's CURRENT.DOSE attribute to the value of NEW.DOSE, where NEW.DOSE is a computed attribute of the attenuate action itself. In the second step, if the attribute of the attenuate action called PERMANENT? has the value *YES*, then the drug's STANDARD.DOSE attribute also is reset to the value of NEW.DOSE. The script thus allows a task-dependent action (attenuating the dose of a drug) to be described in task-independent terms.

161

Table 7.4: PROTÉGÉ Action Primitives

Primitive	Meaning
START	Begin a new process
STOP	Terminate a process
SUSPEND	Suspend a process until a designated condition becomes *true*
RESUME	Resume execution of a suspended process
ALTER ATTRIBUTE	Change a designated attribute of a process to a new value
DISPLAY	Display a message for the e-ONCOCIN user

primitives that users can assemble to denote knowledge-level behaviors. These primitive operations directly modify components of the skeletal plan that e-ONCOCIN is building. The primitives view each plan component as a process that takes place over a discrete interval of time. Regardless of the domain-specific *meaning* of a given process, the knowledge engineer can use the primitives to represent desired alterations in the process' execution or changes in the values of the process' attributes.

There are six primitive operators in PROTÉGÉ (Table 7.4). Four of these (*start, stop, suspend,* and *resume*) directly affect the activity of elements of the current e-ONCOCIN plan. The *start* operator takes as its argument the name of a plan instance to set into execution; *start* causes the new instance to be linked into the planning hierarchy as a component of the plan element associated with the task action. (For example, suppose that a p-OPAL user states that, in a particular circumstance, the drug methotrexate should be administered. This knowledge-level specification implies that an instance of the drug methotrexate should *start* as a component of the currently active chemotherapy.) The *stop* operator terminates execution of a designated planning instance. (For example, *stop* the drug methotrexate.) The *suspend* operator requires two arguments: the plan instance to be suspended and the condition under which the instance should be resumed. (For example, *suspend* VAM chemotherapy until the attribute ON.PROTOCOL in the current protocol instance has the value *YES.*) *Resume* causes the designated instance, if it is suspended, to be reactivated—regardless of whether the condition that would otherwise have terminated the suspended state has been met. (For example, *resume* VAM chemotherapy.)

Knowledge engineers can use the two remaining primitives to accomplish desired side

162

effects. The operator *alter attribute* causes a designated attribute of an entity instance to be set to a particular value. (For example, set the attribute ON.PROTOCOL in the current protocol instance to the value *YES.*) The final operator, *display,* simply prints a message for the benefit of the e-ONCOCIN user.

The language that PROTÉGÉ provides for defining a step is fairly simple. Each primitive operator is treated as a function of one or two arguments. All the primitives (except *display*) require as an argument a planning-entity class, the current instance of which is affected by the operator. The *display* operator, on the other hand, takes as its only argument an *attribute* of the task action of which the *display* operator is a part; when e-ONCOCIN invokes the task action, the value of the designated attribute appears as a message to the user. Apart from *display,* the primitive operators may require the value of one of the attributes of the task action as a second argument. The *start* operator, for example, assumes that this second argument represents the name of the particular plan *instance* to initiate; *alter attribute* treats the second argument as the value with which to update the planning-entity attribute designated by the operator's first argument; *suspend* assumes the additional argument expresses the conditions under which the suspended plan component should later be resumed; the *resume* operator interprets the second argument as the name of the specific *instance* to restart. (If *resume* is not supplied with an instance name, all suspended processes of the designated class are restarted.)

Each step may have a *precondition* that must be satisfied for the step to be executed. The knowledge engineer therefore can indicate that a particular step of the script applies only when a designated attribute of the task action has a specific value. The use of these step preconditions is the only mechanism provided in PROTÉGÉ to modify the sequence of events that takes place when the Reasoner executes a task action. The preconditions in PROTÉGÉ are limited to expressions that check for equality between a given action attribute and some constant.

The script language, like any modeling language, is selective in the concepts that it can express. The primitive operators apply to only those instances of planning entities on which the Reasoner is working currently; procedures that affect entities that will be instantiated at some future time generally cannot be expressed. (Although the *start* and *resume* operators

163

refer to planning entities that have not yet been instantiated by the Reasoner, the indicated entities are required to be descendents of the current planning-entity instance.) There are no provisions either for conditional execution of more than a single step or for more complex procedural specifications such as concurrency. Furthermore, the steps in a script execute sequentially and without delay; there is no mechanism to denote interdependencies among the individual steps.

There are numerous ways in which PROTÉGÉ's script language could be enhanced and extended. Some of the current restrictions, such as the inability of the primitive operators to modify planning entities that already have been fully instantiated by the Reasoner, reflect practical limitations in the present ability of e-ONCOCIN to perform backtracking in a manner that guarantees that constraints among plan components will be satisfied. Yet, for the most part, the script language is restricted merely because the clinical-trial domain does not seem to require additional complexity. The current purpose of PROTÉGÉ is to help people build models of generic clinical trials. To increase the expressive power of the modeling language beyond the requirements of the anticipated application area would be superfluous, and would have the disadvantage of making the language more complicated to use. In the extreme, the language could be augmented to reflect the complete procedural capabilities of a Turing machine. As a result, the expanded language would lose its adaptedness to the problems that PROTÉGÉ has been designed to address; the language would lose its *semantic directness* (Hutchins et al., 1986). In the clinical-trial applications that I have explored, PROTÉGÉ's representation of task actions is sufficient to describe the knowledge-level procedures by which e-ONCOCIN can modify evolving skeletal plans. The practical limitations of the language within PROTÉGÉ's domain, however, will be determined only with more extensive experience.

Specification of Task Actions

As they do when instantiating the other components in PROTÉGÉ's model, knowledge engineers use graphical forms in PROTÉGÉ to describe task actions. Users first select the entry in the PROTÉGÉ main menu (see Figure 7.6) labeled *"Task-Level Actions."* The system then displays the form shown in Figure 7.13, allowing users to enter and to review

164

the names of the actions. Data specified using this form are translated into the ENTITY relation in the database; the *role* of these entities is always set to *ACTION*. Thus, the form in Figure 7.13 would create the following tuples:

SYSTEM	ENTITY-TYPE	ENTITY-ROLE
p-OPAL	ATTENUATE	ACTION
p-OPAL	WITHHOLD	ACTION
p-OPAL	SUBSTITUTE	ACTION
p-OPAL	DELAY	ACTION
p-OPAL	ABORT	ACTION
p-OPAL	REPORT	ACTION
p-OPAL	NEW PROTOCOL	ACTION
p-OPAL	OFF PROTOCOL	ACTION
p-OPAL	DISPLAY	ACTION
p-OPAL	ORDER TEST	ACTION

When the user selects one of the arrows in the form in Figure 7.13, PROTÉGÉ displays the form in Figure 7.14, showing the details of the corresponding task action.

At the top of the form in Figure 7.14, the knowledge engineer enters the name of the planning-entity class with which the particular task action should be associated (for example, the oncology *delay* action is associated with entities of the *chemotherapy* class; *attenuate* is associated with the *drug* class.) The ACTION-INVOKING-ENTITY relation is then updated accordingly. The top portion of the form also allows the knowledge engineer to enter and to review the *attributes* of the particular task action, much as the form in Figure 7.8 allows him to enter and review attributes of planning-entity classes. As with the latter form, the form in Figure 7.14 creates new tuples in the ATTRIBUTE relation to store these data.

As with attributes of planning entities, the roles that attributes of task actions play in problem solving depend on various properties of those attributes. The knowledge engineer can specify the properties of an action attribute by selecting the triangular arrow that appears next to the attribute name. The form in Figure 7.15 then appears on the workstation screen. Analogous to the form in Figure 7.9, this form allows the knowledge engineer to describe the individual attributes of a task action in complete detail. The first two rows of blanks update the ATTRIBUTE relation. At the bottom of the form, the

Figure 7.13: Action-Entities Form

This form allows knowledge engineers to list and to review the task actions for a
particular class of applications. In this example, the user has indicated pertinent
actions for clinical trials in oncology. Selecting one of the triangular arrows opens up
another form that shows the details of a given action.

blanks on the left store data in the DEFAULT-VALUES relation; those on the right update
ATTRIBUTE-METHODS.

The bottom portion of the form in Figure 7.14 allows the knowledge engineer to enter
the script for a task action. Because the syntax of the script language is uncomplicated,
filling out this part of the form is straightforward. Each row of blanks corresponds to a
different step in the script. The description of each step is divided into four parts. First,
the primitive operator for the step is listed. Second, there is an optional precondition

166

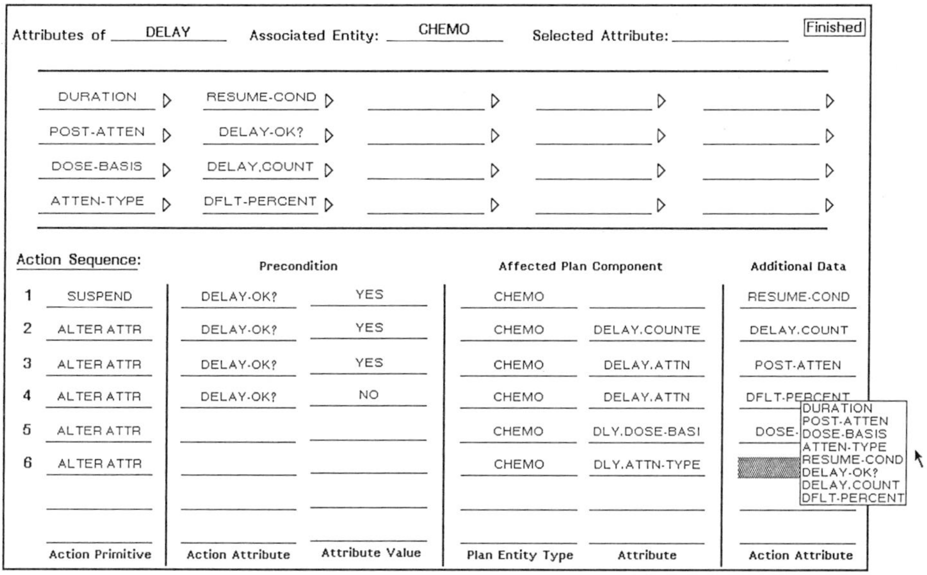

Figure 7.14: Task Actions Form

This form allows knowledge engineers to enter both the attributes and the scripts for task actions. Here, information for the oncology *delay* action is displayed. The script states that, when it is permissible to delay therapy (that is, when the attribute DELAY-OK? has the value *YES*), the current chemotherapy should be suspended and its DELAY.COUNTER attribute incremented. The script also alters attributes of the chemotherapy to establish a drug-dose attenuation that will be applied when the chemotherapy is resumed. If DELAY-OK? has the value *NO* (because the chemotherapy has already been postponed too long), the chemotherapy will not be suspended, but the doses of the chemotherapy's drugs will be attenuated by the user-entered value that the script transfers from the delay action's DFLT-PERCENT attribute. Other attributes of the action specify precisely how these delay-associated dose attenuations should be accomplished.

167

```
                          ┌─────────┐
                          │COMPUTED │
                          │EDITOR   │
        DETAILS OF:       │PREDEFINED│ ↖
        ATTENUATION       │*UNSELECT*│
                          ▓▓▓▓▓▓▓▓▓▓▓      PERCENT           NO
                          How established?   Data Type      Multi-valued?

                                      ATTENUATION
        _____           _____    _____
        INTERVIEWER Display           Flowsheet label              Prompt message

DEFAULT VALUES: _____      METHODS: ____ _____ ▷  ____ _____ ▷

                _____               ____ _____ ▷  ____ _____ ▷  Finished
```

Figure 7.15: Properties of Task Actions

Knowledge engineers use this graphical form to enter and to review the properties
of task-action attributes. This form shows the properties of the attribute ATTEN-
UATION, which belongs to the *attenuate* task action. The knowledge engineer is
about to specify that the value of the attribute should be entered via p-OPAL for
each instance of the *attenuate* action.

for the step, represented as an attribute of the task action in one column followed by a
qualifying value in the next. Third, the step description may contain the name of the
entity class to which the primitive operator is applied, optionally followed by the name of
a specific attribute within that class. Fourth, there is a blank that may optionally contain
the name of an attribute of the task action. The e-ONCOCIN Reasoner may use the value
of this attribute as an argument to the primitive operator.

The knowledge engineer enters the script step by step, filling in the necessary blanks.
Almost always, he makes the entries by selecting values from menus. As each primitive
operator is specified in the first column, PROTÉGÉ prints a step number beside the row
of blanks on the form and enables the user to enter data into other blanks in the particular
row of the step description. As always, PROTÉGÉ's control of which blanks are active is

168

based on the values of form variables; these values are programmed to reflect the evolving semantics of the user's entries. For example, if the knowledge engineer declares that a particular step entails the primitive operator *display,* PROTÉGÉ will not allow him to enter the name of an "affected plan component," because such an argument would be meaningless in this context. The *display* operator takes only one argument—an attribute of the task action, the value of which will be printed for the e-ONCOCIN user. The knowledge engineer can enter only the appropriate attribute name using the last blank in the row, in the column labeled "additional data."

In Figure 7.14, the action attributes and the script specify—in domain-independent terms—the *delay* action in oncology. Understanding how that action is modeled requires understanding the roles that the various attributes play in effecting the required behavior. The DURATION attribute is used to represent the the number of days that chemotherapy should be postponed. The value of this attribute is entered using p-OPAL, and depends on the clincial circumstances that, according to the protocol, are a cause for a delay in treatment. The POST-ATTEN attribute designates a percentage by which the dose of chemotherapeutic drugs should be attenuated following the delay in treatment; the DOSE-BASIS and ATTEN-TYPE attributes allow the p-OPAL user to provide additional information regarding how these post-delay attenuations (if any) should be computed. The DELAY-OK? attribute has a Boolean value computed by e-ONCOCIN; DELAY-OK? has the value *false* if therapy has already been delayed more times than the maximum number specified by the MAX-DELAYS attribute of the associated *chemotherapy;* otherwise, DELAY-OK? has the value *true.* An e-ONCOCIN rule causes the value of the DELAY.COUNT attribute to be set to 1 plus the number of consecutive times that the given chemotherapy has already been delayed; this incremented value then is used by e-ONCOCIN to update the DELAY.COUNTER attribute of the indicated *chemotherapy.*

Entering the script that defines the sequence of operations required to carry out the task action is reminiscent of traditional computer programming. The script for the *delay* action in Figure 7.14, for example, performs the following functions: If DELAY-OK? is *true,* the current *chemotherapy* process is suspended, and the latter's DELAY.COUNTER attribute incremented. The DELAY.ATTEN attribute of the chemotherapy then is set to the value of the POST-ATTEN attribute of the *delay* action. (When the chemotherapy process resumes after the delay, the value of the DELAY.ATTEN attribute will be used to readjust the dosages of the component drugs.) If the value of DELAY-OK? is *false,* then no suspension of the chemotherapy process occurs; the value of the chemotherapy's DELAY.ATTEN attribute, however, is set to the value of the DFLT-PERCENT attribute of the *delay* action. Consequently, when the protocol does not permit additional postponement of therapy, all drugs are given, but the doses of those drugs are attenuated by the percentage specified by the p-OPAL user in the DFLT-PERCENT attribute.

PROTÉGÉ stores each step of the script as a tuple in the ACTION-SEQUENCE relation (see Appendix A). This relation, like a number of other relations in the PROTÉGÉ database, is in *second-normal form* (that is, there are nonkey fields that are interdependent). The relation could easily be further normalized by splitting it into a number of separate relations, removing semantic dependencies among the nonkey fields. Such splitting has the advantage of ensuring that changes to the data reflect these semantic dependencies. Yet, because the data are modified only via this PROTÉGÉ form, and because the behavior of the blanks has been programmed to prevent entries that are semantically inconsistent, full normalization of the relation is not required. In fact, relying on the *form system* to manage some of the dependencies in the data reduces the total number of relations needed in the database, thus simplifying the system and increasing its efficiency.

Summary of Task Actions

PROTÉGÉ's model of skeletal planning makes a distinction between the components of the plan and additional operations that modify the plan components. The latter are referred to as *actions*. Knowledge engineers use PROTÉGÉ's graphical forms to describe these actions at the knowledge level as a sequence of primitive operations in the form of a script.

The steps in a script are based on six primitive operators that form the basis of a simple language for describing processes. Each primitive requires either one or two arguments. One of these arguments may be a variable that is defined as an *attribute* of the task action being specified. Like the values of planning-entity attributes, the attributes of task actions may be established by the knowledge engineer using PROTÉGÉ, by the application specialist using the generated editor, or by e-ONCOCIN in the course of a consultation. As a result, different portions of an action script may be instantiated at each of the three levels.

7.3.3 Input Data

The third component of PROTÉGÉ's model deals with the data that are entered into the advice system. This part of the model allows the knowledge engineer to use PROTÉGÉ to describe the nature of these data. The application expert then can use the PROTÉGÉ-generated editor to create rules that invoke specific task actions when specific conditions involving these data are true. At the lowest level, the e-ONCOCIN Interviewer uses PROTÉGÉ's description of the expected input data to tailor its graphical user interface.

A Model for Input Data

PROTÉGÉ views input data as belonging to discrete *classes*. A data class groups together data items that application specialists tend to regard as related. In ONCOCIN, for example, physicians classify their entries that define the patient's condition and response to treatment using descriptors such as "hematology data" or "chemistry data." Such distinctions among data items are of great practical importance because all the input data cannot fit on the workstation screen at the same time. ONCOCIN necessarily divides the data among separate sections of its graphical flowsheet. There is a "hematology form" for hematology data and a "chemistry form" for serum chemistry data. The various data classes make intuitive sense to the physicians who use ONCOCIN.

All items within a data class have a *data type*—a designation of the particular values that a given data item can acquire legally. The data type is a property of a data item determined by the semantics of the application area. In ONCOCIN, for example, a patient's platelet count is always expressed as an *integer;* a white-blood-cell count is represented by a *real number;* the presence of various kinds of toxicity is represented on an integer scale from 1 to 4.

There are two varieties of data types: *continuous* and *enumerated.* Items with a continuous data type have values that are composed of arbitrary strings of characters. In

PROTÉGÉ-generated editors and advice systems, users enter *continuous* data by composing desired values using registers. *Enumerated* data types, on the other hand, are sets of fixed values. For example, the grade of an ONCOCIN toxicity is always one of 1, 2, 3, or 4; no other possibilities exist. Because the number of choices is finite, users generally enter values for items having an enumerated data type by making a selection from a pop-up menu.

PROTÉGÉ distinguishes between data classes in which *all* data items have an enumerated data type and those in which items have either an enumerated or a continuous type. This distinction becomes important for the knowledge editors that PROTÉGÉ generates, which must determine the appropriate graphical forms with which to display rules that involve data of particular classes. For example, various ordinal scales (and, hence, various data types) may be used for representing different kinds of toxicity, but all items within the *toxicity* data class have an enumerated data type. When the knowledge engineer declares that the toxicity data class is composed exclusively of enumerated data types, p-OPAL can take advantage of that information; it can use a graphical form that lists all possible values for data items in the toxicity class when rules are entered (see Figure 8.6, page 198). The knowledge engineer otherwise declares a data class to be *continuous,* which means that both enumerated and continuous data types may appear in the data class. (In p-OPAL, both the hematology and chemistry data classes are *continuous.*)

In addition to having a name and a data type, the items within a data class possess other properties. All data items have a text string that serves as a label when terse descriptions of the item are printed out. (This string appears as a *label* on the e-ONCOCIN flowsheet.) Furthermore, data items may have a more verbose description that e-ONCOCIN can print in its prompt window for purposes of explanation. Each input item may represent static information that tends to be collected only once (for example, patient demographic data) or, more commonly, the data may vary over time. Although both static and dynamic data can be printed by the e-ONCOCIN Interviewer on the graphical flowsheet, PROTÉGÉ's model also assumes that display of a particular data item can be disabled optionally. Thus, if the *"Show Always?"* property is set to *NO,* the e-ONCOCIN Interviewer will not create a row in which to display the item if there are no data values to display. This property allows the knowledge engineer to distinguish between routine data items that should always appear on the flowsheet (whether any data have been recorded for these items or not) and less customary user entries.

PROTÉGÉ presumes that the name given to the end user's means for acquiring the value of a data item may not be the same as that given to the data item itself. In the clinical-trial domain, for example, physicians frequently order composite laboratory tests that result in the reporting of multiple data items. For example, the values for all the items on the hematology form can be obtained by ordering just a single test: *the complete blood count* (CBC). Thus, if e-ONCOCIN will need the value of the patient's white-blood-cell count at the time of its next consultation, the program should request that a CBC be performed.[10] Accordingly, PROTÉGÉ's model links each data item to a corresponding data source (that is, a laboratory test) that provides the appropriate value.

Data items with *continuous* data types may have additional properties. Because users construct the values for these data via register input devices, it often is desirable to test whether entries are within reasonable ranges. The e-ONCOCIN Interviewer can then inform the user when an entered value appears suspect. PROTÉGÉ thus allows knowledge engineers to place specific upper and lower bounds on the permissible values for numeric data items. Values outside this range are intended to be rejected by e-ONCOCIN. (For example, entering a body weight of less than 0 kg or greater than 500 kg would be a clear error.) PROTÉGÉ's model also presumes that knowledge engineers may want to indicate upper and lower bounds on what are "reasonable" entries for a particular datum. Thus, should an e-ONCOCIN user enter a weight that is, say, less than 40 kg or greater than 100 kg, the system will accept the value but will ask the physician to confirm that the number is correct.

Describing Input Data for PROTÉGÉ

Selecting *"Input Data"* from the PROTÉGÉ main menu (see Figure 7.6) causes the form in Figure 7.16 to appear. The knowledge engineer can use this form to enter and to review

---

[10] Even when physicians are interested in no other values, automated clinical laboratories find it more efficient to perform the entire CBC than to count only the white blood cells in a sample.

Figure 7.16: Data-Classes Form

Knowledge engineers use this form to enter the classes of data items in the application area. The knowledge editor that PROTÉGÉ generates will have a different form for each data class that the user specifies. In addition, the e-ONCOCIN Interviewer will create a separate section of its graphical flowsheet for each class.

the *classes* of data items that are relevant for the application area. This form creates and displays tuples in the ENTITY relation; the ROLE field of each tuple is set to the value *DATUM.*

When the user selects one of the triangular arrows in the form in Figure 7.16, he can then enter and review the individual data items within the data class using the form shown in Figure 7.17. As each new data item is typed in, PROTÉGÉ creates a new tuple in the DATA-ITEM relation. The form in Figure 7.17 also asks the knowledge engineer to indicate

174

| CHEMISTRY | CONTINUOUS | CREATININE | Finished |
Data Class	Data-Type Class	Selected Data Item	
CALCIUM ▷	SGOT ▷	▷	▷
PHOSPHORUS ▷	SGPT ▷	▷	▷
BUN ▷	SODIUM ▷	▷	▷
URIC ACID ▷	POTASSIUM ▷	▷	▷
GLUCOSE ▷	CHLORIDE ▷	▷	▷
TOTAL PROTEIN ▷	CO2 ▷	▷	▷
ALBUMIN ▷	CREATININE ▷	▷	▷
TOTAL BILIRUBIN ▷	▷	▷	▷
CHOLESTEROL ▷	▷	▷	▷
ALK PHOSPHATASE ▷	▷	▷	▷
LDH ▷	▷	▷	▷

Figure 7.17: Data-Items Form

Users enter the list of data items within the designated data class via this form. They also must indicate whether the data types of the members of the data class are exclusively enumerated or whether some data types are continuous.

whether the items in the data class have continuous or enumerated data types; the result is stored in the relation called DATA-CLASS-DATA-TYPE.

By selecting one of the triangular arrows in Figure 7.17, the knowledge engineer can examine and specify the properties of the corresponding data item. For example, Figure 7.18 shows information regarding *serum creatinine*. The entries made using this form update the DATA-ITEM, TESTS, and DATA-TYPES relations.

7.3.4 Data Types

Every attribute of every entity and every data item that the knowledge engineer describes using PROTÉGÉ must have a data type. PROTÉGÉ, the editors that PROTÉGÉ generates, and e-ONCOCIN all use the data-type information to determine the legal operations and functions that may be applied to the particular datum. Each data type is associated

175

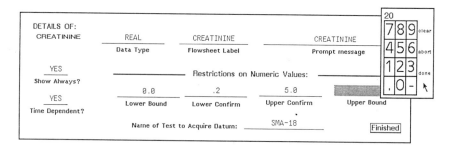

Figure 7.18: Data-Item-Detail Form

PROTÉGÉ allows knowledge engineers to specify the properties of e-ONCOCIN's input data using this graphical form. The "restrictions on numeric values" apply to only those data items having *continuous* data types, and are used by e-ONCOCIN to validate the end user's entries. In this example, the user is about to declare that when an e-ONCOCIN user enters a serum creatinine value that is greater than 20 mg/dl, that value should be rejected by the system.

with a specific *input device,* such as a menu or register. Thus, the data type of an entry provides the basis for programs to determine how new values should be elicited from users.

Some data types are built into the system and are always available when knowledge engineers create new applications. There are three such predefined *continuous* data types: *integer, real,* and *percent.* Each is associated with a different, specialized register input device. There is just one predefined *enumerated* data type in PROTÉGÉ—*Boolean,* which is specified by a menu that has the binary choices *yes* and *no.*

Although they are not predefined, there are other data types that PROTÉGÉ creates on its own. Specifically, PROTÉGÉ requires that the *name* attribute of a planning entity have an enumerated data type, the name of which is the same as the name of the entity. For example, in defining p-OPAL, there is both a *CHEMO* planning entity and a *CHEMO* data type. The CHEMO data type lists all the possible chemotherapy names that the knowledge engineer anticipates. (This list can later be augmented by the p-OPAL user, if necessary.) Similarly, p-OPAL has *XRT* and *DRUG* data types. Each time a new entity is entered into the form in Figure 7.7, the PROTÉGÉ editor automatically assigns the required data type by creating a new tuple in the DATA-TYPES relation.

All other data-type names must be entered explicitly by the knowledge engineer. Whenever he describes a planning-entity attribute using the form in Figure 7.9, or enters an action attribute (Figure 7.15), or defines a data item (Figure 7.18), he must enter a data type. In each case, the knowledge engineer can either select an existing data type from a menu or specify the name of a new data type. If he enters a new data-type name, the DATA-TYPES relation is updated appropriately, making the new data type available for assignment to other attributes and data items.

Of course, for the knowledge engineer to type in only the *names* of the new data types is not enough. For PROTÉGÉ to generate a useful knowledge editor, the knowledge engineer must eventually assign a specific software input device to each data type. Thus, selecting the item labeled *"Data Types"* in the PROTÉGÉ main menu (see Figure 7.6) brings up the form shown in Figure 7.19, which has been designed for the knowledge engineer to make these choices.

At the top of the form in Figure 7.19 is a list of all of the data types that have been declared. When the user selects one of the data types with the mouse, the blank labeled *"Input Format"* becomes active and displays whether input data of the designated type are to be entered via menus (if the data type is enumerated), entered via registers (if the data type is continuous), or simply typed in from the keyboard. The knowledge engineer can change the input format from the default device, if necessary, by selecting the input-format blank and making a choice from a menu. The blank to the right of the input-format blank either displays the name of the register to be used for entering items of the designated data type (as in Figure 7.19), or, if the input device is a menu, displays the optional menu *title* (Figure 7.20).

When the user indicates that data of a particular type are to be entered via menus, the data-type form is used to enumerate all the possible values (Figure 7.20). Each value has an optional associated *prompt message* that provides the end user with an additional explanation of what the value means. The data entered into the form are used to produce all the input menus in e-ONCOCIN and in the PROTÉGÉ-generated editor. PROTÉGÉ stores the data in the MENU-SELECTIONS relation.

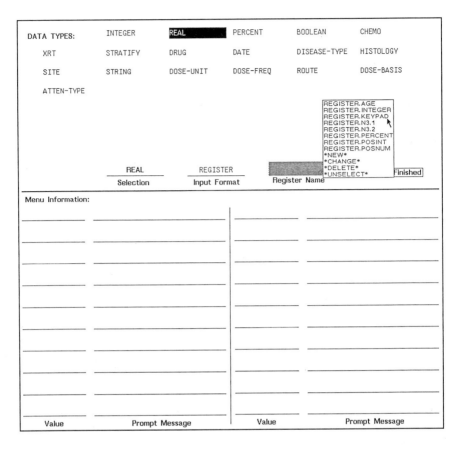

Figure 7.19: Data-Types Form

This form displays all the data types that have been declared for a particular domain. Knowledge engineers specify the software input device for each data type. Here, the user is indicating that *real* data should be elicited using a specific predefined register.

7.4 Conclusion

PROTÉGÉ is built from a series of graphical forms and specialized procedures that operate on a set of database relations. This chapter has described what the forms look like and how they behave. It has provided an overview of how the forms are programmed and how they are linked to the database. My goal has been to provide enough details about the implementation that, in principle, my work can be reproduced by other researchers.

In concentrating on the details, however, it is important not to lose sight of what

178

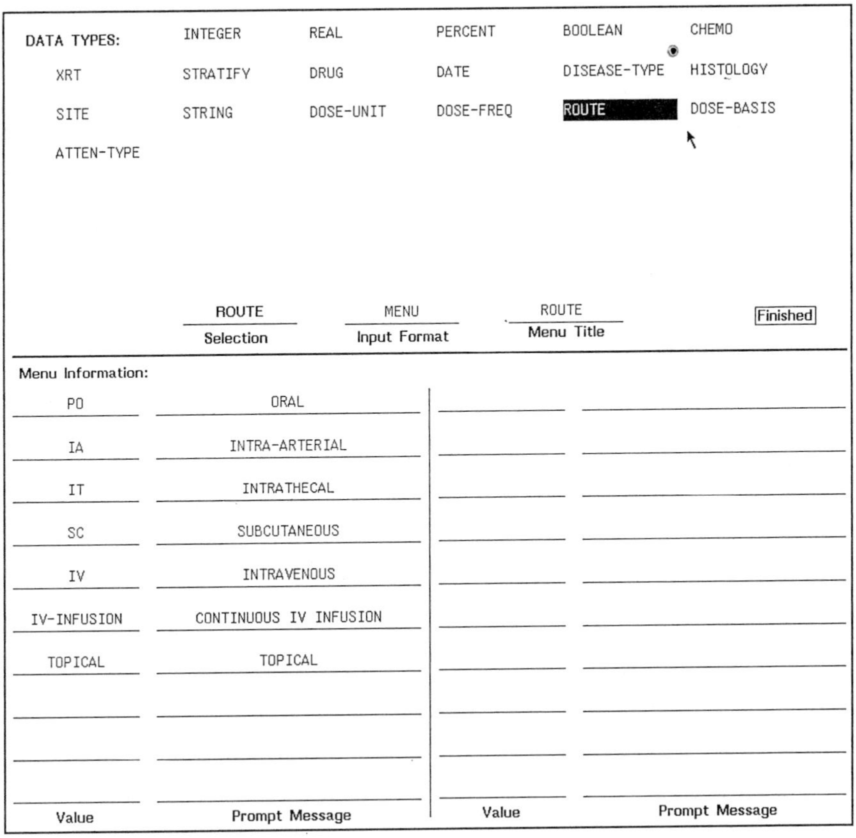

Figure 7.20: Entry of Menu Information

When a knowledge engineer declares that a particular data type is to be entered via a *menu*, the bottom portion of the data-type form allows him to enumerate the possible values. Each value is associated with an optional prompt message, which e-ONCOCIN displays to the end user to provide explanation.

the system is doing in a broader sense: PROTÉGÉ starts with a general model of problem solving and allows a knowledge engineer to instantiate that model for a particular class of application tasks. Both the relations in PROTÉGÉ's database and the blanks in PROTÉGÉ's graphical forms are representative of an underlying model of skeletal planning. The model is in many ways incomplete, requiring the knowledge engineer to descend to the symbol level to express a large number of concepts. The model also is quite broad, encompassing large portions of the behavior needed to carry out planning in a complex

179

clinical application.

The terms and relationships in PROTÉGÉ's model form a systematic domain (see Section 2.2.2). Consequently, the knowledge engineer who fills in the forms must have a clear understanding of what PROTÉGÉ means by *planning entity, action,* or *input data.* Like other knowledge editors based on explicit models of problem solving, PROTÉGÉ requires its users to assimilate the model and to agree to define tasks in the world in terms of the systematic domain. Because novice users cannot be expected to find the systematic domain intuitive, PROTÉGÉ must be regarded as a tool primarily for knowledge engineers, not for application specialists.

When knowledge engineers describe a clinical-trial application for PROTÉGÉ, the terms and relationships that they define represent *yet another* model and another systematic domain—one that pertains to a particular class of clinical trials. As I shall describe in the next chapter, this task-specific model provides the basis for a knowledge editor that PROTÉGÉ creates for use expressly by clinical-trial experts. The resultant knowledge editor allows application experts to extend the task model created using PROTÉGÉ, and thus to define specific task instances. At that stage, knowledge engineers need no longer be involved in the knowledge-entry process.

8 Generation of Knowledge Editors

The AI literature contains reports of dozens of computer programs that have been designed to facilitate knowledge acquisition. Each of these tools in some way helps knowledge engineers and application specialists to build computational models of expert problem solving. Each tool also has its own framework for guiding a user's interaction with the system—a *conceptual model* of the knowledge to be entered. In the case of OPAL, the conceptual model is based on the task of therapy planning in oncology. In the case of PROTÉGÉ, the conceptual model is based primarily on the problem-solving method of skeletal-plan refinement. A key lesson of work described in this book is that a *partial model of expert behavior* entered into one knowledge editor, such as PROTÉGÉ, can in turn be used as the *conceptual model* for another knowledge-editing program, such as OPAL.

This chapter describes the knowledge editors that are created by PROTÉGÉ. It traces the origins of their conceptual models and the transfer of information from PROTÉGÉ down to an executable expert system. For consistency, I shall draw all my examples from p-OPAL, the PROTÉGÉ-generated knowledge editor for clinical trials in oncology that was the focus of the examples in Chapter 7. Before proceeding, however, I shall address a potential ambiguity in language. In this chapter, I shall always use the terms *editor* and *knowledge editor* to denote knowledge-editing tools created using PROTÉGÉ. When referring to the PROTÉGÉ system itself—which, of course, also is a knowledge editor—I shall simply use the name PROTÉGÉ.

8.1 The Knowledge to be Entered

Chapter 7 described the knowledge that users enter into PROTÉGÉ. It is now appropriate to consider the statements that PROTÉGÉ users *cannot* enter. Whereas PROTÉGÉ allows knowledge engineers to describe *classes* of clinical trials, the editors that PROTÉGÉ generates are concerned with clinical-trial *instances*. These editors allow application experts to add additional, instance-specific knowledge to the knowledge already entered using PROTÉGÉ. The latter specifications allow e-ONCOCIN to consult on patients enrolled in the particular clinical trials that the experts describe.

The best way to explore the concepts that must be entered at the editor level is to examine what knowledge is entered into PROTÉGÉ and to ascertain where the gaps are. There are two kinds of omissions: (1) instance-specific relationships that PROTÉGÉ cannot represent, and (2) instance-specific values for task-dependent attributes. I shall now describe each of these notions.

8.1.1 Instance-Specific Relationships

A major purpose of PROTÉGÉ-generated editors is to allow domain experts to describe relationships that are present in specific clinical trials. The PROTÉGÉ user, for example, lists the types of input data that are relevant in the application area (for example, hematology data) and defines carefully, in a generic sense, the task actions that changes in the input data can invoke (for example, attenuating the dose of a drug). Never entered into PROTÉGÉ, however, are the precise relationships between possible data values and *specific* actions (for example, when the white-blood-cell is less than 2000, attenuate methotrexate by 75 percent). These relationships vary from protocol to protocol and are entered at only the knowledge-editor level. PROTÉGÉ-generated editors, like the original OPAL program (see Section 6.2.4), use custom-tailored forms to allow users to define the protocol-specific mappings of potential data values onto appropriate actions.

The other group of relationships that users must describe at the editor level involve the planning hierarchy. In PROTÉGÉ, knowledge engineers enter only the *classes* of entities that may constitute a skeletal plan and the hierarchical relationships among the classes.

182

What is missing is specific knowledge of how one instance of a class in the hierarchy is composed of other instances. Thus, a knowledge engineer can tell PROTÉGÉ that chemotherapies are made up of drugs. He also can enumerate the names of the various chemotherapies and drugs in the application area. What the knowledge engineer *cannot* tell PROTÉGÉ, however, is how *instances* of those drugs such as VP-16, Adriamycin, and methotrexate can be administered in sequence to yield a chemotherapy such as VAM.

The PROTÉGÉ-generated editors assume that instances of each class in the planning hierarchy always are composed of instances of classes at the next level of detail. More important, the component instances are related to form a *procedure* that takes place over time. In OPAL, for example, each *protocol* instance has, as one of its attributes, a procedural specification for the sequence of *chemotherapy* and *radiotherapy* instances that constitute the protocol (see Section 6.2.2). ONCOCIN follows this procedure to determine the particular chemotherapy and radiotherapy treatments to administer at each patient visit. In the editors generated by PROTÉGÉ, I have extended this model so that *every* nonterminal instance in the planning hierarchy has such a procedural attribute. The domain expert must use the knowledge editor to define the necessary procedural relationships when any nonterminal instance is declared. Thus, in both OPAL and p-OPAL, users specify procedures that define how each protocol instance is composed of chemotherapies and radiotherapies; in p-OPAL, however, they must in addition specify procedures that describe how each chemotherapy is composed of individual drugs. (The original OPAL program makes the simplifying assumption that all the drugs in a chemotherapy are given once, concurrently, at the start of each treatment cycle. Explicit definition of a chemotherapy's procedure therefore is not required, or even possible, in OPAL.)

Domain experts enter these procedural specifications into the PROTÉGÉ-generated editors using a modified version of the iconic flowchart language originally developed for OPAL (Musen et al., 1988b). The manner in which the knowledge editors apply this language is outlined in Section 8.3.

8.1.2 Instance-Specific Values

The second group of concepts that must be entered at the editor level involve assumptions that depend on the application area. These entries correspond to those task-specific attributes defined at the PROTÉGÉ level that have values that must be established using the editor. In PROTÉGÉ, there are two kinds of attributes that may have *editor-established* values: (1) attributes of planning entities (for example, the standard dose of a drug) and (2) attributes of task actions (for example, the percentage by which to attenuate a dose). For simplicity, I shall refer to these characteristics as *editor-established attributes,* even though it is the *value,* not the attribute itself, that is defined at the editor level.

Whenever an application specialist uses a knowledge editor to define a new planning-entity instance (for example, a specific *drug*), she must enter a value for each editor-established attribute that was defined for the class at the PROTÉGÉ level. Thus, if the knowledge engineer tells PROTÉGÉ that instances of the *drug* class have an editor-established attribute called *dose*, then, each time a new drug is specified at the editor level, the application specialist must designate the appropriate *dose* value. Knowledge engineers use PROTÉGÉ to define the names and properties of editor-established attributes for each planning-entity class. When domain experts later enter *values* for these attributes, specific instances within the class become distinguishable. For example, the drug named methotrexate, which is administered orally, with a standard dose of 25 mg, can be discerned from the drug named cyclophosphamide, which is administered intravenously, with a standard dose of 100 mg. The editor-established attributes thus represent a set of related terms (a model) that domain experts can instantiate via the editor.

As described in Section 7.3.2, PROTÉGÉ users also declare editor-established attributes for task actions (such as *attenuate*). Each time an application specialist uses an editor to enter a rule that associates a particular set of conditions with a particular task action, she is designating an *instance* of the action. The rule is characterized by the specific conditions that predicate the action and by the values for the editor-established attributes that the user enters to define the action more completely. For example, in one situation, the dose of a drug may be attenuated by 50 percent. In another, the attenuation may be 75 percent. In each case, the percentage is represented as an editor-established

184

attribute of the *attenuate* action. A value must be assigned to this attribute to make the action operational. The editor-established attributes of each action constitute a set of terms (a model) by which the application specialist can describe the specific behaviors she wishes the action to entail.

8.1.3 Summary

Instantiation of a clinical-trial protocol at the editor level requires a number of different specifications. The domain expert must define the associations between possible values of input data with specific actions to take. She must indicate the names of the *instances* within each class in the planning hierarchy that compose other instances. The expert also must establish the *procedures* that determine the order in which these instances become active. Finally, for each entity in the planning hierarchy and for each specific action, the expert must determine the values for the attributes that distinguish one instance from another.

8.2 A System of Generic Forms

Much of the knowledge that users define at the editor level is entered using graphical forms similar to those that were hand-crafted for OPAL. The editor forms, however, are initially void of any application-specific information (Figure 8.1). When PROTÉGÉ generates a knowledge editor for a new task domain, no form objects are created *de novo*. Rather, preexisting form templates are instantiated based on the knowledge entered into PROTÉGÉ.

When an editor form is first opened, the form blanks query the PROTÉGÉ database to determine (1) the annotations to display, (2) the data to accept from the user, and (3) the specific registers and menus to use for input. The database queries instantiate the generic form template so that application specialists can view and edit the pertinent information. As in PROTÉGÉ, instantiation of the forms is controlled by the rebinding of *form variables* (see Section 7.1.1), the values of which are passed to the editor form objects when the forms are opened on the workstation screen. This instantiation of the

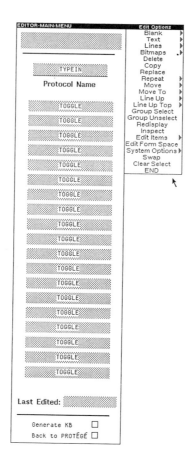

Figure 8.1: A Generic Form

All the forms at the editor level are generic templates, instantiated based on information entered at the PROTÉGÉ level. This figure shows the editor main-menu form as it appeared when it was created using the form-system editor. When this form template is instantiated, the blanks labeled *toggle* display the names of the editor forms that a user can access from this main menu. (Compare with Figure 8.2.)

forms must not be confused with the other kind of instantiation that takes place at the editor level—the instantiation of a *task model* by the user to encode particular clinical-trial protocols.

The software that controls the graphical forms at the editor level is the same program code that controls the forms in PROTÉGÉ. The editor forms access information from the same database that PROTÉGÉ uses, although the editors employ their own set of output relations to *store* data entered by the domain expert (Appendix B). Thus, the structure of the editor form objects can be the same as that of the form objects in PROTÉGÉ. More important, both sets of objects are resident in the workstation's memory at the same time. Toggling the blank labeled *"Invoke Editor"* on the main-menu form in PROTÉGÉ (see Figure 7.6, page 144) (1) closes the PROTÉGÉ form and (2) opens the main-menu form for whichever knowledge editor was selected (Figure 8.2). Toggling the blank labeled *"Back to PROTÉGÉ"* on the editor form returns the user to the PROTÉGÉ main menu. Passage between the two systems thus is fluid and virtually instantaneous.

Although there is no application-specific knowledge incorporated within the generic form objects, the forms do make significant assumptions about the contents of the PROTÉGÉ database, the concepts to be entered at the editor level, and the manner in which users will interact with the system. I shall discuss these assumptions as I describe each of the generic editor forms.

8.2.1 The Editor Main Menu

When a user selects the box labeled *"Invoke Editor"* on the PROTÉGÉ main-menu form (see Figure 7.6, page 144), the system instantiates an editor for the application that currently appears in the PROTÉGÉ blank labeled *"Editor Name."* Accordingly, the editor main-menu form in Figure 8.2 appears on the workstation screen. PROTÉGÉ passes the name of the application (in the case of Figure 7.6, *p-OPAL*) to the editor via a form variable. The value of this variable is then displayed in the topmost blank of the editor main menu.

Just as the PROTÉGÉ main menu is used to enter the name of an application area, the editor main menu is used to select the name of a particular protocol within a given

187

Figure 8.2: Editor Main Menu Form

This form allows the application specialist to enter the name of the particular protocol to be defined and to access the other task-specific forms at the knowledge editor level. The toggle labeled *"PROTOCOL DATA"* allows the user to specify information regarding the designated protocol and the other planning entities in the hierarchy (for example, chemotherapies and drugs). The other toggles in the menu, such as the highlighted blank labeled *"CHEMISTRY,"* represent the data classes that the knowledge engineer defined at the PROTÉGÉ level and denote forms that allow the application specialist to enter protocol-specific rules. When the user selects the box labeled *"Generate KB"*, an e-ONCOCIN knowledge base is created from the specifications that have been entered. The box labeled *"Back to PROTÉGÉ"* closes the editor main menu and returns the user to the PROTÉGÉ environment.

class of clinical trials. The user simply selects the blank labeled *"Protocol Name."* A menu appears, displaying data from the PROTOCOL relation (Appendix B). The user can either select a previously entered protocol from the menu or type a new protocol name into the blank; the PROTOCOL relation is then updated accordingly.

The other blanks in the editor main menu do not accept input, but rather provide access to the other forms in the system. When the user selects one of these toggles with the mouse, the corresponding editor form opens on the display. The first such item in Figure 8.2 opens a form for specifying the details of the *protocol* instance. This *"PROTOCOL DATA"* toggle is always the first selection in the list, regardless of the application area, as PROTÉGÉ predefines the most general component of every skeletal plan to be *protocol.* Once the protocol form is displayed, the user can access other forms for describing the component instances in the planning hierarchy (Section 8.2.3).

The remaining selections in the main-menu list are used to access forms that allow the user to map potential data values onto corresponding actions. These forms have domain-specific counterparts in OPAL (see Figure 6.7 and Figure 6.8, pages 125 and 126); in the PROTÉGÉ-generated editors, however, the form templates are totally generic and are instantiated with the necessary domain-dependent information from the PROTÉGÉ database (Section 8.2.2). The editor main menu is programmed to list a different form for every *class* of data item in the application area that the knowledge engineer has declared at the PROTÉGÉ level. The system determines the names of these data classes by querying the PROTÉGÉ ENTITY relation.

8.2.2   Editor Data Forms

PROTÉGÉ and the editors that it generates incorporate a number of assumptions that were originally made in OPAL. The most restrictive of these assumptions is that actions entered at the editor level are not predicated on *conjunctions* of conditions. This simplifying measure has not yet proved limiting in the clinical-trial domain, and offers the advantage of permitting the knowledge editors to display associations between data and actions using a concise, intuitive syntax. In domains where conjunctions of conditions would need to be specified frequently, however, knowledge entry would require a language that is more

189

complex than the one that I shall describe here.

The knowledge editors created by PROTÉGÉ require only two generic forms to allow application specialists to map input data onto task actions. One of these forms is used for data classes that have both continuous and enumerated data types; the other form is for enumerated data only.

Actions Predicated on Either Continuous or Enumerated Data

Application specialists can use the continuous-data form shown in Figure 8.3 to enter knowledge-level rules that pertain to input data with either continuous or enumerated data types. (When a data class is composed *exclusively* of items with enumerated data types, as is the case with p-OPAL toxicity data, a different form is used, as described subsequently.) The continuous-data form has four major sections. The top section contains a blank that passively displays the name of the form instance—which is, by definition, also the name of the relevant data class. The top section also contains the *"Finished"* blank that closes the form and returns control to the editor main menu. The next section lists, for the given data class, all the data items that the knowledge engineer defined at the PROTÉGÉ level. As with the OPAL form in Figure 6.7 (page 125), the user selects data items from this list one at a time to review and to enter the relevant rules.

Each rule entered into the editor is associated with a precise set of planning-entity instances (or a *context*) that defines the circumstances under which the rule is applicable. In Figure 8.3, for example, the context is "when in Protocol 20-83-1, when administering VAM chemotherapy, when giving the drug methotrexate." Thus, all *attenuate* actions that the user might enter would apply to only the drug methotrexate as it is used in VAM chemotherapy in this protocol; the attenuations would not apply to other drugs, nor would they apply to other uses of methotrexate. Similarly, all *delay* actions declared in this context would apply to only VAM chemotherapy.

The third section of the continuous-data form in Figure 8.3 allows the application specialist to define the planning context for the entered rules. Initially, the context is simply that of the current protocol. The user can refine the context specification by selecting the blank to the right of the *protocol* blank in Figure 8.3, causing the menu in

190

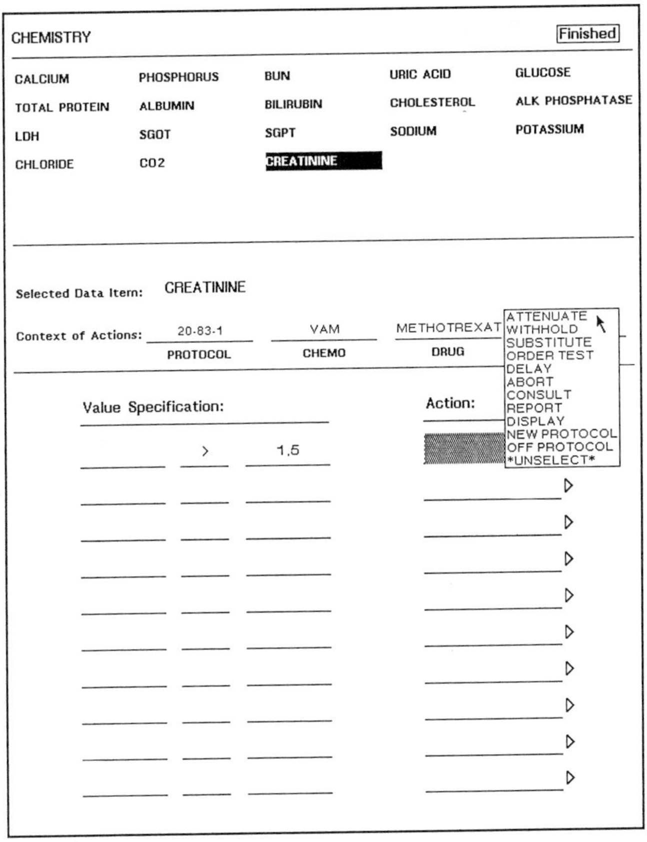

Figure 8.3: Continuous-Data Action Form

This form allows users to indicate the actions to take when input data have specific values or fall into a particular range. The form shows the data items for the entire data class. Only one such data item can be selected at a time, however. The figure shows the form instantiated for serum chemistry data in p-OPAL. The user is about to specify that, when the serum creatinine is greater than 1.5 mg/dl, the drug methotrexate should be attenuated when given in VAM chemotherapy in Protocol 20-83-1.

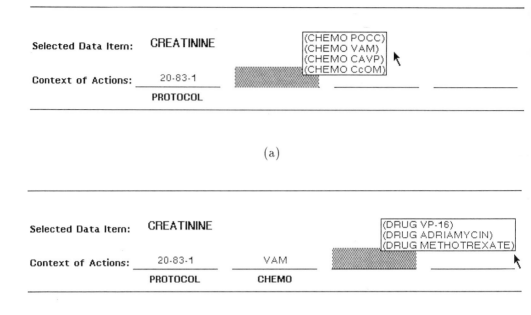

Figure 8.4: Entering the Context for Actions

The editor requires the user to specify the plan *instances* that are affected by particular actions. Consequently, the forms in Figures 8.3 and 8.6 use menus to allow entry of the necessary context description. The preselected protocol name is assumed to be the most general context in which the user's entries apply. (a) The user is about to enter that the context should be narrowed to *VAM chemotherapy* within Protocol 20-83-1. (b) The user is about to refine the context further—to the drug *methotrexate* within VAM chemotherapy in this protocol.

Figure 8.4(a) to be generated. By retrieving data from the the PROTOCOL-COMPOSITION relation, the blank creates a menu listing all the planning-entity instances in the database that are components of the current protocol.[1] If, for example, the user refines the context

---

[1] Generation of the menu actually requires more than a simple selection operation. Instances of planning entities that themselves have no *component* entities, and for which there are no associated task actions, are further selected out of the list displayed in the menu. (For example, *radiotherapies* in p-OPAL fall into this category because they are terminal entities in the planning hierarchy and there are no task actions that affect them.) Such entities would be irrelevant for restricting the context of task actions and would merely make the menu more complicated.

192

to include "VAM chemotherapy," the blank to the right of the *protocol* blank is filled in (Figure 8.4b) and the next blank in the row becomes active. As is seen in the figure, the new blank then allows the user to refine the context to include one of the *drug* instances within VAM chemotherapy.

At any time, the application specialist can update the context shown in the form by changing the blanks in this middle section. Selecting a blank produces a menu that lists the relevant entity instances that constitute whatever instance is displayed to the left of the selected blank. If the user changes the contents of the blank, all blanks to the right of the updated blank are cleared automatically.

Once the application expert has selected a data item and specified the proper planning context, she can begin to enter rules using the blanks provided in the bottom portion of the form in Figure 8.3. On the left, the user enters a statement regarding possible values for the selected data item (a *value specification*); on the right, she enters a task action to take if the value specification is true.

The value specification requires the user to enter both a predicate relation (Table 8.1) and the particular value (or values) that the predicate should take as its arguments. The predicates are represented in the form as simple symbols. Although most of the predicates involve only one argument, four of them take two arguments. These two-place predicates denote *ranges* of data values in which the boundaries at the high end and the low end of the range may (or may not) be specifically included. If the selected data item has an *enumerated,* rather than a continuous, data type, the only predicates that apply are "=" and "<>."

The predicates refer to only the current value of the selected data item. As in OPAL, it is not possible to enter value specifications that refer to past data. A facility for describing time-oriented queries on the patient database would be an obvious and valuable extension to the present system.

When the user wishes to enter the data values that constitute the arguments for a predicate, she selects the appropriate blanks in the columns labeled *"Value Specification."* The knowledge editor queries the DATA-ITEM relation to determine the data type for the selected data item, and then uses the DATA-TYPE relation to determine the correct software

Table 8.1: Predicates on Input Data

Symbol	Meaning
=	Equal to
<>	Not equal to
<	Less than
<=	Less than or equal to
>	Greater than
>=	Greater than or equal to
thru []	Between two values, including both bounds
thru (]	Between two values, not including lower bound
thru [)	Between two values, not including upper bound
thru ()	Between two values, not including either bound

input device needed to enter the values. Note that, when a data item in the second section of the form is selected, not only does the visual appearance of the form change (for example, the user's choice is highlighted), but the *behavior* of the form changes as well (that is, different registers or menus will appear in the fourth portion of the form, depending on the selected item's data type).

Whenever the user enters a value specification on the left side of the form, the corresponding *action* blank on the right side of the form becomes active. When the user selects this blank, she can enter the action to take if the condition represented by the value specification is true. A menu is constructed that lists the names of only those task actions that are germane in the currently specified *context*. For example, if the p-OPAL context specification is limited to "Protocol 20-83-1," the only applicable actions are *end protocol* and *report*. Extending the specification to include "VAM Chemotherapy," as in Figure 8.4(a), adds actions such as *delay* and *abort* to the menu. (It would have been inappropriate for the user to be able to enter these chemotherapy-oriented actions without first indicating which chemotherapy instance should be affected.) Similarly, if the context specification is extended to include a particular *drug* (Figure 8.4b), additional actions such as *attenuate, omit,* and *substitute* become available to the user. Thus, the menu is constantly tailored to display precisely those actions that might be relevant in the designated planning context.

Each time the domain expert enters an action to take, she implicitly identifies an *instance* of the task action. The planning context (for example, when administering methotrexate in VAM chemotherapy in Protocol 20-83-1), the data-item selection (for example, serum creatinine), the value specification (for example, greater than 1.5 mg/dl), and the action name (for example, *attenuate*) are all distinguishing features of the particular action. For convenience, the editor generates a unique identifier that is used internally to refer to each action instance. This computed name—along with the data item, value specification, and context information—is stored in the CONTINUOUS-DATA-ACTION relation.

Task actions frequently have attributes with values that must be established at the editor level. If the user selects such an action from the menu in Figure 8.3, the action-attributes form shown in Figure 8.5 immediately appears on the screen. Like the OPAL form in Figure 6.6 (page 123), this generic form allows the user to enter the required attribute values. A blank at the top of the form passively displays the action name. The active blanks in the form allow the user to enter the values for all the editor-established attributes. Beneath each active blank is a passive "label" blank for the attribute—a label that changes depending on the action being instantiated. Thus, in the case of the *attenuate* action, the topmost active blank in the form solicits the percentage by which to reduce the dose of the drug; in the case of the *delay* action, the same physical blank solicits the number of days to delay chemotherapy.

The action-attributes form in Figure 8.5 solicits values for all the editor-established attributes of the designated task action. When the user selects one of the active blanks, the specific register or menu that accepts the input value is determined from the data type of the corresponding attribute. Whenever the application specialist enters a value for one of these action attributes, the ATTRIBUTE-INSTANTIATIONS relation is updated. After entering the necessary values, the user selects the blank labeled *"Finished."* The form closes and the continuous-data form (Figure 8.3) is again available for use. If the application specialist ever wishes to review or change any of the attribute values for an action instance that was entered previously, she simply selects the triangular arrow next to the relevant action in Figure 8.3. The action-attributes form (Figure 8.5) then reappears on the screen.

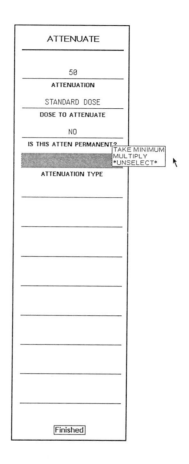

Figure 8.5: Action-Attributes Form

This form allows the application specialist to enter the editor-established attributes for a task action. The form in the figure has been instantiated for the p-OPAL *attenuate* action. The user has indicated that the current drug dose should be lowered by 50 percent. She is about to specify that, if the current dose has already been reduced for any other reason, that reduced dose should be *multiplied* by the 50-percent attenuation.

Actions Predicated on Enumerated Data Only

Whereas the continuous-data form in Figure 8.3 allows entry of rules predicated on input data with both continuous and enumerated data types, the form in Figure 8.6 serves the same function for data classes having *enumerated* data types only. Whenever the user selects a data item from the list at the top of the enumerated-data form, all permissible values for the datum are displayed automatically at the bottom of the form, one per row in the column labeled *"Value."* (The form object obtains these data values by querying the MENU-SELECTIONS relation.) The form displays up to three task actions for e-ONCOCIN to take whenever the value of the data item selected at the top of the form is equal to the value at the start of a given row. (Compare the p-OPAL form in Figure 8.6 with the OPAL form in Figure 6.8, page 126.)

As in Figure 8.4, the user must specify the *planning context* for the actions in the third portion of the enumerated-data form by choosing the names of the appropriate planning-entity instances from menus. Then, when the user selects one of the blanks for entering actions at the bottom of the form, the menu that appears displays only those task actions that are germane in the context. As before, the application specialist can change the context at any time; the menu of possible actions and the action instances that appear in the form change accordingly.

When new actions are entered into the blanks at the bottom of the form (Figure 8.6), the editor creates new tuples in the ENUMERATED-DATA-ACTION relation. Each tuple corresponds to a different action *instance* (for example, a specific circumstance when a drug should be attenuated or chemotherapy should be delayed). As she does when entering actions predicated on *continuous* data, once an action instance is defined, the user enters the values for any editor-established attributes of the instance via the action-attributes form in Figure 8.5. In this manner, the user can specify the percentage to attenuate or the period of time by which to delay.

When the user wishes to review the enumerated-data form in Figure 8.6, she can inspect the editor-established attributes for any of the actions simply by selecting the triangular arrow adjacent to the blank. The action-attributes form in Figure 8.5 reappears, displaying the values for the designated action.

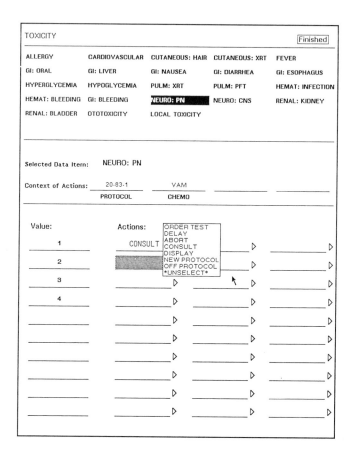

Figure 8.6: Enumerated-Data Action Form

This form allows the application specialist to enter rules that relate task actions to potential values of data items that have enumerated data types. The current form shows actions to take if peripheral-nervous-system toxicity occurs when administering VAM chemotherapy. Note that because this context specification does not mention the name of a specific drug, the menu of available actions is different from that in Figure 8.3.

8.2.3 Editor Planning-Entity Forms

Entering task rules is only a part of what the application expert must do to specify a new protocol. She also must describe the instances of the components in the planning hierarchy (for example, the specific chemotherapies and drugs in p-OPAL) and indicate their procedural relationships (for example, the sequence of drugs in a given chemotherapy). By selecting the blank labeled *"Protocol Data"* in the editor main menu (Figure 8.2), the user can open a generic form used to instantiate the elements of the planning hierarchy (Figure 8.7). The form itself is set up to acquire data regarding the *protocol* entity at the top of the hierarchy. In Figure 8.7, for example, the form is labeled with the word *protocol* and shows the *name* of the protocol as well. (The protocol name was entered previously into the editor main menu, and was passed to the new form via a form variable.) Like the action-attributes form in Figure 8.5, the generic entity form in Figure 8.7 is predominantly composed of two kinds of blanks: (1) passive blanks that display the *labels* for the editor-established attributes that pertain to the class (for example, the label for the protocol's "Revision Date"), and (2) active blanks that the user can select to enter the instance-specific values for those attributes (for example, the inverted blank above the revision-date label in Figure 8.7).

Figure 8.7 displays for the *protocol* class the attributes that knowledge engineers at the PROTÉGÉ level declared to require value definitions by application specialists at the editor level. The form has been instantiated for acquiring the values needed to define a particular instance of a particular planning entity (that is, "Protocol 20-83-1"). Although the appearance and outward behavior of the form in Figure 8.7 obviously are tailored for entering information about this specific protocol, the procedural methods associated with the individual blanks are *generic* and thus are independent of the form's instantiation. When the application specialist selects one of the active blanks in the form, the DATA-TYPES relation provides the name of the required input mechanism. If the entry is to be selected from a menu, the blank queries the MENU-SELECTIONS relation to obtain the list of possible values. The datum that the user enters into the blank is then stored in the ATTRIBUTE-INSTANTIATIONS relation. Because knowledge entry at the editor level is simply a matter of providing values for pre-established attributes, there is no need to create

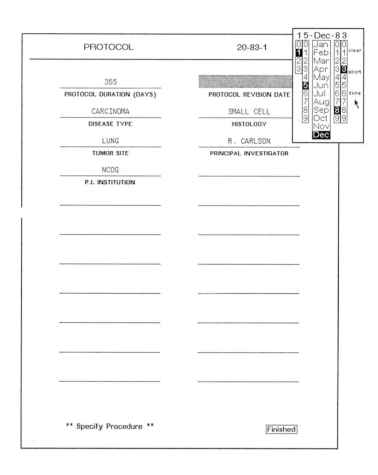

Figure 8.7: Generic Planning-Entity Form

This form allows application specialists to enter the values for attributes of planning-entity instances. Here, the form is instantiated to show attributes of *protocol 20-83-1*. Because protocols are composed of other plan elements that are at the next level down in the planning hierarchy, the user can select the blank labeled *"Specify Procedure"* to close the form and to invoke the special visual language required to enter the sequence of the components (Section 8.3).

200

distinct relations in the database to store information that pertains to specific entity classes (such as *protocol*); the single ATTRIBUTE-INSTANTIATIONS relation contains the values for all the attributes of all the entities that the application specialist may define.

At the PROTÉGÉ level, knowledge engineers define the hierarchy of classes that potentially constitute a plan in a particular application area. At the knowledge-editor level, domain experts define the instances of these classes and specify the time-oriented, procedural relationships among the instances. The way an expert instantiates the *protocol* class at the top of the hierarchy is simple: She selects the blank labeled *"PROTOCOL DATA"* in the editor main menu to access the form in Figure 8.7. Instantiating the rest of the plan also is straightforward, and requires *interleaving* form-based entry of attribute values with the entry of procedural specifications using a visual flowchart language. (I shall describe the syntax and semantics of this language in Section 8.3.) Thus, when the user selects the blank labeled *"Specify Procedure"* in Figure 8.7, the *protocol* form is closed, and a new environment is entered that allows the user to draw a flowchart that describes the protocol in terms of the plan components that it comprises. (This environment is much like the procedural portion of OPAL described in Section 6.2.2.) For example, in Figure 8.8, the user has indicated that protocol 20-83-1 comprises a particular sequence of *chemotherapy* and *radiotherapy* instances. When she selects one of the planning instances in the flowchart graph with the mouse, the graph disappears and the generic entity form in Figure 8.7 is instantiated for the selected plan component. Figure 8.9 shows the form instantiated for VAM chemotherapy.

As in OPAL, the PROTÉGÉ-generated editors allow the application specialist to use the icons in the graph (for example, a *VAM* box in Figure 8.8) as a menu by which to access the forms that describe the planning instance with which the icons correspond (for example, the details of how VAM should be administered; Figure 8.9). Thus, selecting an icon opens the generic planning-entity form, instantiated for the designated class and instance. If the selected entity is itself composed of a sequence of plan instances, the new form will have a blank labeled *"Specify Procedure"*, which, when toggled, causes the editor to display yet another flowchart—one describing how the components of *that* entity should be administered. The graph that appears, in turn, serves as a menu by which to access

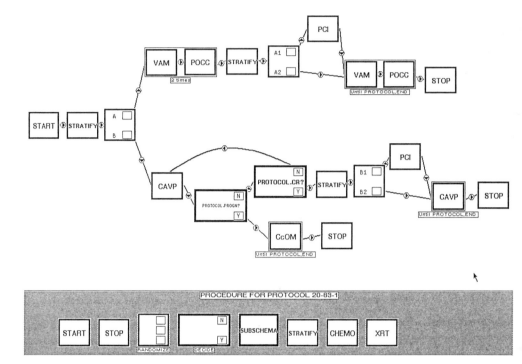

Figure 8.8: Procedural Specification for Protocol 20-83-1

This p-OPAL graph shows the sequence of planning instances to apply when carrying out the procedure for protocol 20-83-1. Selecting one of the instances in the graph allows the user to define the attributes of that instance. In this diagram, the expert has specified that patients are to be stratified and then randomly assigned to either Arm A, which tests the chemotherapies VAM and POCC, or Arm B, which tests the chemotherapy CAVP. Patients who respond to either treatment may be randomly assigned to receive prophylactic cranial irradiation (PCI).

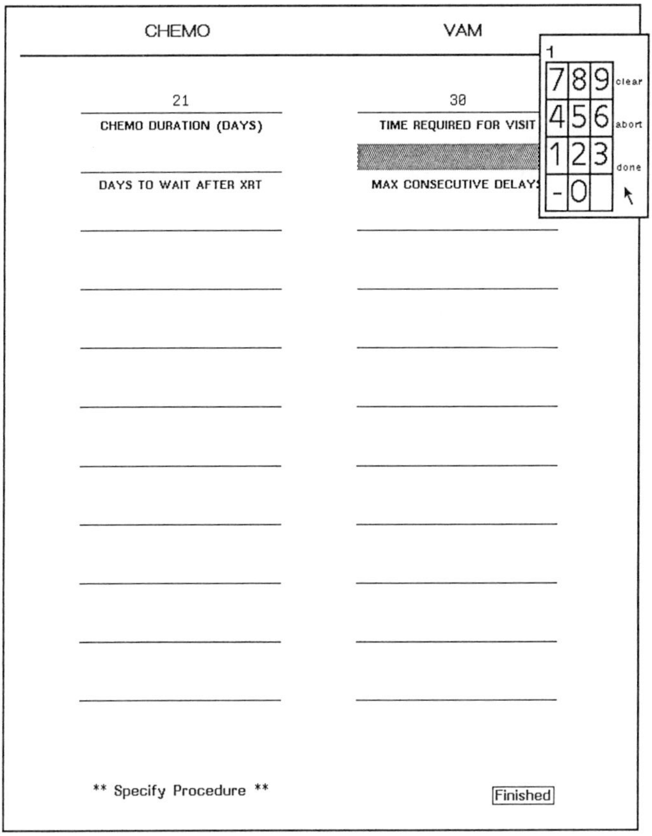

Figure 8.9: Generic Form Instantiated for Chemotherapy VAM

This is the same generic form as that shown in Figure 8.7, but it now shows the attributes of VAM chemotherapy. The user accessed the form by selecting one of the icons labeled *VAM* in the graph in Figure 8.8. Choosing the blank labeled *"Specify Procedure"* allows the application specialist to describe the manner in which the component *drugs* in VAM should be administered.

other forms to instantiate the lower-level planning entities that appear in the new diagram (Figure 8.10).

A menu accessible from the flowchart environment allows the user to move back up to the form that describes the entity the procedure for which is depicted in the graph (for example, from the graph describing the procedure for VAM in Figure 8.11, the user could return to the form for that chemotherapy in Figure 8.9). If the user selects the *"Finished"* blank in that form, she is returned to the graph from which the form was originally invoked (for example, from the VAM form in Figure 8.9, the user would be transferred back to the protocol graph in Figure 8.8). It is then possible to select another icon in the higher-level flowchart and thus to explore a different portion of the planning hierarchy (for example, POCC chemotherapy). Alternatively, the user can move up to the form instance from which the current graph was itself invoked (for example, the protocol form in Figure 8.7). This hierarchy of forms and graphs encourages the application specialist to instantiate the protocol in a top-down manner. Regardless of whether the tree of planning instances is "bushy" or deep, the organization imposed by the editor makes it straightforward for the user to locate the particular forms and graphs that she may need to enter instance-specific information.

8.3   Entry of Procedural Knowledge

PROTÉGÉ makes the assumption that each element of a skeletal plan may be composed of other plan instances, and that there is always some longitudinal, time-ordered procedure that must be followed involving the component instances. For example, in the oncology domain, a predefined algorithm always governs the administration of the chemotherapies and radiation treatments within a protocol, whereas additional algorithms govern the administration of the drugs within the chemotherapies. The knowledge editors that PROTÉGÉ generates require application experts to make these algorithms explicit at every level of the planning hierarchy.

The language with which users describe such procedural knowledge is based on the visual flowchart language developed for OPAL (see Section 6.2.2). In the PROTÉGÉ-

204

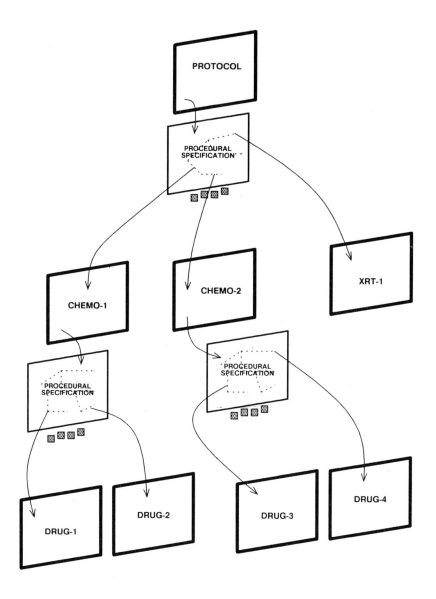

Figure 8.10: Instantiating the Planning Hierarchy

Starting with the *protocol* entity, users instantiate a hierarchical plan by interleaving form-based and icon-based knowledge entry. The protocol form (Figure 8.7) provides an entrée into the flowchart language that specifies the sequence of instances that constitutes the longitudinal plan of the protocol (Figure 8.8). Selecting one of the icons in the graph opens a form for entering the values of the attributes of that entity. The new form, in turn, may be used to access a flowchart that describes how this component is itself defined, and so on. The figure shows an example of this process when using p-OPAL.

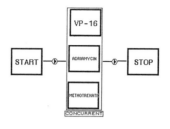

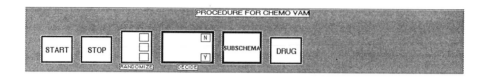

Figure 8.11: Procedural Specification for VAM Chemotherapy

VAM involves the simple, concurrent administration of three drugs. *VP-16,* '*dria-mycin,* and *methotrexate* are all instances of the *drug* class. Because chemotherapies are composed of only sequences of drugs, there is but one domain-dependent icon in the palette of reference icons beneath the graph, namely, DRUG. Compare with Figure 8.8.

generated editors, however, this iconic language adapts itself to the particular types of procedures that users enter in different planning contexts. For example, when the domain expert must enter the sequence of chemotherapies and radiotherapies that define a given protocol, the workstation screen appears as in Figure 8.8. The palette of reference icons that is used to construct the flowchart contains five basic control elements (START, STOP, RANDOMIZE, DECIDE, and SUBSCHEMA) followed by three additional icons that are specific to the current context (CHEMO, XRT, and STRATIFY). The latter three icons appear in the palette because the knowledge engineer declared at the PROTÉGÉ level that instances of protocols are composed of chemotherapies, radiotherapies, and stratification steps. (The editor obtains these data from the COMPOSITION relation.) On the other hand, when the application specialist (1) selects a *VAM* icon from the graph in Figure 8.8, (2) accesses the form in Figure 8.9, and then (3) toggles *"Specify Procedure,"* she can enter a flowchart such as the one in Figure 8.11. This time, the expert uses the iconic language to enter the sequence of drugs in VAM chemotherapy. Although the same five *control* icons appear

206

in the palette, the CHEMO, XRT, and STRATIFY icons have been replaced by a single icon labeled DRUG. Thus, the editor restricts the domain-specific processes that are available to the user to those plan components that can legally appear in the flowchart.

8.3.1   The Environment for Entering Procedural Specifications

As in the OPAL flowchart language, when the application specialist selects one of the reference icons in the palette, a copy of the icon appears in the main graph region. By moving the mouse, the user can then position the new icon anywhere in the graph. When the user selects one of the domain-dependent icons (such as CHEMO or DRUG), a menu is displayed that allows her to select the name of the *instance* within the class that the new icon will represent (such as *VAM* for the chemotherapy class in Figure 8.8 or *methotrexate* for the drug class in Figure 8.11).[2] The indicated name then appears as a label for the icon.

As in OPAL, when the user creates a DECIDE node, she is presented with a menu of possible choices on which to predicate the corresponding decision point. The menu is a list of those planning-entity attributes that were defined at the PROTÉGÉ level to have both a data type of *Boolean* and a value that is computed by e-ONCOCIN. The name of the attribute that the expert selects is then used to annotate the icon.

The direct-manipulation interface (Shneiderman, 1983) in the flowchart environment permits the user easily to add new icons to the graph, to adjust their position, and to link them to one another. The result is a "what you see is what you get" visual programming language for describing procedures. Although the various processes represented in the flowchart are necessarily application-dependent, the language for describing the sequencing of these processes is universal. In the next section, I shall describe this visual language in detail.

---

[2]The editor generates the list of possible instances from data in the MENU-SELECTIONS relation. When the user indicates her choice, the PROTOCOL-COMPOSITION relation is updated to reflect that the selected instance is now part of the entity being diagrammed. If the user later erases the icon, the PROTOCOL-COMPOSITION relation is updated to reflect the deletion of the component.

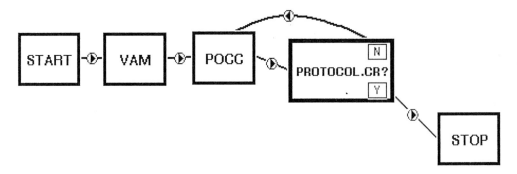

Figure 8.12: Conditional Loop

This procedure calls for a single cycle of VAM chemotherapy to be administered, followed by cycles of POCC chemotherapy until the *CR* attribute of the current protocol instance becomes *true*.

8.3.2   The Iconic Language

A complete procedural specification is represented by a deterministic finite-state diagram with a single START node and one or more STOP nodes. In general, the application specialist specifies the flow of control using the directed links that connect the icons in the graph. She may represent the concept of iteration, however, in a more abstract way, discussed in Section 8.3.2.

Conditionality

As in typical flowchart languages, the links between icons are unlabeled. The user expresses *conditionality* by placing DECIDE nodes in the graph that she labels with Boolean attributes of planning entities, the values of which are used to determine the flow of control. For example, as part of the procedure diagrammed in Figure 8.12, POCC chemotherapy is administered one cycle at a time until e-ONCOCIN can conclude that an attribute of the *protocol* class called *CR* (complete response to treatment) has the value *true*. (This flowchart is analogous to the OPAL graph shown in Figure 6.4, page 120.)

A special form of conditionality is represented by the RANDOMIZE icon. Such a node allows application experts to indicate conveniently when patients are to be assigned ran-

208

domly to alternative treatments. Although a physician could theoretically represent the same flow of control by using one or more DECIDE nodes, I have chosen to tailor the visual language more specifically to the clinical-trial domain. This consideration is important because the editors generated by PROTÉGÉ are intended to be used by doctors, not by programmers.

Iteration

Early experience with OPAL demonstrated that application specialists who are not familiar with computers have difficulty thinking about iterative sequences (as in Figure 8.12) in terms of explicit branch points and state transitions. These experts prefer flowcharts in which the concept of iteration either is ignored or at best is represented as an annotation to the graph. Accordingly, the iconic language insulates its user from the details needed to specify the flow of control for iteration. To specify a repeating sequence of operations, the application specialist enters the basic sequence of nodes and then draws a box around the relevant icons with the mouse. A menu then asks the user whether the enclosed sequence is to be repeated (1) a fixed number of times; (2) until a condition occurs; (3) a fixed number of times *then* until a condition occurs; or (4) a fixed number of times *or* until a condition occurs, whichever happens first. Further menus solicit the number of iterations or the precise condition to test. The editor then replaces the original sequence of icons with a single icon the image of which is a graph of the procedure to be repeated. The new REPEAT icon is annotated with a phrase describing the test that determines when the iterative loop should terminate. The process of specifying repeating elements graphically is shown in Figure 8.13.

An icon representing a repeating sequence of operations can be manipulated like any other node in the graph. The user thus can include a REPEAT icon among those nodes designated as part of some higher order repeating sequence. The superimposition of icons in the graph adds a third dimension to the visual representation, defining a hierarchy of nested operations. Iteration can be nested to any level (Figure 8.14).

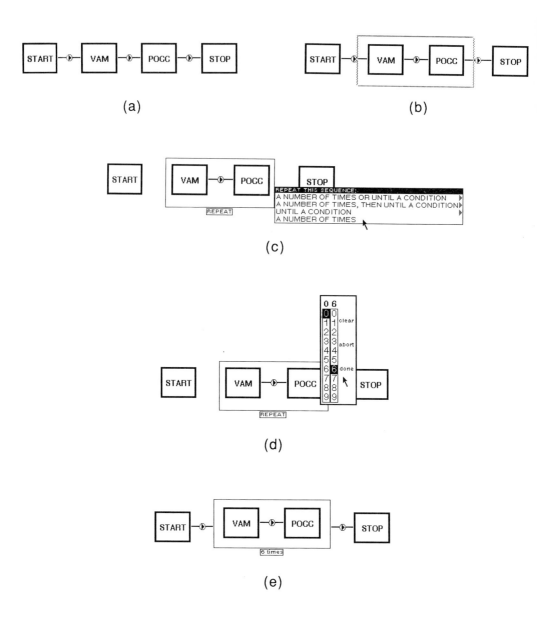

Figure 8.13: Specifying a Repeating Sequence

(a) The user enters the basic icons. (b) The user delimits the iterative sequence by using the mouse to draw a box around the involved nodes. (c) The user selects the type of iteration from a menu. Sequences may repeat a fixed number of times, until a condition becomes true, or a combination of both. (d) The user enters the values for the terminating conditions. (e) The system annotates the REPEAT icon with the specific terminating condition.

210

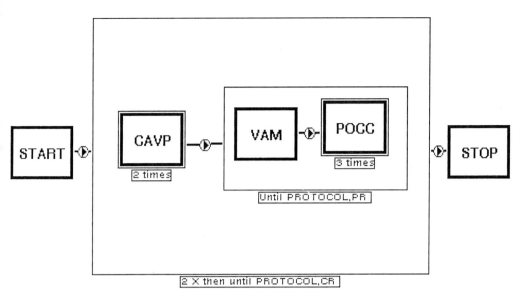

Figure 8.14: Nested Iterative Sequences

Iterative sequences may be nested to any level. Each loop has its own terminating condition with which the corresponding REPEAT icon is annotated.

Concurrency

An application specialist can designate two or more sequences as concurrent by using the mouse to draw a box around the corresponding groups of nodes, similar to the way she specifies repeating sequences. The concurrent sequences can be of any complexity and can themselves specify concurrent sequences (Figure 8.15).

The semantics are such that the individual operations drawn within the CONCURRENT icon proceed independently in parallel; when all the simultaneous sequences within the box have terminated, control passes to the node in the graph that follows the CONCURRENT icon.

Abstraction

The readability and modifiability of programs written in textual languages depend to a large extent on the languages' ability to represent control structures and data at an adequate level of abstraction. Because the PROTÉGÉ-generated editors are intended

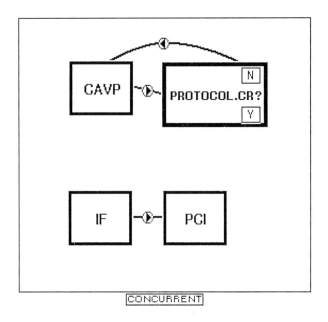

Figure 8.15: Concurrent Sequences

In this example, cycles of CAVP chemotherapy are administered until the *CR* (complete response) attribute of the current protocol becomes *true*. Simultaneously, two radiation treatments are given: involved field (IF) followed by prophylactic cranial irradiation (PCI).

to be used by nonprogrammers, removing unnecessary procedural detail is a particularly important goal.

I have already described how the iconic language facilitates *control abstraction* through its ability to denote iteration without the user having to specify the precise transitions back to a loop's starting point. A further degree of abstraction often is necessary, however, because iterative sequences may be more complicated than standard "DO WHILE" loops. Some procedures may call for exiting a loop *whenever* a condition becomes true, regardless of whether an iteration has completed. Hence, before making any transitions within the loop, the program must test a condition to determine whether premature termination should occur. Application specialists may not want to be concerned with such procedural details, but the details still have to be represented somehow.

A solution to this problem is achieved by an approach that is equivalent to *exception handling* in traditional programming languages such as PL/I. The user can create an iterative sequence and specify that the termination condition is to be checked *implicitly* before any transitions within that sequence are made; if at any time the condition becomes *true*, control passes out of the loop. A nested iterative sequence inherits any exceptions that might apply to the enclosing loops and may, of course, have a local terminating condition of its own.

Procedural abstraction is achieved by use of auxiliary graphs called *subschemas*. These graphical subroutines make the representation of complex procedures easier, particularly when a visual program might otherwise be too big to fit in one graph. Similar constructs have been used in other graphical languages (Wasserman, 1985; Jacob, 1985).

Specifically, if the user selects the reference SUBSCHEMA icon with the mouse, she can position a copy of that icon in the current graph. The user then assigns a name to the icon. Whenever a SUBSCHEMA node in the graph is selected, one of the choices in the resultant menu allows the user to specify the details of the subschema procedure. The current graph is then replaced with a new graph (initially blank) corresponding to the particular subschema. Once the procedure for the subschema has been diagrammed, the user simply returns to the original graph.

A graph may have multiple instances of the same subschema, each referring to the identical procedural specification. In this manner, redundant portions of a flowchart only need to be entered once. Subschemas may call other subschemas to any level of nesting. However, the user is prevented from allowing subschemas to call themselves recursively, either directly or via another subschema. Otherwise, the application specialist might inadvertently create a procedure that would never terminate.

8.3.3 A Hierarchy of Time-Ordered Processes

There are several issues regarding the semantics of the iconic language that are important for e-ONCOCIN. Of particular concern is the manner in which the language deals with the passage of time.

Each application-specific icon in the flowchart (for example, each instance of a *drug, chemotherapy,* or *laboratory test*) denotes a process that takes place over a discrete time

213

interval. A process may be instantaneous (for example, a *test*) or may take place over many days or weeks (for example, the administration of a *chemotherapy*). The precise duration is determined by factors intrinsic to the process. From the perspective of the flowchart graph, all that is represented is the order in which one process follows another. The flowchart views each individual process as a black box. The specific properties of the process do not become relevant until the application specialist uses the form-based part of the editor to instantiate the description for the process' class, which was entered at the PROTÉGÉ level.

The algorithm expressed by the flowchart is ultimately converted to an e-ONCOCIN *generator* (see Figure 5.4, page 105). As a result, the semantics of the flowchart representation are defined operationally, by the manner in which the e-ONCOCIN Reasoner interprets the corresponding generator.

Each time the Reasoner invokes a generator at the advice-system level, the program traverses *state descriptions* in the generator that represent the nodes in the flowchart. Eventually, the Reasoner either encounters a state description that indicates the name of some process to perform or reaches the generator's terminal state. In the case of *concurrent* operations, however, the Reasoner traverses separate *subgenerators* for each simultaneous sequence that was diagrammed within the CONCURRENT icon of the original flowchart; each subgenerator independently determines a different process for e-ONCOCIN to execute. The Reasoner suspends its traversal of a generator (or subgenerator) as soon as it encounters a process to initiate. It then turns its attention to refinement of that skeletal process in light of current circumstances.

The Reasoner will not reexamine a generator until the process that was last initiated by the generator has halted. Thus, whenever a new e-ONCOCIN consultation begins, the Reasoner must determine whether that process still is *active* (in which case the skeletal process undergoes refinement) or whether the process is *terminated* (in which case, the Reasoner refers back to the generator to determine the *next* process in the sequence to initiate). Control can not pass from one process to the next until the first process has finished. More important, the actual transitions between processes occur only when the Reasoner invokes the generator. The start of a new process must thus coincide with the occasion of an e-ONCOCIN consultation. Therefore, at the conclusion of every session, the Reasoner informs the user of the earliest time that one of the currently active processes will terminate. A patient visit (hence, an e-ONCOCIN consultation) will be scheduled for that date, in anticipation that a subsequent process will begin then.[3]

In constructing the flowchart, the application specialist must view each transition between processes as being accompanied by an e-ONCOCIN consultation. The consultation determines the values for those attributes of the process that vary depending on current circumstances regarding the patient or the protocol. The values of the attributes remain in effect until either the process completes or the values are altered during an intervening e-ONCOCIN consultation. Such a pre-emptive consultation could occur because either (1) the Reasoner has resumed this process after previously suspending it, or (2) there is a process of finer granularity farther down in the planning hierarchy that some other flowchart has initiated. Thus, in Figure 8.8, the user would expect a new consultation to begin at the start of each *chemotherapy* and *radiotherapy* node in the flowchart. Consultations could occur more frequently, however, if any of the processes in the graph were composed of complex lower-level procedures. For example, oncologists administer drugs in POCC chemotherapy *twice* during each course of treatment (Figure 8.16). There thus are two e-ONCOCIN consultations during each cycle of POCC.

The planning hierarchy that the application specialist creates at the editor level thus consists of a three-dimensional space. Each plan instance includes a set of attributes, plus an algorithm that sequences the process' subcomponents over time. Each subcomponent contains its own set of attributes and, possibly, a time-oriented algorithm of more primitive subcomponents. The temporal and compositional relationships among these entities correspond to the pathways within the editor that application specialists use to access the various forms and flowcharts (see Figure 8.10). It is this homology between the functional constituents of the plan and the structure of the editor's user interface that makes entry of these complex procedural relationships straightforward.

---

[3]If any process that is currently *suspended* is slated to resume before that date, the next patient visit will be scheduled accordingly.

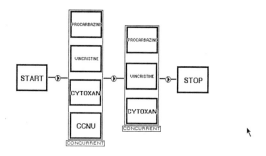

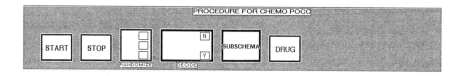

Figure 8.16: Procedural Specification for POCC Chemotherapy

POCC chemotherapy is administered over the course of two patient visits. On the first visit, four drugs are given in combination. Two weeks later, three of those drugs are repeated.

8.4   Creation of a Knowledge Base

After the domain expert has defined the knowledge for a new protocol, selecting the blank labeled *"Generate KB"* on the editor main menu causes the system to generate a knowledge base that can be used directly by e-ONCOCIN. Translating the user's entries into the editor to a usable knowledge base requires mapping items from the database into appropriate objects in the OZONE programming language (Lane, 1986). The required kinds of objects, the links among them, and the objects' slot names are governed by the requirements of the e-ONCOCIN Reasoner and Interviewer.

The translation programs contain knowledge both of the syntax of the objects in the e-ONCOCIN knowledge base (that is, the frames, rules, and generators) and of the relations in the PROTÉGÉ database. The code extracts values from the database and constructs the necessary data structures. I shall not describe the mechanics of this translation in great detail because the transformations depend heavily on satisfying the requirements of e-ONCOCIN syntax—which is in many ways quite arcane. The syntax at the symbol level is relatively unimportant. What *does* matter is that the translation routines incorporate the semantics of PROTÉGÉ's model of skeletal planning to transform the instantiations of that model in the database into appropriate symbol-level entities.

I shall now provide a synopsis of the events that take place when the editor generates an e-ONCOCIN knowledge base. (The various structures in the knowledge base were described in Chapter 5.)

8.4.1 Translating Data Classes

In the first phase of translation, the program constructs a parameter object for each possible data item that might be entered into the advice system. The appropriate data type, menu selections, and display information are copied from the database and are stored in the parameter objects.

The translation programs also create objects that describe the various data classes that were entered into PROTÉGÉ. The data-class objects are used to create the necessary flowsheet sections for the e-ONCOCIN Interviewer.

8.4.2 Translating the Planning Hierarchy

The translation routines create an object in the knowledge base for each planning-entity class defined at the PROTÉGÉ level. An object also is produced for each *instance* of the class specified at the editor level.

Each attribute of each type of entity becomes a separate *parameter*. The translation routines generate a parameter object to store the data type and menu information. Slots also are created within the planning-entity *class* and *instance* objects to refer to the newly created parameter. Attributes with values that were predefined at either the PROTÉGÉ level or entered at the editor level, however, are treated as *constants* by e-ONCOCIN. The values are stored in slots in either the corresponding *class* objects or *instance* objects, depending on which tool was used to establish the values. (Values that are predefined at the PROTÉGÉ level always pertain to the entire class.)

Another set of functions traces the icons in each graphical flowchart diagram to build appropriate generator objects. These functions create a parameter object for the state variable and loop counters in each generator, and link each generator object to the planning-instance object to which it corresponds.

8.4.3   Translating Task Rules

Finally, there is the question of how to represent the task rules that application specialists enter at the editor level. For each such rule, the translation programs generate a symbol-level rule object (Figure 8.17). The *condition* of the rule is an expression in the e-ONCOCIN rule language that tests the value of the parameter corresponding to the data item designated in the task rule. The *action* of the translated rule contains the script for the task action (see Section 7.3.2). In the translated rule, each step of the script is represented as a call to a specific function that can effect the primitive operator (for example, *start* or *alter attribute*) designated in that step. The translation routines instantiate the function call to reflect the values for those action attributes that have already been established at either the PROTÉGÉ or the editor level. The values of any *computed* attributes of the action, however, cannot be established until the time of a consultation. They consequently are encoded as *nongoal* parameters of the planning instance with which the task action is associated (see Section 7.3.1). The values of these parameters will be computed by the appropriate e-ONCOCIN rules when the script is processed.[4]

Because the e-ONCOCIN Reasoner performs all its activities in response to the need to conclude values for parameters, there must be some parameter associated with each planning-instance object to cause the symbol-level rules derived from the task rules to execute. Just having the translated rules present in the knowledge base is not sufficient. Consequently, the translation programs add a multivalued parameter called ACTIONS.TO.TAKE to each planning-instance object. The *methods* for this parameter are the translated task rules that apply to that instance. Thus, when e-ONCOCIN instantiates the associated planning

---

[4] *Editor-established* attributes of the action also are translated into nongoal parameters of the planning instance. Creating these parameters allows the e-ONCOCIN rules that are invoked when the script is executed to locate the values for these editor-established attributes, if necessary. Because the editor-established attribute values to which the parameters correspond vary from action to action, the translated rule ensures that these parameters are reset to the values specific to the action instance before the script is executed.

218

PRECONDITION:

CONDITION: (NCOMPARE CHEMISTRY.CREATININE 1.5)

CONCLUSION: (DRUG.ACTIONS.TO.TAKE 'ATTENUATE0086)

ACTION: ((CONCLUDE ATTENUATE.ATTENUATION '50)
                  (CONCLUDE ATTENUATE.DOSE.BASIS 'STANDARD DOSE)
                  (CONCLUDE ATTENUATE.PERMANENT? 'YES)
                  (CONCLUDE ATTENUATE.ATTEN-TYPE 'MULTIPLY)

                 (ALTER.ATTR DRUG METHOTREXATE DRUG.CURRENT.DOSE
                       ATTENUATE.NEW.DOSE NIL NIL)
                 (ALTER.ATTR DRUG METHOTREXATE DRUG.STANDARD.DOSE
                       ATTENUATE.NEW.DOSE 'YES 'YES))

Figure 8.17: Translated Task Rule

This symbol-level expression corresponds to the task rule entered at the top of Figure 8.3: "If the serum creatinine level is greater than 1.5 mg/dl, then attenuate the dose of methotrexate to 50 percent of the previous dose." In the translated rule, the first step of the action script in Figure 7.12 (page 161) has been replaced by a call to a function that sets the value of the parameter DRUG.CURRENT.DOSE to that of the parameter ATTENUATE.NEW.DOSE. Because the p-OPAL user indicated that, in the future, the attenuated dose should be used as the *standard* dose for this drug, the second step of the script is translated into a function call that resets the DRUG.STANDARD.DOSE parameter.

entity for a particular context, all the rules linked to the relevant ACTIONS.TO.TAKE parameter will be invoked automatically. In fact, the only purpose of this parameter is to force the Reasoner to evaluate these rules. If the *condition* of any of the rules is satisfied, the corresponding *script* will be executed.

Although this mechanism allows the knowledge in the task rules to be translated and executed by e-ONCOCIN in a domain-independent manner, there are major disadvantages to the approach. In particular, when multiple task rules are applicable in a specific situation, there is no explicit way to control the order in which the rules are applied; the rules are simply executed sequentially in the order in which they are listed in the knowledge base. Although this lack of specific control may not lead to difficulty in simple application areas, it will cause potential problems when multiple rules may apply in particular circumstances. For example, one rule may call for a plan component to be suspended in the current situation whereas a second rule may call for the plan to be terminated. At present, there is no explicit way of indicating which of these rules should have precedence. In the current e-ONCOCIN implementation, the behavior of the Reasoner can depend on the *order* in which the rules are evaluated.[5] Although knowledge engineers can always alter the rules or change the rules' ordering, tinkering with the knowledge base at the symbol level is not a satisfactory solution. Nevertheless, PROTÉGÉ has been designed to interface with the existing e-ONCOCIN control structure and thus has to accept these limitations. Our laboratory is developing a new version of e-ONCOCIN that addresses many of the present system's difficulties in controlling inference.

8.4.4 The Generated Knowledge Base

After the translation programs have finished (typically within a few minutes on a Xerox 1186 workstation), the user has immediate access to the hierarchy of OZONE objects that constitutes the knowledge base for the given application. This collection of objects must be written to a temporary file and then subsequently loaded by a user running e-ONCOCIN. Because of the programs' requirements for memory, it is unfortunately not practical to run PROTÉGÉ, the knowledge editor of interest, and e-ONCOCIN in the same workstation environment.

Running an e-ONCOCIN consultation is straightforward, and involves the same startup procedure as in ONCOCIN. If a physician desires a consultation regarding a patient already known to the system, he simply selects that patient's name from a menu. If the patient is new, the user enters the patient's name and indicates the protocol in accordance with which the patient should be treated. The e-ONCOCIN Interviewer then constructs a custom-tailored flowsheet and requests the necessary input data. After the physician enters the data, the e-ONCOCIN Reasoner generates a recommendation based on its knowledge of the particular protocol. The program fills in the therapy sections of the flowsheet automatically

---

[5]The current version of ONCOCIN has the same problem (Tu et al., 1989). Programmers have had to adjust the order in which many of ONCOCIN's rules are invoked specifically to avoid these kinds of interactions.

to convey its treatment advice to the user.

8.5   Conclusion

The knowledge editors created by PROTÉGÉ generalize many of the features that were developed for OPAL. The editors instantiate a system of generic forms that allow application specialists to enter knowledge-level rules and to establish values for the instance-specific attributes of task actions and planning entities. The iconic language used in OPAL has been expanded to allow domain experts to specify the procedures that apply at all levels of the planning hierarchy. Additional programs transform the protocol descriptions entered in the editors into usable e-ONCOCIN knowledge bases, in a domain-independent fashion.

Rather than concentrating on the individual forms and the icons, however, it is important to view the PROTÉGÉ-generated editors as *languages*. Each editor represents a unique language for describing clinical trials in a particular application area. That language, of course, is derived from the entries made by a knowledge engineer at the PROTÉGÉ level. The language deals only with those concepts that distinguish one clinical trial from another within the application area; the features shared by all protocols within the class need not (and cannot) be discussed. Each editor provides a language that allows the application specialist to enter statements primarily about the *content* of specific protocols. For example, users may enter statements about the attributes of particular plan components or may list actions that need to be taken. Yet knowledge of the *process* of refining the plan or of the steps that are required *to carry out* specific actions is largely implicit at the editor level. Knowledge engineers must specify this process knowledge using PROTÉGÉ.

PROTÉGÉ is used to model the structure of the application area and the treatment-planning procedures for classes of clinical trials. The editors that PROTÉGÉ generates are used to enter the content knowledge for specific instances of clinical trials. Because the two types of knowledge-editing tools have different purposes, they each adopt different conceptual models for the knowledge entered by their respective users. Whereas the conceptual model in PROTÉGÉ is based to a large extent on a model of skeletal-plan refinement, the model at the editor level is framed by the task-specific knowledge entered at the PROTÉGÉ level. Like OPAL, the editors generated by PROTÉGÉ ask their users to enter knowledge using terms that directly reflect the application task. As I shall demonstrate further in Chapter 9, the use of such task-oriented knowledge-editing tools can greatly facilitate the development of certain classes of expert systems.

9 A New Application Area: Hypertension

In the preceding two chapters, I have described PROTÉGÉ in detail and have discussed the manner in which the system is used to build special-purpose knowledge-editing tools. My examples have come from oncology, the application domain for which ONCOCIN and OPAL were developed. PROTÉGÉ, however, has been designed to allow construction of knowledge-editing programs for a variety of clinical-trial areas, and potentially for skeletal-planning problems beyond medicine. I have not yet documented the generalizability of the PROTÉGÉ approach to an area other than oncology, however. In this chapter, I shall therefore demonstrate how PROTÉGÉ has been used to develop a new knowledge editor, called HTN, that is custom-tailored for entry of clinical trials in a *different* medical field—namely, antihypertensive drug studies.[1]

In contrast to protocols in oncology, protocols for the control of high blood pressure that are sponsored by pharmaceutical companies tend to be relatively simple. Consequently, it will be possible for me to show completely how HTN was used to define a hypertension trial on the basis of specifications entered into PROTÉGÉ. By demonstrating the entire methodology—from definition of the hypertension task model using PROTÉGÉ, to entry of a particular protocol using HTN, to patient-specific consultations with e-ONCOCIN—I intend to show the scope and generalizability of these techniques.

---

[1]Physicians often abbreviate the term *hypertension* as *HTN*.

Table 9.1: Phases of a Hypertension Drug Study

Phase		Actions
1	Observation	No active medication; placebo may be prescribed
2	Titration	Drug dose is adjusted
3	Maintenance	Drug dose is held constant
4	Washout	Drug is withdrawn

9.1 Hypertension Protocols

The clinical trials for which HTN was designed tend to be randomized, double-blind studies that compare a new drug with some standard therapy or with inactive, placebo treatment. These protocols generally are administered by pharmaceutical companies as part of their Phase III testing of new drugs (see Section 4.1.1). In most of these RCTs, only one drug is given at any time. In some studies, however, additional medications are added when a patient's blood pressure fails to respond to maximal doses of single-agent therapy.

Hypertension protocols customarily are divided into several phases (Table 9.1). Almost always, there is an initial period of observation during which the patient's blood pressure is monitored while he is off of all medication. During this time, the patient may be given either no drugs at all or a placebo. After the observation period, the patient is started on standardized medication that is furnished directly by the drug company. All tablets have a uniform appearance that prevents their identification by inspection alone; thus, neither the physician nor the patient knows whether the drug is the experimental preparation or a traditional treatment. During this second phase, the dose of the drug to which the patient has been assigned may be adjusted in attempts to bring the patient's blood pressure into the normal range. At the same time, the patient is monitored for side effects. The protocols therefore require the patient to have frequent laboratory testing during this period in an effort to discover asymptomatic toxicity. After a predefined time interval, the dose-titration period ends and the patient enters a maintenance phase, during which he is observed while on a constant dose of the medication. Some protocols also have a final washout phase, during which the physician stops the medication completely and documents the expected rise in the patient's blood pressure or other withdrawal phenomena.

The medical tests that are required during hypertension drug trials tend to be studies that are routinely available in almost all clinical laboratories. These include chest radiographs, electrocardiograms, complete blood counts (CBCs), standard blood-chemistry tests, and urinalyses. The hypertension protocols indicate specific times during the clinical trial when physicians should order particular laboratory tests and record the results. At each patient visit, physicians must record other data regarding the patient, including findings on physical examination, reports of possible side effects to the medication, and, of course, the patient's blood pressure and other vital signs.

9.2   Modeling the Hypertension Domain

I shall now describe how PROTÉGÉ was used to develop a model of the hypertension domain. I do not claim that the model is sufficient to represent all clinical trials that involve antihypertensive medications; it can be applied, however, to many typical protocols in this application area. (There are some unusual hypertension protocols that would require a different model.)

Creating the task model for hypertension was straightforward. I first spent approximately 6 hours reviewing 10 protocol documents from different drug companies, studying four of the protocols in depth. I was able to design a conceptual model for hypertension and then enter it into PROTÉGÉ in about 3 hours.[2] I subsequently refined the model in several ways, but these changes were relatively minor. Together, the subsequent revisions required no more than 30 minutes to perform.

9.2.1   Planning Entities

The planning entities in the hypertension domain are shown in Figure 9.1. In the model, *protocols* are composed of three classes of more primitive elements: *tablets, tests,* and *wait* periods. I use the generic word *tablet* to denote the administration of any agent by mouth—

---

[2]Dr. Peter Rudd served as my domain expert during these experiments.

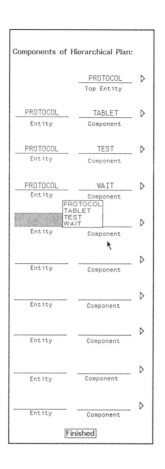

Figure 9.1: Planning Entities in the Hypertension Domain

This PROTÉGÉ form shows the planning entities in the hypertension model. *Protocols* are composed of *tablets, tests,* and *wait* periods. Compare this form with Figure 7.7 (page 151), which shows the planning entities in the oncology domain.

either an active drug or a placebo. A *test* refers to any specially timed laboratory study mandated by a hypertension protocol (for example, blood work and electrocardiograms). Routine physical examinations and the recording of vital signs (such as blood pressure and pulse) are not modeled explicitly as *tests*, because these are not data that the physician must request from a third party such as a clinical laboratory. A *wait* simply constitutes a discrete interval of time during which no active therapy takes place. The *wait* component is needed to model those periods when hypertensive patients are observed but when no

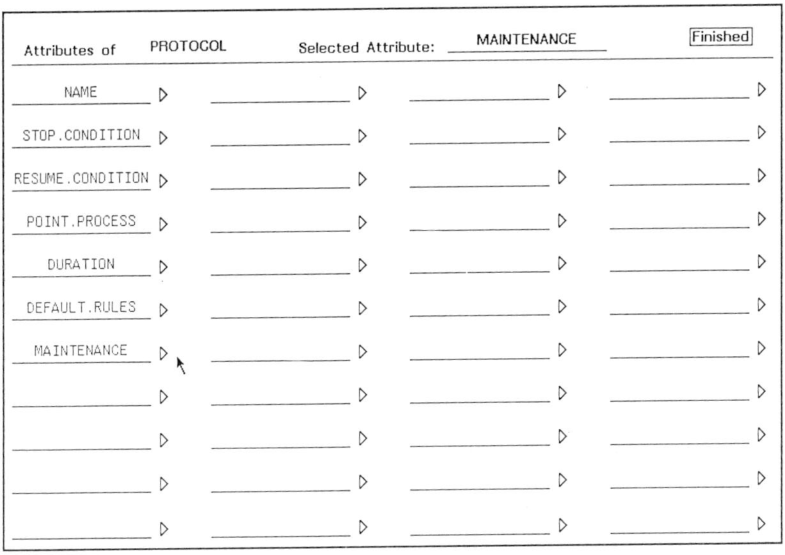

Attributes of PROTOCOL   Selected Attribute: ___MAINTENANCE___   [Finished]

```
    NAME           ▷ _____ ▷ _____ ▷ _____ ▷
STOP.CONDITION     ▷ _____ ▷ _____ ▷ _____ ▷
RESUME.CONDITION   ▷ _____ ▷ _____ ▷ _____ ▷
POINT.PROCESS      ▷ _____ ▷ _____ ▷ _____ ▷
    DURATION       ▷ _____ ▷ _____ ▷ _____ ▷
DEFAULT.RULES      ▷ _____ ▷ _____ ▷ _____ ▷
MAINTENANCE        ▷ _____ ▷ _____ ▷ _____ ▷
_____        ▷ _____ ▷ _____ ▷ _____ ▷
_____        ▷ _____ ▷ _____ ▷ _____ ▷
_____        ▷ _____ ▷ _____ ▷ _____ ▷
_____        ▷ _____ ▷ _____ ▷ _____ ▷
```

Figure 9.2: Attributes of Hypertension Protocols

This graphical form allows knowledge engineers to review all the attributes of hypertension *protocol* entities. Compare this form with the oncology specifications in Figure 7.8 (page 153). Protocols have an attribute called MAINTENANCE, the value of which is established at the editor level, defining the time after which physicians may no longer titrate the patient's drug dose. All other attributes of a hypertension *protocol* are the standard ones that PROTÉGÉ creates for every entity. The knowledge engineer specifies the properties of the MAINTENANCE attribute using the form in Figure 9.3.

tablets are given. (An alternative way of implementing the same concept would have been to create the notion of a *null* tablet. The use of an explicit *wait* period seemed more natural, however.)

Defining a task model with PROTÉGÉ requires that the attributes of these planning entities be defined. Figure 9.2 shows the attributes of the *protocol* entity in the hypertension domain. The only user-specified attribute, called MAINTENANCE, refers to the time in the protocol (measured in weeks) when the patient enters *maintenance phase* and no further adjustments in drug dose are allowed. Figure 9.3 shows how the MAINTENANCE

```
  DETAILS OF:
  MAINTENANCE        EDITOR          INTEGER                              NO
                   How established?   Data Type      REASONER Priority  Multi-valued? Time varying?

                   WEEK MAINTENANCE BEGINS        WEEK THAT MAINTENANCE PHASE BEGINS
  INTERVIEWER Display    Flowsheet label                   Prompt message

  DEFAULT VALUES:

  METHODS:          ____  ____ ▷  ____  ____ ▷  ____  ____ ▷  ____  ____ ▷

                    ____  ____ ▷  ____  ____ ▷  ____  ____ ▷  ____  ____ ▷   │Finished│ ↖
```

Figure 9.3: Properties of HTN Protocol MAINTENANCE Attribute

This form allows knowledge engineers to enter properties of the attributes of planning entities. Here, the user has specified that the MAINTENANCE attribute of HTN protocols is an integer that is defined at the knowledge-editor level. This attribute corresponds to the week of the protocol when the patient enters the "maintenance phase," the period during which the physician no longer adjusts the dose of the tablet administered to the patient.

attribute has been defined using PROTÉGÉ; because the *"How Established?"* property is set to *editor*, the value for this attribute will be solicited by HTN each time a hypertension protocol is entered. HTN will print the *"Interviewer Label"* for the MAINTENANCE attribute ("Week Maintenance Begins") as the label for the blank in the HTN *protocol* form that requests this information.

Similarly, the attributes for the other entities in the model must be declared. *Tablets* have three special attributes: INITIAL DOSE, CURRENT DOSE, and DOSE FREQUENCY (Figure 9.4). The INITIAL DOSE is the number of tablets prescribed for the patient to take before the physician starts to titrate the dose. The DOSE FREQUENCY refers to the number of times per day that the patient takes the tablets. For example, physicians may prescribe that a tablet be taken daily (*qd*), twice daily (*bid*), or three times per day (*tid*). The model assumes that the INITIAL DOSE and DOSE FREQUENCY are attributes the values of which are defined at the knowledge-editor level (Figure 9.5). These attributes define properties of the tablet that do not change over time. CURRENT DOSE, however, is a computed attribute; its value can vary from visit

228

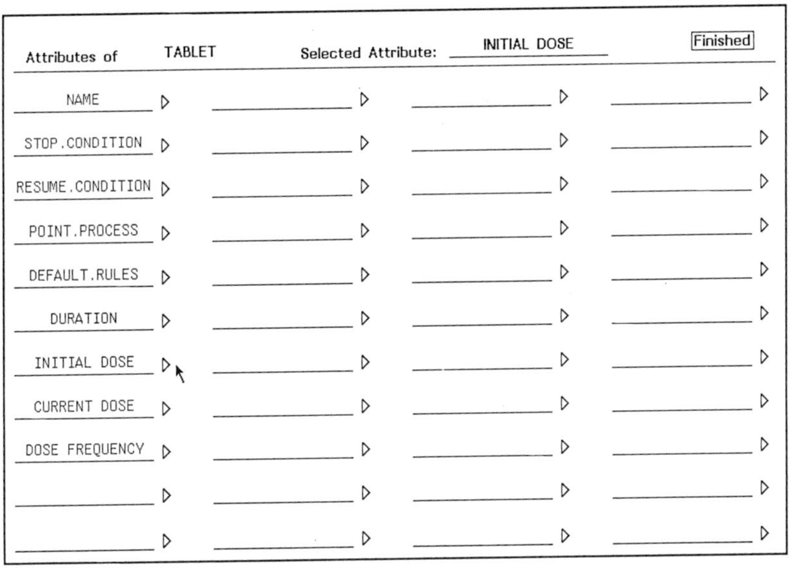

Figure 9.4: Attributes of Tablets

In the hypertension model, tablets have a three special attributes: INITIAL DOSE, CURRENT DOSE, and DOSE FREQUENCY. The details of these attributes are given in Figure 9.5.

to visit. Because, in the absence of rules to the contrary, the current dose of a tablet is always the same as the previous dose, CURRENT DOSE is defined as a *frame* attribute (Figure 9.5(c); see also Section 7.3.1). In this manner, HTN will automatically add a rule to the e-ONCOCIN knowledge base asserting that, by default, CURRENT DOSE does not change unless explicitly altered by some other rule.

9.2.2 Task Actions

The second part of the model defined with PROTÉGÉ involves task actions. In oncology protocols, such actions alter the manner in which chemotherapies and drugs are administered. In hypertension protocols, these actions affect *tablets* and *tests*. Figure 9.6 shows the particular actions required in the hypertension domain: the protocol can be terminated, tablets can be either started or discontinued, tablet doses can either be increased

DETAILS OF:
INITIAL DOSE

EDITOR	INTEGER		NO	NO
How established?	Data Type	REASONER Priority	Multi-valued?	Time varying?

	INITIAL DOSE TO GIVE	INITIAL TABLET DOSE TO GIVE
INTERVIEWER Display	Flowsheet label	Prompt message

DEFAULT VALUES: _____ _____ _____

METHODS: ____ ____ ▷ ____ ____ ▷ ____ ____ ▷ ____ ____ ▷

____ ____ ▷ ____ ____ ▷ ____ ____ ▷ ____ ____ ▷ [Finished]

(a)

DETAILS OF:
CURRENT DOSE

COMPUTED	INTEGER	GOAL	NO	FRAME
How established?	Data Type	REASONER Priority	Multi-valued?	Time varying?

FLOWSHEET	DOSE TO GIVE	NUMBER OF TABLETS TO GIVE
INTERVIEWER Display	Flowsheet label	Prompt message

DEFAULT VALUES: _____ _____ _____

METHODS: RULE DOSE01 ▷ ____ ____ ▷ ____ ____ ▷ ____ ____ ▷

____ ____ ▷ ____ ____ ▷ ____ ____ ▷ ____ ____ ▷ [Finished]

(b)

DETAILS OF:
DOSE FREQUENCY

EDITOR	DOSE FREQ		NO	YES
How established?	Data Type	REASONER Priority	Multi-valued?	Time varying?

FLOWSHEET	DOSE FREQUENCY	DOSE FREQUENCY
INTERVIEWER Display	Flowsheet label	Prompt message

DEFAULT VALUES: _____ _____ _____

METHODS: ____ ____ ▷ ____ ____ ▷ ____ ____ ▷ ____ ____ ▷

____ ____ ▷ ____ ____ ▷ ____ ____ ▷ ____ ____ ▷ [Finished]

(c)

Figure 9.5: Details of Tablet Attributes

This figure shows how attributes of the *tablet* entity are defined using PROTÉGÉ: (a) the INITIAL DOSE attribute, (b) the CURRENT DOSE attribute, and (c) the DOSE FREQUENCY attribute. The latter two attributes have values that appear on the Interviewer flowsheet.

230

Task-Level Actions:

END PROTOCOL ▷

INCREASE DOSE ▷

DECREASE DOSE ▷

ADD TABLET ▷

STOP TABLET ▷

ORDER TEST ▷

▷

▷

▷

▷

▷

▷

▷

▷

▷

▷

Finished

Figure 9.6: Task Actions in the Hypertension Domain

Task actions in hypertension protocols include ending the study, increasing and decreasing the dose of a tablet, starting a new tablet or discontinuing an existing one, and ordering tests. Compare these actions with those for oncology in Figure 7.13 (page 165).

or decreased, and new tests can be ordered.

For each task action, PROTÉGÉ requires a *script* that defines how to bring about that action in domain-independent terms (see Section 7.3.2). Figure 9.7(a), for example, shows the form that defines the script for the *add tablet* action. Administration of a new tablet is effected by starting a new process of the *tablet* class. The name of the specific tablet to start is determined by the value of an attribute called TABLET NAME, the value of which is established at the editor level. Thus, if a physician at the editor level uses HTN to specify

(a)

Attributes of __ADD TABLET__   Associated Entity: [____]   PROTOCOL / TABLET / TEST / WAIT / *UNSELECT*   ...ted Attribute: _____   [Finished]

TABLET NAME ▷ _____ ▷ _____ ▷ _____ ▷ _____ ▷
_____ ▷ _____ ▷ _____ ▷ _____ ▷ _____ ▷
_____ ▷ _____ ▷ _____ ▷ _____ ▷ _____ ▷
_____ ▷ _____ ▷ _____ ▷ _____ ▷ _____ ▷

Action Sequence:

	Precondition		Affected Plan Component		Additional Data
1 START			TABLET		TABLET NAME
Action Primitive	Action Attribute	Attribute Value	Plan Entity Type	Attribute	Action Attribute

(b)

Attributes of __INCREASE DOSE__   Associated Entity: __TABLET__   Selected Attribute: __INCRMNT.OK?__   [Finished]

INCREMENT ▷ _____ ▷ _____ ▷ _____ ▷ _____ ▷
NEW DOSE ▷ _____ ▷ _____ ▷ _____ ▷ _____ ▷
INCRMNT.OK? ▷ _____ ▷ _____ ▷ _____ ▷ _____ ▷
_____ ▷ _____ ▷ _____ ▷ _____ ▷ _____ ▷

Action Sequence:

	Precondition		Affected Plan Component		Additional Data
1 ALTER ATTR	INCRMNT.OK?	YES	TABLET	CURRENT DOSE	NEW DOSE
Action Primitive	Action Attribute	Attribute Value	Plan Entity Type	Attribute	Action Attribute

Figure 9.7: Scripts for Task Actions

This figure shows the scripts that define how to effect two of the task actions in the hypertension domain. (a) The *add tablet* action has an attribute, TABLET NAME, the value of which is entered by the application specialist at the editor level to establish the particular tablet *instance* that should be started. (b) The *increase dose* action raises the dose of the associated tablet by whatever INCREMENT is entered at the editor level. The values of the attributes NEW DOSE and INCRMT.OK? are concluded by specific e-ONCOCIN rules.

232

situations when the *add tablet* action should take place, she must enter the appropriate tablet names in each instance. Figure 9.7(b) shows the script for the *increase dose* action. This task action, which alters the CURRENT DOSE attribute of a given tablet, has three attributes itself. The first attribute of the *increase dose* action is INCREMENT, the value of which must be entered into HTN for each instance of the *increase dose* action in a given protocol. The second attribute is NEW DOSE, the value of which is *computed.* Consequently, the knowledge engineer must enter an e-ONCOCIN rule into PROTÉGÉ (using the form in Figure 7.11, page 158) that states that the NEW DOSE is the sum of the CURRENT DOSE of the tablet plus the editor-entered INCREMENT. The action script for *increase dose* simply replaces the CURRENT DOSE of the tablet with the computed NEW DOSE—provided that the third attribute, INCRMT.OK?, has the value *YES.* The value of INCRMT.OK? is concluded by another e-ONCOCIN rule entered into PROTÉGÉ. INCRMT.OK? will have value *YES* only during a protocol's titration period, when physicians may legally adjust the dose of a tablet; during the maintenance phase, this attribute will have the value *NO.* The rule that concludes the value of INCRMT.OK? must examine the MAINTENANCE attribute of the current *protocol* to determine whether the patient has reached the maintenance phase (see Figure 9.3).

The scripts for the other task actions in the hypertension domain (*end protocol, stop tablet, decrease dose,* and *order test*) are of a complexity similar to that of the examples in Figure 9.7. There are no intricate sequences of operations, as is sometimes needed to represent task actions in oncology.

9.2.3   Input Data

The third component of PROTÉGÉ's model includes the data that are input from the environment that can affect the advice system's behavior. In hypertension applications, these data include vital signs (including blood pressure), different kinds of laboratory data (blood chemistry, hematology, and urinalysis results), physical-examination data, and reports of side effects that either are volunteered by the patient or are elicited or observed by the physician (Figure 9.8).

As in oncology, the data items in each class must be enumerated using PROTÉGÉ

Figure 9.8: Data Classes in the Hypertension Domain

This form shows the classes of input data that are relevant for hypertension protocols. Compare these classes with those for oncology in Figure 7.16 (page 174).

(Figure 9.9). Not surprisingly, hypertension protocols require the physician to follow carefully various aspects of a patient's blood-pressure status. Both systolic and diastolic blood pressure must be recorded.[3] More important, the physician often must measure the vital signs with the patient in different *positions*. As seen in Figure 9.9(a), hypertension protocols may require the physician to record systolic blood pressure, diastolic blood pressure, and pulse with the patient standing, sitting, and lying down.

---

[3]The *systolic blood pressure* is the pressure in the arteries when the heart contracts, whereas the *diastolic blood pressure* is the pressure when the heart relaxes. When a physician says, for example, that a patient's blood pressure is "120/80," the systolic pressure is 120 mm Hg and the diastolic pressure is 80 mm Hg.

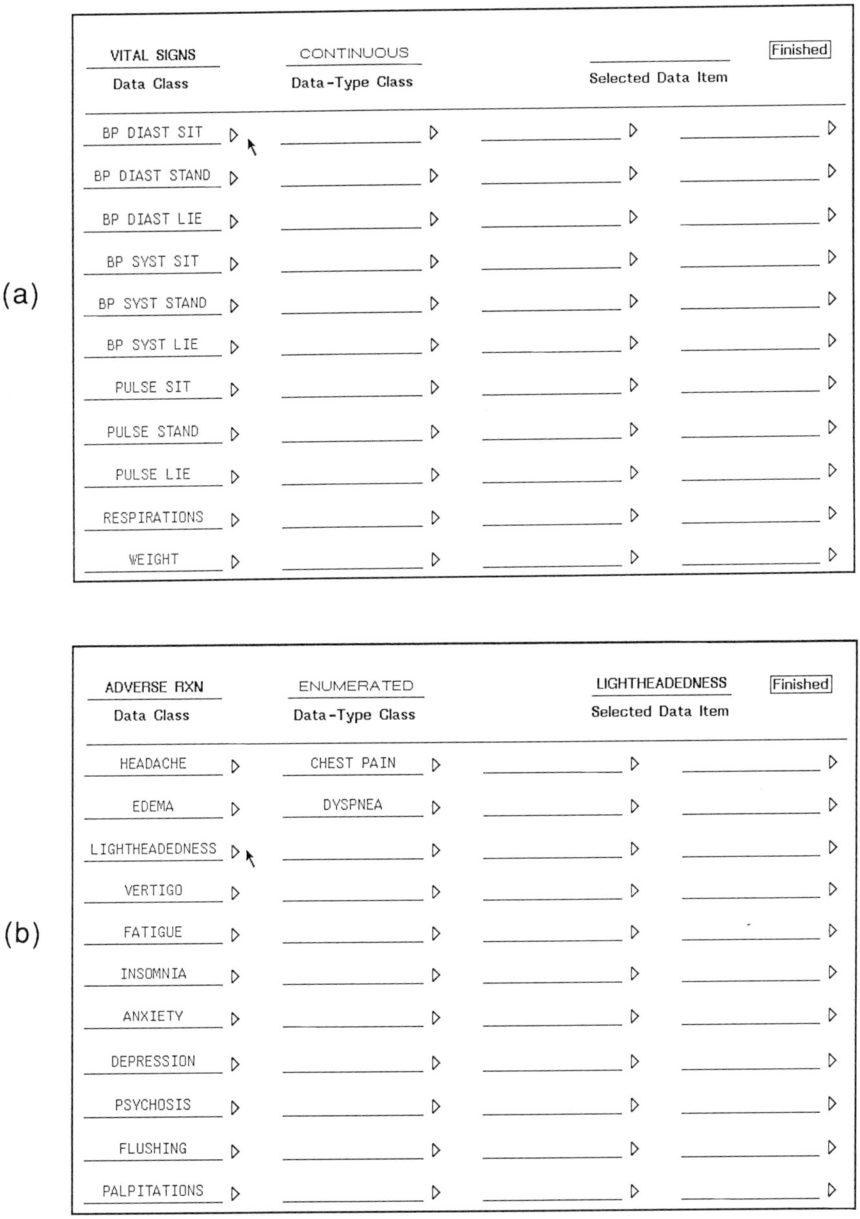

(a)

VITAL SIGNS Data Class	CONTINUOUS Data-Type Class	Selected Data Item		Finished
BP DIAST SIT ▷	▷	▷	▷	
BP DIAST STAND ▷	▷	▷	▷	
BP DIAST LIE ▷	▷	▷	▷	
BP SYST SIT ▷	▷	▷	▷	
BP SYST STAND ▷	▷	▷	▷	
BP SYST LIE ▷	▷	▷	▷	
PULSE SIT ▷	▷	▷	▷	
PULSE STAND ▷	▷	▷	▷	
PULSE LIE ▷	▷	▷	▷	
RESPIRATIONS ▷	▷	▷	▷	
WEIGHT ▷	▷	▷	▷	

(b)

ADVERSE RXN Data Class	ENUMERATED Data-Type Class	LIGHTHEADEDNESS Selected Data Item		Finished
HEADACHE ▷	CHEST PAIN ▷	▷	▷	
EDEMA ▷	DYSPNEA ▷	▷	▷	
LIGHTHEADEDNESS ▷	▷	▷	▷	
VERTIGO ▷	▷	▷	▷	
FATIGUE ▷	▷	▷	▷	
INSOMNIA ▷	▷	▷	▷	
ANXIETY ▷	▷	▷	▷	
DEPRESSION ▷	▷	▷	▷	
PSYCHOSIS ▷	▷	▷	▷	
FLUSHING ▷	▷	▷	▷	
PALPITATIONS ▷	▷	▷	▷	

Figure 9.9: Data Class Items for Hypertension Protocols

These forms show the individual items for (a) vital signs and (b) adverse reactions. The vital signs include diastolic blood pressure, systolic blood pressure, and pulse, recorded when the patient stands, sits, and lies down. The adverse reactions include various side effects that the patient may volunteer, or that may be elicited or observed by the physician.

Figure 9.9(b) shows the data items for the *adverse reactions* data class. Using the same data-item-detail form that is shown in Figure 7.18 (page 176) for oncology data, each of these side effects is given a special data type called ADVERSE RXN. The PROTÉGÉ data-types form (Figure 9.10) then permits the knowledge engineer to enter the potential values that constitute this new data type. These values define the contents both of the menu that will be made available to the application experts who use HTN to declare how adverse reactions are to be handled in specific hypertension protocols, and of the menu that will be made available to e-ONCOCIN users who must record the actual adverse reactions experienced by patients enrolled in the HTN-entered protocols.

9.2.4 Data Types

Every data item, every planning-entity attribute, and every task-action attribute must be given a data type (for example, *integer* or *real*). The data-type information is required to produce the necessary software input devices (that is, menus and registers) that users will employ when interacting with both the PROTÉGÉ-generated knowledge editor and e-ONCOCIN. Every menu and register displayed by these programs is derived from the entries made into the form in Figure 9.10. If the knowledge engineer wants to change a particular menu or register at either the editor or advice-system level, he needs only to update this form. Both the knowledge editor and e-ONCOCIN then make the appropriate adjustments.

PROTÉGÉ automatically creates a data type for each planning-entity class in the user's model. Thus, the menu of data types at the top of Figure 9.10 includes the data type *tablet,* to which the user assigns the possible values *PLACEBO* and *DRUG*. (Recall that physicians in this application area never know the actual *name* of the drug given to a particular patient; these clinical trials are double-blind.) The data type *test* has possible values such as *CXR* (chest X-ray examination), *ECG* (electrocardiogram), *CBC* (complete blood count), *U/A* (urinalysis), and *SMA-18* (sequential multianalysis of 18 different blood-chemistry tests). Other data types in HTN, such as *URINE PH* and *URINE MICRO,* represent special enumerated data types created by the user to describe certain input data in this domain (in this case, parts of a urinalysis). Other data types, such as

236

DATA TYPES: INTEGER   REAL   PERCENT   BOOLEAN   TABLET

    TEST   URINE SG   URINE pH   ++++   URINE MICRO   **ADVERSE RXN**

    WAIT   DOSE FREQ   ▴

            ADVERSE RXN   MENU   ADVERSE RXN   [Finished]
            ‾‾‾‾‾‾‾‾‾‾‾   ‾‾‾‾   ‾‾‾‾‾‾‾‾‾‾‾
              Selection   Input Format   Menu Title

Menu Information:

  ABSENT   ABSENT
  ‾‾‾‾‾‾   ‾‾‾‾‾‾   ‾‾‾‾‾‾‾   ‾‾‾‾‾‾‾‾
  ELICITED   ELICITED W/ DIRECT QUESTIONING
  ‾‾‾‾‾‾‾‾   ‾‾‾‾‾‾‾‾‾‾‾‾‾‾‾‾‾‾‾‾‾‾‾‾‾‾   ‾‾‾‾‾‾‾   ‾‾‾‾‾‾‾‾
  VOLUNTEERED   VOLUNTEERED BY PATIENT
  ‾‾‾‾‾‾‾‾‾‾‾   ‾‾‾‾‾‾‾‾‾‾‾‾‾‾‾‾‾‾‾‾‾‾   ‾‾‾‾‾‾‾   ‾‾‾‾‾‾‾‾
  OBSERVED   OBSERVED BY PHYSICIAN
  ‾‾‾‾‾‾‾‾   ‾‾‾‾‾‾‾‾‾‾‾‾‾‾‾‾‾‾‾‾   ‾‾‾‾‾‾‾   ‾‾‾‾‾‾‾‾

  Value   Prompt Message   Value   Prompt Message

DOSE FREQ, list potential values for user-defined attributes of planning entities (here, the DOSE FREQUENCY attribute of *tablets*, which takes on values such as *qd, bid,* and *tid*).

9.3   Entering a Specific Protocol

Given the model of hypertension clinical trials entered into PROTÉGÉ, creating a knowledge editor for this domain is simply a matter of selecting the *"Invoke Editor"* box on the PROTÉGÉ main menu (see Figure 7.6, page 144). The form in Figure 9.11 appears on the workstation screen, serving as the main menu for the HTN editor. The blank at the top of the form allows the user to edit an existing protocol or to enter a new hypertension study. The toggle labeled *"Protocol Data"* allows a physician to describe the protocol and other components of a treatment plan. Those labeled *"Adverse Reactions," "Urinalysis,"* and so on display forms that allow entry of protocol-specific rules pertaining to each of the data classes declared at the PROTÉGÉ level.

9.3.1   Sandoz Protocol 331

A representative hypertension drug study, which I have encoded for e-ONCOCIN using HTN, is Study 331 from Sandoz Research Institute (East Hanover, New Jersey). This RCT, which is still under active investigation at the time of this writing, tests the safety and efficacy of treating high blood pressure with an experimental drug compared to a conventional agent.[4] Because the Sandoz study will serve as the basis for the extended example in this chapter, I shall describe this clinical trial in detail (Figure 9.12).

The Sandoz protocol first has an observation period during which study physicians follow their patients weekly for three visits. During this time, the physicians give the patients supplies of a placebo and instruct them to take one capsule twice daily. This

---

[4]The experimental preparation is a calcium-channel blocking drug that Sandoz demonstrated to be a potent vasodilator in laboratory animals. The control drug is a common angiotensin-converting-enzyme inhibitor. Study 331 is one of several Phase III trials that the company has conducted to evaluate the drug in humans. I selected this study for entry into HTN purely out of interest, as Dr. Peter Rudd had a number of patients at the Palo Alto Veterans' Administration Medical Center enrolled in this protocol at the time that I was developing PROTÉGÉ.

Figure 9.11: HTN Main Menu

After the hypertension domain is modeled at the PROTÉGÉ level, selecting the box labeled *"Invoke Editor"* on the PROTÉGÉ main menu (see Figure 7.6, page 144) causes the main menu for the HTN editor to appear on the workstation screen. In the figure, physicians have already entered portions of two hypertension protocols into HTN. The pop-up menu allows the user to choose to work on one of these existing treatment plans or to enter a new protocol. Compare this form with the main menu for p-OPAL (see Figure 8.2, page 188).

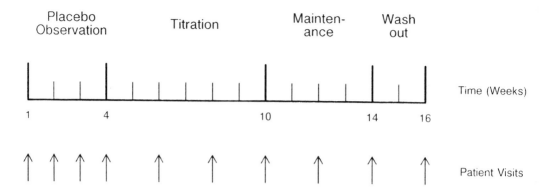

Figure 9.12: Sandoz Research Institute Study Number 331

This randomized clinical trial (RCT) studies the safety and efficacy of an experimental drug versus a standard drug in treating hypertension. After a 3-week period on placebo, patients are prescribed one of the two drugs at random. The patients are then seen biweekly during the 6-week titration period and 4-week maintenance period. A 2-week period off medication completes the study.

first part of the study is thus *single-blind:* The physicians are aware that the patients are not yet taking active medication. Next comes the double-blind titration period, during which either the experimental preparation or the control drug is dispensed to the patients in unlabeled capsules; the physicians are thus unaware of which patients receive which treatment until the study has been completed. The patients start out taking a single dose of their assigned drug twice daily, visiting their physicians at biweekly intervals. During the titration period, the protocol calls for the physicians to increase the dose of the drug any time that a patient's diastolic blood pressure in the sitting position is greater than 90 mm Hg (torr). If the blood pressure is 90 mm Hg or less, the previous dose of the drug is continued. After the tenth week of the protocol, the patient enters the maintenance phase, during which the protocol forbids further adjustments to the patient's dose. At the end of the fourth week of the maintenance period, the physician discontinues the medication and observes the patient for the final 2 weeks of the study.

In addition to mandating the drugs that patients receive, the Sandoz protocol also requires that physicians order a number of laboratory tests. These tests are done before the patient starts the placebo phase, before the titration phase, before and after the mainte-

240

nance phase, and again after completion of the study. At every patient visit, the physician must examine the patient, measure the blood pressure and pulse with the patient both sitting and standing, and determine whether the patient has experienced any side effects of treatment. For any adverse reaction, the physician must note whether the presence of the condition was volunteered by the patient, elicited only with direct questioning, or observed objectively.

9.3.2 Describing the Plan Components

I shall now show how Sandoz Research Institute Study Number 331 was entered into HTN. After typing in the new protocol number into the HTN main menu (see Figure 9.11), we selected the blank labeled *"Protocol Data,"* causing the form in Figure 9.13 to be displayed. The only editor-established attribute of hypertension protocols that I had declared at the PROTÉGÉ level was MAINTENANCE (see Figure 9.3). The top blank of the HTN protocol form is thus labeled *week maintenance begins* and solicits the required value. Because I gave the MAINTENANCE attribute a data type of *integer,* HTN can produce the appropriate register input device when physicians select this blank. As entered into the form in Figure 9.13, the maintenance period for Sandoz protocol 331 begins at week 10. When HTN generates an e-ONCOCIN knowledge base, the rules in the system that determine whether it is appropriate to alter the dose of a tablet will use this datum to determine whether a patient enrolled in the Sandoz study is in the titration period or in the maintenance period of the protocol.

When users select the blank labeled *"Specify Procedure"* in the protocol form in Figure 9.13, they can then enter the procedure that is associated with that protocol. The protocol form is closed, and a graphical programming environment that has been tailored for entry of the constituents of hypertension protocols appears on the screen (Figure 9.14). The palette of reference icons along the bottom of the graph includes the TABLET, TEST, and WAIT entities that were declared at the PROTÉGÉ level to compose hypertension protocols. Although the graphical *syntax* is the same as that used in p-OPAL (see Figure 8.8, page 202), the semantics of the flowchart language now concern elements from the hypertension domain. In Figure 9.14, the graph for the Sandoz protocol calls for patients

241

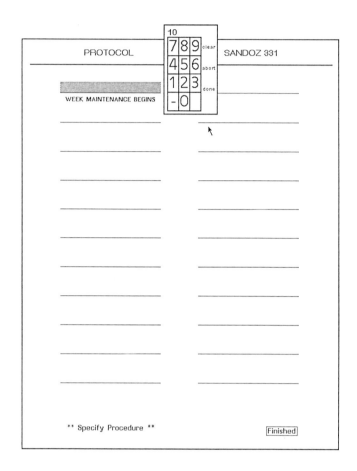

Figure 9.13: HTN Protocol Form

HTN instantiates this generic form to allow entry of information concerning the *protocol* entity in hypertension clinical trials. The only editor-established attribute for this entity that was declared at the PROTÉGÉ level is MAINTENANCE. Accordingly, this form solicits a value representing the week of the protocol when the patient enters the maintenance phase.

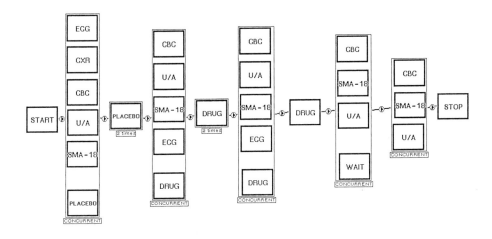

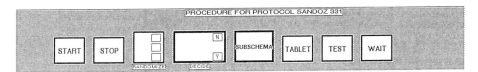

Figure 9.14: Procedural Specification for Sandoz Protocol 331

The flowchart shows the procedure required in the execution of Sandoz Protocol 331. Patients receive only placebo therapy for three 1-week intervals, during which time their blood pressure is observed. Then, for five 2-week intervals, they receive therapy with either the experimental drug or a standard treatment. Throughout the study, a number of specific laboratory tests must be ordered. Compare this diagram with the oncology flowchart in Figure 8.8 (page 202).

o receive placebo therapy for three treatment intervals, followed by five intervals of treatment with an active drug (either the experimental agent or the control drug). At specific imes in the protocol, laboratory tests are performed, concomitant with the administration of either a drug or placebo tablet. At the end of the study, there is a WAIT period during which the physicians give no tablets and simply monitor the patient, who is now receiving no medication.

As described in Figure 8.10 (page 205), each flowchart at the editor level serves as a

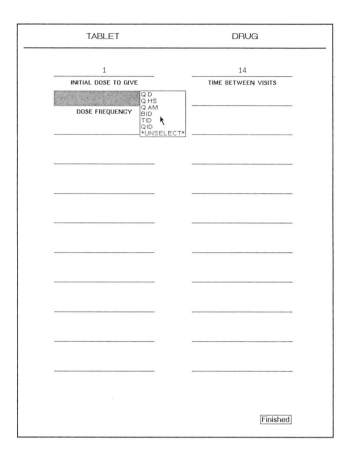

Figure 9.15: HTN Tablet Form

In the hypertension domain, *tablet* entities have three editor-established attributes: INITIAL DOSE, DURATION, and DOSE FREQUENCY. HTN solicits values for these attributes for each tablet instance that the physician declares. In this example, the generic form allows the HTN user to describe the *drugs* that are given as part of the Sandoz protocol.

menu by which the user can access the forms that describe the components of the graph. Thus, selecting any one of the icons labeled DRUG in Figure 9.14 causes the flowchart to be erased and the form shown in Figure 9.15 to be displayed. The form solicits values for those editor-established attributes of tablet entities that were declared at the PROTÉGÉ level (namely, INITIAL DOSE, DURATION, and DOSE FREQUENCY). Because there were no subcomponents of tablet entities described using PROTÉGÉ, there is no *"Specify Procedure"* blank at the bottom of the tablet form (unlike the *protocol* form in Figure 9.13).

When users select the *"Finished"* blank in Figure 9.15, they return to the flowchart graph in Figure 9.14. When users select any of the icons labeled PLACEBO, the graph disappears again and a form similar to that in Figure 9.15 appears on the screen, but this other form allows the users to edit the values for attributes of the PLACEBO tablets in this protocol. Users then can return to the flowchart via the *"Finished"* blank to access the forms for the other nodes in the graph (for example, the WAIT icon or the icons for the individual laboratory tests). From the graph, it also is possible to go back to the form that describes the protocol itself (see Figure 9.13). If users then select *"Finished"* in the protocol form, that form disappears and the HTN main menu is again accessible (see Figure 9.11).

9.3.3 Entering Rules

Once HTN users have defined the structure of the protocol by creating the flowchart and entering values for the editor-established attributes of the treatment-plan components, they can specify the task rules that can modify execution of the protocol. As in p-OPAL, selecting a data class in the HTN main menu causes the corresponding form to be displayed for entry of rules that pertain to that class.

The form shown in Figure 9.16, for example, allows the user to enter actions to take if the patient is observed to have *anxiety* as a possible adverse reaction of treatment. Like the p-OPAL form for enumerated data (see Figure 8.6, page 198), all potential values for the selected data item are listed at the left side. Figure 9.17 shows the HTN form for entry of rules that are predicated on a patient's vital signs. Here, the HTN user is specifying the rule from the Sandoz protocol that states that, if a patient's diastolic blood pressure (measured in the sitting position) is greater than 90 mm Hg, the current dose of the drug to which the patient has been assigned should be increased. Because the *increase dose* action has the editor-established attribute called INCREMENT (see Figure 9.7b), the HTN user must further specify that, in this situation, the dose of the drug should be increased by *one capsule* (Figure 9.18). Because Sandoz Protocol 331 is so simple, this rule concerning diastolic blood pressure is the only task rule that HTN users must specify in this clinical trial.

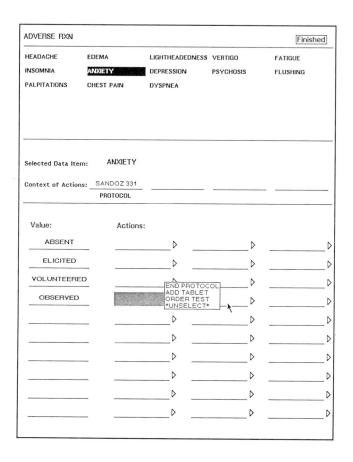

Figure 9.16: HTN Form for Adverse Reactions

This form allows users to enter task rules for hypertension protocols related to adverse reactions to therapy. Because adverse reactions have an enumerated data type, this form is able to list all potential values for a selected data item. Here, the user is about to select an action to take if the treating physician observes that the patient is suffering from *anxiety*. The actions on the menu are limited to those that are relevant in the planning context that the user has specified (namely, a particular protocol).

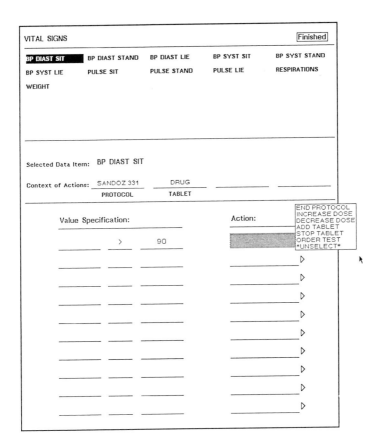

Figure 9.17: HTN Form for Vital Signs

This form allows users to enter task rules for hypertension protocols related to a patient's vital signs. Here, the user is about to enter the rule from Sandoz Protocol 331 that states that if a patient's diastolic blood pressure (measured in the sitting position) is greater than 90 mm Hg, the dose of the drug should be increased by one capsule.

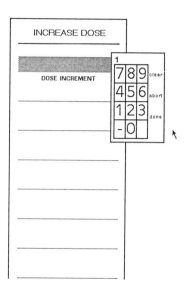

Figure 9.18: Attributes of the Increase-Dose Action

Each time a user specifies a situation in which a dose should be increased, HTN will ask the number of tablets by which to raise the dose. This form is displayed because the knowledge engineer at the PROTÉGÉ level declared that the *increase dose* action has an editor-established attribute called INCREMENT.

9.4 Creating an Advice System

After creating the model of the hypertension domain using PROTÉGÉ, generating HTN, and then entering the Sandoz protocol into HTN, the user can now generate an e-ONCOCIN knowledge base. All that the hypertension expert needs to do is to select the box labeled *"Generate KB"* in the HTN main menu (see Figure 9.11). HTN then transforms the specifications entered into the database into the particular data structures required to drive an e-ONCOCIN consultation. In the case of Sandoz Protocol 331, the resulting knowledge base is a set of 177 objects in the OZONE programming language.

The knowledge base created by HTN serves as the basis for the e-ONCOCIN Reasoner's treatment advice and fashions the e-ONCOCIN Interviewer for consultations in the hypertension domain (Figure 9.19). Each section of the Interviewer flowsheet displays information concerning one of the data classes or planning entities that I described using

PROTÉGÉ. Consequently, there are sections of the flowsheet for recording adverse reactions, urinalysis results, hematology data, chemistry data, and vital signs. Another section shows the tablets to give and their corresponding doses; another shows laboratory tests that must be ordered according to the protocol.

After a user enters a patient's vital signs and test results into the sections of the flowsheet where such data are recorded, e-ONCOCIN can fill out the *recommendation* sections of the flowsheet automatically with the therapy and laboratory studies currently required by the hypertension protocol. If the physician disagrees with e-ONCOCIN's suggestions, he can enter a different treatment plan manually.

Figure 9.19 shows an e-ONCOCIN Interviewer flowsheet for a patient with high blood pressure who has been treated for several weeks on Sandoz Protocol 331. The patient has been seen weekly during the placebo phase and biweekly during the period of drug therapy. (These intervals reflect the DURATION of the *placebo* and *drug* entities, entered using the form in Figure 9.15.) In accordance with the procedure diagrammed in Figure 9.14, the patient received three intervals of placebo therapy before starting on the drug to which he was assigned. The various laboratory tests that e-ONCOCIN recommends also are derived from the HTN flowchart. Because of the rule entered in Figure 9.17, the patient's dose of the drug is increased during the titration phase any time that his diastolic blood pressure is greater than 90 mm Hg.

Thus, the model of the task domain entered into PROTÉGÉ, coupled with the protocol knowledge entered into HTN, is sufficient to create knowledge bases that successfully drive e-ONCOCIN consultations in this new application area. Although the advice system for hypertension protocols has not yet been implemented for clinical use, the ease with which the knowledge base was constructed validates the utility of the PROTÉGÉ approach.

9.5 Extensions to Other Domains

In this chapter, I have shown how PROTÉGÉ can be used to construct advice systems in new application areas. Although the hypertension domain is relatively simple, it represents a manageable substrate for demonstrating a PROTÉGÉ application in its entirety. I have

Vital Signs	BP SYST LIE							
	BP SYST SIT	150	156	155	154	140	138	125
	BP SYST STAND							
	BP DIAST LIE							
	BP DIAST SIT	100	105	103	103	95	92	85
	BP DIAST STAND							
	PULSE LIE							
	PULSE SIT							
	PULSE STAND							
	RESPIRATIONS							
	WEIGHT							
Tablets	TABLET	PLACEBO	PLACEBO	PLACEBO				
	DOSE TO GIVE	1	1	1				
	DOSE FREQUENCY	BID	BID	BID				
	TIME BETWEEN VISITS	7	7	7				
	TABLET				DRUG	DRUG	DRUG	DRUG
	DOSE TO GIVE				1	2	3	3
	DOSE FREQUENCY				BID	BID	BID	BID
	TIME BETWEEN VISITS				14	14	14	14
Tests	TEST	ECG			ECG			ECG
	TEST	CXR						
	TEST	CBC			CBC			CBC
	TEST	U/A			U/A			U/A
	TEST	SMA-18			SMA-18			SMA-18
	Urinalysis							
	Hematology							
	Adverse Reaction							
	Chemistry							
Time	Day	12	19	26	2	16	30	13
	Month	Jul	Jul	Jul	Aug	Aug	Aug	Sep
	Year	87	87	87	87	87	87	87

Figure 9.19: An Advice System for Hypertension Protocols

Domain-independent programs translate the hypertension task model entered into PROTÉGÉ, and the specific protocols entered into HTN, into knowledge bases that can drive e-ONCOCIN consultations. This figure shows the resulting e-ONCOCIN Interviewer for hypertension protocols. Each section of the flowsheet corresponds to a distinct planning entity or data class that was defined at the PROTÉGÉ level. The *tablet* form shows part of e-ONCOCIN's treatment recommendations over time. Note that, in accordance with the procedure entered in Figure 9.14, this patient has received placebo treatment for three 1-week intervals, followed by therapy with an active drug. In accordance with the rule entered in Figure 9.17, any time during the titration phase that the patient's diastolic blood pressure was greater than 90 mm Hg, e-ONCOCIN appropriately recommended that the physician increase the dose.

250

shown how I rapidly modeled a class of hypertension drug studies with PROTÉGÉ to produce a custom-tailored editor called HTN. I then used HTN to enter knowledge about an actual clinical trial (Sandoz 331), and generated a knowledge base that e-ONCOCIN can use to provide data management and treatment advice for patients enrolled in that trial.

There are many other domains to which PROTÉGÉ also should be applicable. PROTÉGÉ will be useful for building models in any domain in which tasks can be solved via the method of skeletal-plan refinement (so that backtracking to satisfy constraints is not a major concern) and in which time is measured in discrete intervals—with no interval having a duration shorter than the time between e-ONCOCIN consultations. PROTÉGÉ thus should be practical for describing a number of clinical-trial areas, such as organ transplantation, diabetes control, rheumatology studies, hematology studies, and other cardiovascular drug testing. The current program probably would not be helpful in defining *inpatient* protocols, such as those relating to hemodialysis techniques or to management of patients having acute cardiac emergencies, as it is difficult to separate time into discrete intervals in these settings.

PROTÉGÉ also could be applied to planning problems outside of clinical medicine. In Friedland's MOLGEN system (1979), for example, experiments in molecular genetics are rendered as problems in skeletal-plan refinement that have discrete steps. It would be valuable to learn to what degree *classes* of such experiments could be modeled using PROTÉGÉ, so that molecular biologists could then use PROTÉGÉ-generated editors to encode knowledge of specific laboratory procedures. If successful, the approach would allow advice systems based on e-ONCOCIN to aid research assistants in the execution of those experiments.

In Chapter 10, I shall discuss the specific limitations of PROTÉGÉ that would impede use of the program in its current form in certain application areas. These restrictions occur because PROTÉGÉ, the editors that it generates, and e-ONCOCIN all contain significant assumptions about planning, about time, and about the process of knowledge entry. These assumptions need to be addressed in future research. Despite these limitations, the system that I have described is capable of modeling clinical trials in oncology and hypertension, and presumably other domains as well. These results demonstrate that model-based knowledge-editing tools can be constructed from metalevel specifications, and that an editor for those specifications, such as PROTÉGÉ, can greatly facilitate production of custom-tailored tools.

10 A Methodology for Knowledge Engineering

In this book, I have presented a methodology for knowledge acquisition for expert systems. The methodology advocates that knowledge engineers, in conjunction with experts, use metalevel knowledge-editing tools to create domain models and to enter process knowledge for new application areas. The models then are used to generate *task-specific* knowledge editors, which application specialists can employ to enter the content knowledge for specific advice systems. This approach consolidates at the metalevel the work that knowledge engineers do best—helping experts to build models; it consolidates at the editor level the knowledge-entry work that experts can most readily perform on their own—specifying the *content*.

When there are multiple, related tasks within the application area, the divide-and-conquer strategy offers a considerable advantage. The difficult problem of creating a computational model of the domain will not disappear, but system builders need to confront only a single bottleneck. If knowledge engineers can help application experts to build domain models by using tools such as PROTÉGÉ, those experts then can go to work on their own, defining all the individual tasks to which the models might apply. Each time knowledge engineers construct a single domain model using PROTÉGÉ, application experts then can create multiple related advice systems using the knowledge editor that PROTÉGÉ generates. To date, I have explored the feasibility of this methodology in two clinical-trial areas: oncology and hypertension. In this chapter, I shall discuss both the implications of my results and the limitations of PROTÉGÉ that constitute an agenda for future research.

10.1 The Art of Knowledge Engineering

For as long as there have been expert systems, workers in AI have tried to define what makes knowledge engineering different from the construction of conventional computer programs. Although the field still lacks consensus, I have found the positions articulated by Clancey (1986) and other researchers (Regoczei and Plantinga, 1987; Morik, 1987) to be particularly helpful. For these authors, knowledge engineering is the process of creating and encoding qualitative (nonnumeric) models of systems in the world. In this light, knowledge bases are not unorganized collections of heuristics. They are not chunks of knowledge that correlate directly with the facts and strategies used by human beings in solving problems. And they certainly are not like experts. Knowledge bases are models that abstract some reality. They are selective in what they contain. Because they make assumptions about the world, knowledge bases also fail.

The recognition that knowledge bases are only models is not a basis for pessimism, however. On the contrary, in viewing knowledge engineering as the construction of qualitative models, workers in AI can think more clearly about what they do. Knowledge engineers certainly acquire heuristics and encode rules, but they also do much more than that: Knowledge engineers build models. With this new perspective, knowledge engineers can begin to relate their development of models for expert systems to other kinds of modeling activities. In particular, modeling tools and techniques that have been developed outside of AI suddenly can be applied to the problem of knowledge-base construction. The design of databases, for example, is well recognized as a problem in modeling (Date, 1986; Wiederhold, 1983). PROTÉGÉ, which owes much of its implementation to the use of standard database techniques, is a good example of how viewing knowledge bases as models can suggest new approaches to knowledge engineering that are derived from other disciplines.

This book has described a methodology for generating tools that simplify the construction of knowledge-base models in particular application areas. Each of the tools generated by PROTÉGÉ (knowledge editors such as p-OPAL and HTN) incorporates an explicit model of the tasks that experts in a given application area should want to specify. Because the models are incomplete, experts must instantiate them for particular tasks. Once the task models have been fully defined, however, generating usable knowledge bases is merely a matter of performing syntactic manipulations that involve the various entities, attributes, and values in the models. The frames and rules in an e-ONCOCIN knowledge base denote the same model that is constructed using p-OPAL or HTN and that is stored in their corresponding output database. The model is the same; the symbols that are used to encode the model are different.

10.2 Languages for Building Models

Knowledge acquisition can be defined as the process by which an application specialist and a knowledge engineer work together to build a model of expertise. The model that they build is never preexistent, because much of what an expert knows is initially tacit (Johnson, 1983). Instead, the model must be *created*. The expert first develops a *mental model* of her own professional behavior (Norman, 1983). Simultaneously, the knowledge engineer forms a mental model of what he perceives the expert to be doing when she solves problems. As the knowledge engineer interviews the expert, performs protocol analyses, or reviews the expert's entries into an automated interviewing tool, he may encounter instances in which his mental model does not explain the expert's behavior. Similarly, as the expert is asked to consider new problem-solving situations or to comment on the performance of a prototype system, she may want to reformulate her own mental model. These breakdowns are important, as the identification of incongruities causes *both* the expert and the knowledge engineer to refine their particular mental models. The knowledge engineer and the application specialist eventually agree on a common abstraction. That model, which neither person could imagine initially, becomes the knowledge base.

10.2.1 Choosing a Notation

Tools for building knowledge bases are thus tools for building models. What expert-system builders may need more than anything else are techniques by which domain experts and knowledge engineers can write down descriptions of their mental models, allowing these models to be examined, compared, and discussed. Traditionally, the medium with which the models are recorded is the representation language of the expert-system shell. Some workers, however, have experimented with other methods. For example, the KADS system (Breuker and Wielinga, 1987) and *ontological analysis* (Alexander et al., 1986) make use of special model-building languages that allow knowledge engineers to define the entities, relationships, and transformations among entities in a given domain. Although many researchers have found it adequate to write down textual descriptions of the elements in the model, visual representation of the entities may be even more useful. In designing the MEDAS system, for instance, Naeymi-Rad and colleagues (1986) first modeled part of the knowledge base on paper using entity–relationship (E–R) diagrams similar to those commonly used by database designers.[1] The MEDAS developers found that these simple diagrams facilitated expression of ideas about the knowledge being modeled in a domain-independent and implementation-independent manner.

PROTÉGÉ allows knowledge engineers to model clinical-trial applications using the entity-relationship approach. Although PROTÉGÉ's form-based interface does not currently permit users to create arbitrary E–R diagrams on the workstation screen, PROTÉGÉ does allow knowledge engineers to specify explicitly the entities in the domain, the entities' attributes, and their hierarchical relationships. PROTÉGÉ, like other knowledge-entry systems, is not just a computer program; it is a modeling language. PROTÉGÉ differs from other knowledge-acquisition tools, however, in its clear adoption of the E–R approach. When knowledge bases are viewed as collections of discrete entities and relationships, knowledge engineers can begin to draw on model-building techniques from outside of AI. Moreover, the clarity of the E–R approach helps to make a model's assumptions become apparent.

Before discussing PROTÉGÉ any further, I should note that standard object-oriented languages are based on data structures (namely, *objects*) that also can be used to model entities in the world. Programmers can link objects conveniently to represent relationships such as abstraction and composition. Given this built-in ability to construct E–R models,

---

[1] An E–R diagram contains a separate box for each entity being modeled. The user draws special connections between the boxes to show the relationships among the entities.

256

it is no wonder that object-oriented languages have become so popular for implementing knowledge-based systems. Many workers in AI advocate the routine use of such languages as tools for exploratory programming (Stefik and Bobrow, 1986)—that is, as vehicles for building initial knowledge-base models. The difficulty of using these programming languages to create models, however, is not a matter of abstractive power; rather, it is one of *selectivity.*

General-purpose object-oriented languages treat all properties of an object equally; users cannot easily control which properties are displayed when they create or edit objects; they typically must examine entire data structures *en masse.* Specifically, such languages do not distinguish between the substance of the user's model and those syntactic elements that must be added simply to allow object-oriented programs to *run.* At the same time, establishing the relationship between an object-based task model and a well-defined problem-solving method is almost always left as an exercise for the user—who must work things out for himself at the symbol level. Object-oriented languages are a clear advance over other knowledge-representation schemes. They have even been used independently by physicians in the development of certain clinical applications (Tuhrim et al., 1988). Such languages, however, provide no direct assistance to system builders during the modeling process.

In this book, I have explored the generation and use of modeling languages designed specifically for knowledge acquisition. In particular, I have used PROTÉGÉ to produce p-OPAL and HTN—task-dependent languages that can later be translated into more generic object-oriented representations. My contention, which also has been articulated by other researchers (Gruber and Cohen, 1987; McDermott, 1986; Phillips et al., 1985), is that useful knowledge-acquisition languages must provide sufficient abstraction. Thus, the conceptual model projected by a knowledge-acquisition tool should attempt to match the mental model of the user. Gruber and Cohen, for example, argue that knowledge engineers should "design task-level representational primitives to capture important domain concepts defined by the expert" (Gruber and Cohen, 1987, p. 145). The knowledge-acquisition interface they propose for a medical expert system called MU deals with issues such as *diseases, tests, intermediate diagnoses,* and *efficacy of treatment.* Developing such task-level primitives, however, is *itself* a problem in knowledge acquisition. Knowledge engineers cannot possibly provide experts with a task-based language with which to express domain facts until the engineers understand something about the task. To implement Gruber and Cohen's recommendation in a general sense would require that knowledge acquisition be viewed as a two-step process: (1) developing a task model, followed by (2) using the model to acquire domain facts. This is precisely the strategy that has been automated in PROTÉGÉ.

10.2.2 Two Kinds of Knowledge

At the PROTÉGÉ level, knowledge engineers work with physicians to create models of clinical-trial application areas. These models then serve as the foundation for custom-tailored knowledge-editing tools. PROTÉGÉ is used to map out the structure of the domain and, consequently, the *process* of determining treatment plans when the method of skeletal-plan refinement is applied to individual protocol descriptions. The editors that PROTÉGÉ generates, on the other hand, acquire knowledge about the *content* of specific protocols.

Other workers in AI also have noted a distinction between process knowledge and content knowledge, but all have used different terminology. The developers of NEOMYCIN, for example, contrast the *strategic* knowledge of medical diagnosis with the *domain* knowledge of specific diseases (Hasling et al., 1984). Gruber (1988) speaks of *strategic* knowledge and *substantive* knowledge when he points out much the same divergence. Georgeff and Bonollo (1983) discuss *procedural* knowledge versus *declarative* knowledge (which they are careful to distinguish from procedural and declarative knowledge *representations*). Swartout (1981) refers to process knowledge as *domain principles* and describes content knowledge as a *domain model*.

Not surprisingly, all these authors seem to have had to struggle more to acquire process knowledge than they did to capture content knowledge. Gruber points out that, "It is difficult for experts to explicitly *formulate* their strategic knowledge in a representation that satisfies the requirements for an expert system: the knowledge must be operational (capable of being executed to achieve the desired performance) and general (applying to cases not yet seen)" (Gruber, 1988, p. 580). As described in Section 2.2.1, the process knowledge

258

possessed by experts is, unfortunately, both tacit and context-dependent. Acquiring models of process knowledge should *always* be difficult.

In this book, I make no presumption that the process knowledge that users enter into PROTÉGÉ reflects the precise way physicians think about therapy planning for clinical trials. I do claim, however, that regardless of how physicians themselves may perform therapy planning, PROTÉGÉ provides a useful language with which to model how a *machine* might approach such tasks. More important, I see the separation of task models into a *process* component and a *content* component—with special knowledge-acquisition languages for each—to be a major advantage in developing generalized environments for the construction of expert systems.

10.2.3   The Language at the PROTÉGÉ Level

The forms-based language in PROTÉGÉ allows knowledge engineers to define classes of plans. The language is used to represent the entities and relationships that can constitute a plan, the actions that can modify the plan, and the input data that can predicate those actions. For the most part, PROTÉGÉ elicits only the *process* of arriving at a treatment plan. The language provides no facility to discuss any one plan in particular. When users do enter *content knowledge* at the PROTÉGÉ level (for example, descriptions of the input data), that knowledge applies to all possible plans in the application area.

The knowledge specified using PROTÉGÉ is always explicit. The structure provided by the graphical forms makes apparent both what knowledge PROTÉGÉ expects and where the user should enter that knowledge. The hierarchical arrangement of the forms and the dynamic activation and deactivation of the blanks guide the user's entries. When the knowledge engineer moves down in the hierarchy, he can review and edit details of finer and finer granularity. By moving up in the hierarchy, he can deal with concepts at higher levels of abstraction. Most important, the user frequently can think in terms of knowledge-level constructs, independent of how those constructs might be encoded in a functional e-ONCOCIN knowledge base. (PROTÉGÉ's need for users to enter symbol-level rules that conclude the values of certain attributes is a significant exception.)

The ability to deal with knowledge at appropriate levels of abstraction is widely recognized as a desirable property of languages for defining expert systems. PROTÉGÉ, like knowledge editors such as ROGET, SALT, and MOLE, obtains much of its abstractive power by incorporating an explicit model of problem solving (McDermott, 1988). The conceptual model in PROTÉGÉ is based on the method of skeletal-plan refinement. Knowledge entry is thereby a matter of relating the task at hand to the terms and relationships in the problem-solving model. This model-based approach is viable only when the user understands the model's semantics and can recognize how the model may apply to a given task.

I make the strong assumption in my research that knowledge engineers will be able to apply PROTÉGÉ's model to a variety of clinical-trial applications. To date, I have demonstrated the model to be valid for a subset of both oncology protocols and hypertension drug studies. The utility of the model in these two domains suggests that there are yet other kinds of medical experiments that can be defined suitably using PROTÉGÉ. Learning the bounds of PROTÉGÉ's modeling language, however, will require empirical examination of more types of applications. As Clancey (1986) points out, unlike structural engineers who have theories that can help them to predict the circumstances under which models of bridges or buildings may give way, knowledge engineers currently have no principled mechanisms to determine the limitations of an expert-system model.

Although I have described PROTÉGÉ as a tool for defining knowledge about clinical trials, PROTÉGÉ's model of problem solving undoubtedly extends to other kinds of tasks. The difficult problem, of course, is to be able to predict what those tasks might be. It is possible, for example, that the Digitalis Therapy Advisor (Silverman, 1975) or portions of the MOLGEN program (Friedland, 1979) could be entered into PROTÉGÉ, as both expert systems perform tasks that can be solved using skeletal-plan refinement. PROTÉGÉ's inability to ascribe meaning to planning-entity attributes at the knowledge level (thus requiring the user to enter symbol-level rules) becomes an *advantage* if the goal is to test the system in a large number of unrelated domains. Because PROTÉGÉ makes no suppositions about the semantics of planning-entity attributes, knowledge engineers can write rules that define these attributes to mean anything desired. The language's weakness in abstractive power is thus balanced by increased flexibility.

260

The factors that will most limit the use of PROTÉGÉ beyond certain clinical-trial applications, however, lie not in the language itself, but rather in the restrictive assumptions that are currently made by the editors that PROTÉGÉ generates and by e-ONCOCIN. I shall discuss many of these limitations in the sections that follow.

10.2.4 The Language at the Editor Level

Like OPAL and the other tools discussed in Section 3.3.3, each knowledge editor that PROTÉGÉ generates is based on a model of a class of application *tasks*. The problem-solving method by which those tasks are accomplished is implicit in the model. Thus, the terms and relationships that the user sees deal with only the features that distinguish one task from another—the *content* knowledge that makes each task unique. Empirical experience with OPAL, as well as theoretical arguments from cognitive psychologists (see Section 2.2.1), suggest that domain experts can more readily—and more reliably—volunteer content knowledge than they can provide process knowledge. The primary purpose of PROTÉGÉ is to produce knowledge-editing tools that application experts can use autonomously to enter the content knowledge for new clinical protocols.

The task-dependent languages that PROTÉGÉ produces are analogous to the domain-specific languages that are used in many applications of computer-aided design (CAD). In CAD, when a user confronts similar types of problems repetitively, and the problems are sufficiently constrained, custom-tailored design methods may greatly enhance a system's utility (Majchrzak et al., 1987). Such methods may apply to only the layout of particular kinds of printed circuits or the construction of particular kinds of mechanical parts, but it is precisely this lack of generality that simplifies the CAD languages and makes such systems easier to use. The additional expense of developing special-purpose CAD languages is offset when it is anticipated that the languages will be used repeatedly.

In the case of PROTÉGÉ, each knowledge editor that the program generates represents a custom-tailored language for describing a particular class of clinical trials. Within each class, there are multiple protocols that medical researchers might want to encode (for example, multiple oncology protocols, multiple hypertension drug studies). Like programs for the computer-aided design of physical objects, the editors generated by PROTÉGÉ

261

gain power by restricting their language to task-specific concepts. Because the difficult problem of modeling the process knowledge for the entire class of protocols has already been solved using PROTÉGÉ, users at the editor level need only to determine the relevant task-specific content knowledge. The entry of individual protocols is thus accelerated. More important, clinical-trial experts can enter new protocols themselves without having to rely on knowledge engineers to help them to build an initial task model, because the model will have already been created using PROTÉGÉ.

The knowledge editors generated by PROTÉGÉ are based on visual metaphors that were developed for use in OPAL. The graphical forms and iconic flowcharts simplify knowledge entry by organizing information for the user, by making it obvious what knowledge is expected by the system, and by allowing direct manipulation of images on the workstation screen. Note, however, that whereas the visual metaphors are important, it is not the use of computer graphics or direct manipulation per se that gives these editors their power; the *semantics* of the graphical images are paramount (see Hutchins et al., 1986). In the knowledge editors, the semantics come primarily from the task models entered into PROTÉGÉ. If the portions of these task models that are visible at the editor level are self-explanatory, then the corresponding editors should be easy to use. Computer graphics, however, will not help to clarify an opaque or ambiguous model.

In addition to the task model created with PROTÉGÉ, the generic forms at the editor level carry significant semantic assumptions. Unlike the task models, which can be edited and revised at will, the physical layout of the forms cannot be changed without reprogramming. As I discussed in Chapter 8, the forms make a number of limiting suppositions. For example, the forms for entering the associations between input data and corresponding actions presume that these task rules will reference only the "current" values of data items, and that the user will not predicate task actions on *conjunctions* of conditions (see Figures 8.3 and 8.6, pages 191 and 198). These assumptions are made by the original OPAL system as well. In most clinical-trial applications, where such assumptions generally are valid, domain specialists can examine all the task-level rules that apply in a particular context by viewing a single graphical form. All the knowledge relevant to a particular topic can be perused simultaneously, and distracting details are eliminated. The editors thus choose to sacrifice expressive power for simplicity of presentation.

In other application areas, and in other clinical-trial domains, these simplifying assumptions may not hold. To accommodate such circumstances, the present system of generic forms would have to be extended. For example, new blanks could be added to the forms for users to indicate whether specifications for data-item values refer to either past or present entries. Appending this capability to the editor language would be straightforward, but the graphical forms would have to be made more complicated. A central problem would be precisely *how complicated* to make the forms. Although simple temporal qualifiers such as *current* or *last* might sometimes be sufficient, the e-ONCOCIN rule language can support more intricate retrospective queries on the patient database (Kahn, M.G. et al., 1985). Although some users might want access to all of this expressive power, the added capabilities would come at the cost of making the editor interface more complex. There is a tradeoff between epistemological adequacy and knowledge-presentation clarity.

Similarly, the knowledge editors could be modified to permit users to enter task-level rules predicated on *conjunctions* of conditions, but only if the users were willing to forego the simplicity of viewing multiple, related rules simultaneously. The knowledge editors could provide a variety of menus and registers to help the user to piece together the necessary conjuncts, instantiating a separate graphical form for each task-level rule.

Thus, even though PROTÉGÉ allows the knowledge engineer to custom-tailor each of the task models that are used at the editor level, there are still many semantic assumptions in the editor languages over which the PROTÉGÉ user has no control. These are the suppositions that are built directly into the generic form templates and the iconic flowchart language, dictating the manner in which the editors present and acquire knowledge from domain experts. These assumptions concern the fundamental appearance and behavior of all knowledge editors, and do not depend on the particular task model with which an editor is instantiated. If these additional editor-level assumptions were represented declaratively, they too could be *edited* using PROTÉGÉ. Knowledge engineers then could use PROTÉGÉ to select those simplifying epistemological assumptions that seem reasonable, given the application tasks at hand. There will always be some set of semantic primitives, however, that must remain at the editor level and that is not part of the task model.

Although there are clear restrictions on the knowledge that application specialists can enter currently, the editor-level assumptions nevertheless simplify the job of the *knowledge engineer* who must use PROTÉGÉ to define the task model. Just as enhancing the expressive power of the PROTÉGÉ-generated editors must be tempered by the consequences of making those editors more complicated, offering the knowledge engineer many more options at the metalevel would make PROTÉGÉ itself more difficult to use. In both situations, what is urgently needed is a methodology for helping system builders to know when they have struck the right balance between expressiveness and complexity.

10.2.5   The Influence of the Performance Element

PROTÉGÉ and the editors it generates treat e-ONCOCIN as an expert-system shell. All the assumptions that e-ONCOCIN makes about the world consequently percolate up to models that are created using PROTÉGÉ. The way that e-ONCOCIN represents time, the way that the program instantiates skeletal plans, the way it attempts to satisfy constraints, even the way e-ONCOCIN interacts with its users, all influence the kinds of models that knowledge engineers and domain experts can build with the tools that I have described in this book. Although my work has concentrated on issues of knowledge acquisition and not on AI planning techniques, it is clear that the models created with PROTÉGÉ ultimately are constrained by e-ONCOCIN's limitations. Knowledge engineers who use PROTÉGÉ must understand the assumptions made by e-ONCOCIN, just as they would need to recognize the bounds of any expert-system shell that they might use. The ability of e-ONCOCIN to execute protocols in both the oncology and the hypertension domains indicates that the shell has a degree of generality. Much could be done, however, to enhance e-ONCOCIN's problem-solving method to handle alternative planning situations (Tu et al., 1989).

As e-ONCOCIN evolves, the knowledge-acquisition techniques that I have described will still apply. Yet knowledge engineers have no *meta*-metalevel editor with which to revise PROTÉGÉ itself if the built-in assumptions about e-ONCOCIN no longer hold. Thus, a significant change to e-ONCOCIN would necessitate reprogramming parts of PROTÉGÉ. If programmers were to alter the syntax of e-ONCOCIN's internal knowledge representation, the routines that generate e-ONCOCIN knowledge bases from specifications entered into the task-oriented knowledge editors would need to be updated. If e-ONCOCIN's problem-solving method were to be modified, knowledge engineers would want to change the modeling language at the PROTÉGÉ level to reflect the new semantics. The database schema would have to be changed to reflect the new problem-solving model, and the appropriate forms and blanks (with the required attached procedures) would need to be created to communicate with the database. Although it would thus be necessary to revise portions of PROTÉGÉ to conform with a new problem-solving method, the amount of work involved probably would be small in relation to the number of new knowledge bases that could be generated using the revised knowledge-acquisition tools. More transparent mechanisms to extend PROTÉGÉ to performance elements other than e-ONCOCIN and to problem-solving methods other than skeletal-plan refinement should be the subject of future research.

If PROTÉGÉ were adapted for a performance element such as EMYCIN (van Melle, 1979) or KAS (Reboh, 1981), it would be desirable to incorporate a problem-solving model based on heuristic classification (Clancey, 1985). Knowledge engineers then would use PROTÉGÉ to create models of classification tasks, rather than models of planning tasks. For example, a knowledge engineer might use PROTÉGÉ to describe the class of classification problems that are encountered during geological mineral exploration, as was done in the PROSPECTOR system (Reboh, 1981). A knowledge editor generated by PROTÉGÉ then could be used by expert geologists to enter specific *ore deposit models*. The ore deposit models could be converted to KAS knowledge bases for use by workers in the field who need to determine the most favorable drilling sites for particular minerals.

Although methods that can perform classification according to a preenumerated solution set are well understood by workers in AI, few generic methods that can *construct solutions* to problems have been proposed (Clancey, 1985). Skeletal-plan refinement and the propose-and-revise strategy used in SALT (Marcus, 1988) are two exceptions. In PROTÉGÉ, the database schema contains the terms and relationships of a general model of problem solving (namely, one of skeletal-plan refinement). Adapting PROTÉGÉ for use with another planning technique would require researchers to derive an appropriate set of terms and relationships to describe the problem-solving method of the target performance system. Developing this model of problem solving would probably be the most significant obstacle—and the most important research result—associated with such an effort.

10.3   Summary of this Research

The work that I have described in this book makes contributions to both AI and medical informatics. Although I have attempted to point out the important lessons of this research in the preceding chapters of this document, it will be useful for me to recapitulate the key conclusions here.

- I have pointed out the *conceptual models* that govern the presentation of knowledge by knowledge-editing systems. Knowledge editors may base their conceptual models on (1) symbol-level entities (for example, production rules in EMYCIN), (2) models of problem solving (for example, the classification model in ROGET), or (3) models of the application task (for example, the cancer-therapy model in OPAL).

- I have shown that, in selecting one of these types of conceptual models for a knowledge-editing tool, system builders implicitly determine who will be responsible for guiding the knowledge-level modeling that is required to understand an application task. Thus, when a knowledge editor's conceptual model is based on symbol-level entities (as in EMYCIN), the entire modeling problem is left to the user. When the conceptual model is based on the method of problem solving used by the target advice system (as in ROGET), the knowledge-editing system itself guides the user in analyzing the application. When the conceptual model is based on a predefined model of the application task (as in OPAL), the system designers must perform the knowledge-level analysis.

- My research demonstrates how knowledge engineers can represent the conceptual model for a knowledge-editing program as a precise set of terms and relationships. When the conceptual model is made explicit, a metalevel tool such as PROTÉGÉ can *edit* that model.

266

- The separation of knowledge acquisition into two phases—(1) development a general task model by knowledge engineers and domain experts, followed by (2) instantiation of that model by experts working alone—allows system builders to concentrate on what they do best. In application areas where multiple, related tasks must be encoded, the PROTÉGÉ approach should facilitate development of large numbers of knowledge-based systems.

- In the domain of clinical trials, my methodology should allow systems such as ONCO-CIN to be applied in different areas of medicine. Clinical research often is impeded when physicians misinterpret or otherwise fail to follow protocol guidelines, and when health-care workers fail to collect necessary patient data. Advice systems created using the editors generated by PROTÉGÉ could thus improve protocol-based patient care in a wide range of medical disciplines.

- Just as health-care providers may need help in keeping track of all the stipulations mentioned in certain protocols, the specialists who write the protocols may need assistance in organizing the various specifications and in ensuring that there are no ambiguities or inconsistencies. Thus, tools such as those produced by PROTÉGÉ can serve not only as knowledge editors for expert systems, but also as authoring environments in which clinical researchers can design new protocols productively. Such protocols then could be disseminated to other health-care workers as expert-system knowledge bases, rather than as textual documents. As I shall describe in the next section, the benefits of communicating information using tools based on PROTÉGÉ should extend well beyond clinical-trial applications.

10.4   Facilitating the Authoring of Advice Systems

The tools that I have described in this book have been created to help both knowledge engineers and application specialists to construct models of specific systems in the world—namely, clinical trials. PROTÉGÉ and the editors it generates are design aids. Unlike programs that assist in the design of physical objects such as printed circuits or machine parts, the programs that I have described here have a less tangible end product: The generation of advice.

The knowledge-acquisition tools created by PROTÉGÉ are perhaps most analogous to the many automated tools that can assist educators in the development of programmed curricula (*courseware*) for computer-aided instruction (CAI; Kearsley, 1982). Such authoring systems allow an instructor to specify the particular content knowledge to be taught and the algorithms with which to teach it. The authoring systems then generate executable program code that corresponds to the instructor's lesson plan. Tools for the development of courseware are just one example of *automatic programming systems* (Partsch and Steinbruggen, 1983)—programs that generate other programs on the basis of a user's high-level specifications. Automatic programming systems allow software developers to concentrate on the specifications, rather than on the programming details needed to implement the specifications. In the case of CAI, some workers have reported that, compared with conventional programming languages, special-purpose courseware-authoring systems can reduce the time needed to create computer-based curricula by one order of magnitude (see Kearsley, 1982).

To my knowledge, no one has done similar timing studies of computer-based knowledge-acquisition systems. Workers in AI have always assumed that such tools represent an advance. This lack of formal evaluation makes it difficult to measure progress precisely, but is often understandable. For example, once OPAL was put into routine use, system builders could not imagine returning to their onerous manual techniques. The obvious rapidity with which oncology protocols could be encoded using OPAL made knowledge engineers unenthusiastic, to say the least, about engaging in academic experiments to quantify the relative speedup over traditional knowledge entry. Similarly, I have not performed controlled evaluations of the degree to which PROTÉGÉ expedites the construction of knowledge editors such as p-OPAL and HTN. The limited anecdotal evidence that I report in this book suggests that experienced users can create new knowledge editors with PROTÉGÉ in a few days—and possibly in a few hours. (For comparison, OPAL required 3.5 person-years to build from scratch; much of that time, of course, was devoted to developing an appreciation of the problems to be solved.)

The knowledge editors that are created using PROTÉGÉ, like systems for designing courseware, provide a mechanism for authorities in an application area to communicate their knowledge to other people. In the domain of clinical trials, these knowledge-editing tools allow clinical researchers to transmit their interpretations of medical protocols to the physicians who ultimately must care for the patients being studied. Unlike many textual protocol documents (Musen et al., 1986), the knowledge bases that are generated by these editing tools can relate the precise behaviors that expert physicians would prescribe in various circumstances. The knowledge bases convey much the same information as do the written protocols, but they do so more succinctly and often more clearly. As Winograd and Flores (1986) emphasize, the computer is fundamentally a *structured dynamic communication medium* that is qualitatively different from other media such as the printed page. In their view, languages such as those generated by PROTÉGÉ define systematic domains in which conversations can take place between individual practitioners and the knowledge-base authors.

Using tools and engaging in conversations are fundamentally human behaviors. Since the beginning of written language, the process of communicating via printed media has changed markedly as people have developed new tools to facilitate the use of written discourse. From styli for inscribing cuneiform, to the printing press, to workstations for assisting desktop publishing, tools have changed the ease with which we can communicate in print by orders of magnitude. Yet, over the centuries, the kinds of ideas that people have been able to express via printed media have changed little. Despite our tools, we have come to recognize that there are inherent limitations in the conversations that we can have via printed text, and we have learned to accept these constraints. We know when it is reasonable to communicate in writing and when we should pick up the telephone or pay a visit to someone.

Expert systems represent a new form of communication channel. Most application specialists have few intuitions about how this medium shapes the conversations that are possible with the people who ultimately use expert systems. Just as the ancients relied on scribes to help them to produce their manuscripts, most professionals remain dependent on knowledge engineers to help them to master this new form of communication. But, as the printing press facilitated written discourse, the advent of new tools, such as the ones produced using PROTÉGÉ, may greatly increase the ease with which experts can create knowledge bases on their own. Systems such as PROTÉGÉ, which can, in turn, ease development of these knowledge-base authoring tools, should help us to widen further this communication channel.

Reducing the need for knowledge engineers in the construction of expert systems will not, however, break the fabled bottleneck completely. Designing a knowledge base, like writing a book or preparing a lecture, is a creative process. As Brooks points out, "Great designs come from great designers .... Sound methodology can empower and liberate the creative mind; it cannot inflame or inspire the drudge" (Brooks, 1987, p. 18). PROTÉGÉ's limitations are ultimately those of its human users. Although the system can help people to build models of clinical trials, PROTÉGÉ certainly cannot formulate those models on its own. The development of models is, fundamentally, a human activity; like all creative endeavors, the development of models is difficult.

Just as word processors can do nothing to cure writer's block, computer-based tools such as PROTÉGÉ cannot eliminate all the obstacles to building expert systems. Such tools can, however, streamline much of the knowledge-engineering process. By separating the hard problems of creating a task model (at the PROTÉGÉ level) from those of applying the model (at the editor level), we can greatly simplify the operation of creating knowledge bases for multiple, related tasks. At the same time, by making the terms and relationships of the model explicit, tools such as PROTÉGÉ can help system builders to identify more easily the limitations of their models and the assumptions that their models make.

270

Appendices

Appendix A PROTÉGÉ Database Relations

SYSTEMS

SYSTEM	name of knowledge editor
DATE-CREATED	date first defined
DATE-EDITED	date last revised
DATE-TRANSLATED	date e-ONCOCIN KB generated

ENTITY

SYSTEM	name of knowledge editor
ENTITY-TYPE	planning-entity class
ROLE	PLAN, ACTION, or DATUM

COMPOSITION

SYSTEM	name of knowledge editor
ENTITY-TYPE	planning-entity class
COMPONENT	planning-entity subclass

ATTRIBUTE

SYSTEM	name of knowledge editor
ENTITY-TYPE	planning-entity class
ATTRIBUTE-NAME	attribute of planning entity
PRIORITY	GOAL, NON-GOAL, or DEFAULT
DATA-TYPE	data type of attribute
MULTI-VALUED?	YES or NO
TIME-VARYING?	YES, NO, or FRAME
USER-DISPLAY	display on FLOWSHEET or SPECIAL-MSG?
INTERVIEWER-LABEL	short descriptive label
PROMPT	long descriptive label

DATA-CLASS-DATA-TYPE

SYSTEM	name of knowledge editor
DATA-CLASS	data class; TOXICITY, etc.
DATA-TYPE-CLASS	ENUMERATED or CONTINUOUS

DATA-ITEM

SYSTEM	name of knowledge editor
DATA-CLASS	data class of item; TOXICITY, etc.
DATA-ITEM	name of data item
INTERVIEWER-LABEL	short descriptive label
DATA-TYPE	data type of data item
PROMPT	long descriptive label
TIME-VARYING?	YES or NO
SHOW-ALWAYS?	YES or NO
TEST-NAME	source of data item
LOWER-BOUND	smallest possible value
LOWER-CONFIRM	questionable lower limit
UPPER-BOUND	largest possible value
UPPER-CONFIRM	questionable upper limit

DEFAULT-VALUES

SYSTEM	name of knowledge editor
ENTITY-TYPE	planning-entity class
ATTRIBUTE-NAME	name of attribute of planning-entity class
DEFAULT-VALUE	default value for attribute

TESTS

SYSTEM	name of knowledge editor
DATA-CLASS	data class; TOXICITY, etc.
TEST-NAME	possible data source within data class

ATTRIBUTE-METHODS

SYSTEM	name of knowledge editor
METHOD-TYPE	RULE, FUNC, GEN, or ASK
METHOD-NAME	name of method
ENTITY-TYPE	planning-entity class
ATTRIBUTE-NAME	attribute value of which is concluded

RULE-PRECONDITION

SYSTEM	name of knowledge editor
METHOD-NAME	name of rule
CLAUSE-NUMBER	line number of precondition
CLAUSE	text string

RULE-PREMISE

SYSTEM	name of knowledge editor
METHOD-NAME	name of rule
CLAUSE-NUMBER	line number of condition
CLAUSE	text string

RULE-CONCLUSION

SYSTEM	name of knowledge editor
METHOD-NAME	name of rule
CLAUSE-NUMBER	line number of conclusion
CLAUSE	text string

MENU-SELECTIONS

SYSTEM	name of knowledge editor
DATA-TYPE	name of data type
SELECTION	possible data value
PROMPT STRING	verbose explanation of data value

DATA-TYPE

SYSTEM	name of knowledge editor
DATA-TYPE	name of data type
INPUT-DEVICE	MENU, REGISTER, or TYPEIN
NAME	name of input device

ACTION-INVOKING-ENTITY

SYSTEM	name of knowledge editor
ACTION-NAME	name of task-level action
ENTITY-TYPE	associated planning-entity class

ACTION-SEQUENCE

SYSTEM	name of knowledge editor
ACTION-NAME	name of task-level action
STEP-NUMBER	step number in script
CONDITION-ATTRIBUTE	attribute of step precondition
CONDITION-VALUE	required value for precondition attribute
ACTION-PRIMITIVE	START, STOP, RESUME, SUSPEND, etc.
AFFECTED-ENTITY	first argument of primitive operator
AFFECTED-ATTRIBUTE	attribute of first-argument entity
ATTRIBUTE-ARG	2nd argument of operator, an action attribute

Appendix B Editor Database Relations

PROTOCOL

SYSTEM	name of knowledge editor
PROTOCOL	name of protocol instance
DATE-CREATED	date protocol first defined
DATE-EDITED	date last revised

PROTOCOL-COMPOSITION

SYSTEM	name of knowledge editor
PROTOCOL	name of protocol instance
ENTITY-TYPE	planning-entity class
ENTITY-NAME	planning-entity instance
COMPONENT-TYPE	class of planning-entity subcomponent
COMPONENT-NAME	instance of planning-entity subcomponent
REFERENCE-COUNT	total instances of subcomponent in protocol

ENUMERATED-DATA-ACTION

SYSTEM	name of knowledge editor
PROTOCOL	name of protocol instance
CONTEXT-TYPE-1	a planning-entity class
CONTEXT-NAME-1	a planning-entity instance
CONTEXT-TYPE-2	a planning-entity class
CONTEXT-NAME-2	a planning-entity instance
CONTEXT-TYPE-3	a planning-entity class
CONTEXT-NAME-3	a planning-entity instance
DATA-CLASS	data class of premise data item
DATA-ITEM	name of premise data item
DATA-VALUE	value of premise data item
ACTION-NAME	task-level action if premise satisfied
ACTION-IDENTIFICATION	instance of task-level action

CONTINUOUS-DATA-ACTION

SYSTEM	name of knowledge editor
PROTOCOL	name of protocol instance
CONTEXT-TYPE-1	a planning-entity class
CONTEXT-NAME-1	a planning-entity instance
CONTEXT-TYPE-2	a planning-entity class
CONTEXT-NAME-2	a planning-entity instance
CONTEXT-TYPE-3	a planning-entity class
CONTEXT-NAME-3	a planning-entity instance
DATA-CLASS	data class of premise data item
DATA-ITEM	name of premise data item
DATA-VALUE-1	value of data item
RELATION	predicate of data item value
DATA-VALUE-2	2nd data item value for 2-place predicates
ACTION-NAME	task-level action if premise satisfied
ACTION-IDENTIFICATION	instance of task-level action

ATTRIBUTE-INSTANTIATIONS

SYSTEM	name of knowledge editor
PROTOCOL	name of protocol instance
ENTITY-TYPE	entity class
ENTITY-INSTANCE	class instance
ATTRIBUTE-NAME	attribute name within class
ATTRIBUTE-VALUE	editor-assigned value for attribute

GENERATORS

SYSTEM	name of knowledge editor
ENTITY-TYPE	planning-entity class
ENTITY-NAME	planning-entity instance
GENERATOR	name of generator object for instance

Bibliography

Addis, T. R. (1987). A framework for knowledge elicitation. In *Proceedings of the First European Workshop on Knowledge Acquisition for Knowledge-Based Systems*, Reading University, Reading England.

Aikins, J. S., Kunz, J. C., Shortliffe, E. H., and Fallat, R. J. (1983). PUFF: An expert system for interpretation of pulmonary function data. *Computers and Biomedical Research*, 16:199–208.

Alexander, J. H., Freiling, M. J., Shulman, S. J., Staley, J. L., Rehfuss, S., and Messick, S. L. (1986). Knowledge level engineering: Ontological analysis. In *Proceedings AAAI-86*, pages 963–968, Philadelphia, Pennsylvania. American Association for Artificial Intelligence, Morgan Kaufmann Publishers.

Anderson, J. R. (1987). Skill acquisition: Compilation of weak-method problem solutions. *Psychological Review*, 94:192–210.

Armitage, J. O. and Corder, M. P. (1982). Reasons for failure of MOPP to cure Hodgkin's disease. *American Journal of Clinical Oncology*, 5:315–319.

Begg, C. B., Carbone, P. P., Elson, P. J., and Zelen, M. (1982). Participation of community hospitals in clinical trials: Analysis of five years experience in the Eastern Cooperative Oncology Group. *New England Journal of Medicine*, 306:1076–1080.

Belkin, N. J., Brooks, H. M., and Daniels, P. J. (1987). Knowledge elicitation using discourse analysis. *International Journal of Man–Machine Studies*, 27:127–144.

Bennett, J. S. and Engelmore, R. S. (1984). Experience using EMYCIN. In *Rule-Based Expert Systems: The MYCIN Experiments of the Stanford Heuristic Programming Project*, pages 314–328. Addison-Wesley, Reading, Massachusetts.

Bennett, J. S. (1985). ROGET: A knowledge-based system for acquiring the conceptual structure of a diagnostic expert system. *Journal of Automated Reasoning*, 1:49–74.

Blum, B. I. (1983). A data model for patient management. In *Proceedings of MEDINFO 83*, pages 748–751, Amsterdam. Fourth World Conference on Medical Informatics, Elsevier Science Publishers.

Bonollo, U. and Georgeff, M. P. (1983). Peritus: A system that aids the construction of procedural expert systems. Technical Report 39, Monash University, Clayton, Victoria, Australia.

Boose, J. H. (1985). A knowledge acquisition program for expert systems based on personal construct psychology. *International Journal of Man–Machine Studies*, 23:495–525.

Boose, J. H. and Bradshaw, J. M. (1987). Expertise transfer and complex problems using AQUINAS as a knowledge acquisition workbench for knowledge-based systems. *International Journal of Man–Machine Studies*, 26:3–28.

Brachman, R. J. and Levesque, H. J., editors (1985). *Readings in Knowledge Representation*. Morgan Kaufman Publishers, Los Altos, California.

Breuker, J. and Wielinga, B. (1987). Use of models in the interpretation of verbal data. In Kidd, A. L., editor, *Knowledge Acquisition for Expert Systems: A Practical Handbook*, pages 17–44. Plenum, London.

Brodie, M. L. and Mylopoulos, J., editors (1986). *On Knowledge Base Management Systems*. Springer-Verlag, New York.

Brooks, F. P. (1987). No silver bullet: Essence and accidents of software engineering. *Computer*, 20:10–19.

Buchanan, B. G., Barstow, D., Bechtal, R., Bennett, J., Clancey, W., Kulikowski, C., Mitchell, T., and Waterman, D. A. (1983). Constructing an expert system. In *Building Expert Systems*, pages 127–167. Addison-Wesley, Reading, Massachusetts.

Buchanan, B. G. and Shortliffe, E. H. (1984). *Rule-Based Expert Systems: The MYCIN Experiments of the Stanford Heuristic Programming Project*. Addison-Wesley, Reading, Massachusetts.

Buchanan, B. G., Sutherland, G., and Feigenbaum, E. A. (1969). Heuristic Dendral: A program for generating explanatory hypotheses in organic chemistry. In *Machine Intelligence*, pages 209–254. Edinburgh University Press.

Bundy, A., editor (1986). *Catalogue of Artificial Intelligence Tools*. Springer-Verlag, New York, 2nd edition.

Bylander, T. and Chandrasekaran, B. (1987). Generic tasks for knowledge-based reasoning: The 'right' level of abstraction for knowledge acquisition. *International Journal of Man–Machine Studies*, 26:231–243.

Chandrasekaran, B. (1986). Generic tasks in knowledge-based reasoning: High-level building blocks for expert system design. *IEEE Expert*, 1:23–30.

Charness, N. (1979). Components of skill in bridge. *Canadian Journal of Psychology*, 33:1–16.

Chase, W. G. and Simon, H. A. (1973). Perception in chess. *Cognitive Psychology*, 4:55–81.

Chi, M. T. H., Feltovich, P. J., and Glaser, R. (1981). Categorization and representation of physics problems by experts and novices. *Cognitive Science*, 5:121–152.

Clancey, W. J. (1984). Knowledge acquisition for classification expert systems. In *Proceedings of the ACM Annual Conference*, pages 11–14. Association for Computing Machinery.

Clancey, W. J. (1985). Heuristic classification. *Artificial Intelligence*, 27:289–350.

Clancey, W. J. (1986). Viewing knowledge bases as qualitative models. Technical Report KSL-86-27, Knowledge Systems Laboratory, Stanford University, Stanford, California.

Clancey, W. J. and Shortliffe, E. H., editors (1984). *Readings in Medical Artificial Intelligence: The First Decade*. Addison-Wesley, Reading, Massachusetts.

Cleaves, D. A. (1987). Cognitive biases and corrective techniques: Proposals for improving elicitation procedures for knowledge-based systems. *International Journal of Man–Machine Studies*, 27:155–166.

Cohen, N. J. (1984). Preserved learning capacity in amnesia: Evidence for multiple memory systems. In *Neuropsychology of Memory*, pages 83–103. Guilford Press, New York.

Combs, D. M., Musen, M. A., Fagan, L. M., and Shortliffe, E. H. (1986). Graphical specification of procedural and inferential knowledge. In *Proceedings of AAMSI Congress 86*, pages 298–302, Anaheim, California. American Association for Medical Systems and Informatics.

Combs, D. M. (1988). ODIE: A system for design and management of form-based interfaces. Technical Report 225, Medical Computer Science Group, Knowledge Systems Laboratory, Stanford University, Stanford, California.

Combs, D. M. (1989). A database-management system for Interlisp-D. Technical Report 243, Medical Computer Science Group, Knowledge Systems Laboratory, Stanford University, Stanford, California.

Conklin, J. (1987). Hypertext: An introduction and survey. *Computer*, 20(3):17–41.

Cooke, N. M. and McDonald, J. E. (1987). The application of psychological scaling techniques to knowledge elicitation for knowledge-based systems. *International Journal of Man–Machine Studies*, 26:533–550.

Coughlin, L. and Patel, V. L. (1985). Adapting a paradigm from cognitive science to medical education: Problems and possible solutions. In *Proceedings of the Twenty-Fourth Annual Conference on Research in Medical Education*, pages 97–102, Washington, DC. American Association of Medical Colleges.

Cox, B. J. (1986). *Object-Oriented Programming: An Evolutionary Approach*. Addison-Wesley, Reading, Massachusetts.

Date, C. J. (1986). *An Introduction to Database Systems*, volume 1. Addison-Wesley, Reading, Massachusetts, 4th edition.

Davis, C. K. (1985). The impact of prospective payment on clinical research. *Journal of the American Medical Association*, 253:686–687.

Davis, R. (1976). *Applications of Meta Level Knowledge to the Construction, Maintenance, and Use of Large Knowledge Bases*. PhD thesis, Stanford University, Stanford, California. Rep. No. STAN-CS-76-564.

de Greef, P. and Breuker, J. (1985). A case study in structured knowledge acquisition. In *Proceedings of the Ninth International Joint Conference on Artificial Intelligence*, pages 390–392, Los Angeles, California.

de Groot, A. D. (1965). *Thought and Choice in Chess*. Basic Books, New York.

Deitterich, T. G. (1986). Learning at the knowledge level. *Machine Learning*, 1:287–315.

Dietterich, T. G. and Bennett, J. S. (1986). The test incorporation theory of problem solving (preliminary report). In *Proceedings of the Workshop on Knowledge Compilation*, pages 145–159, Corvallis, Oregon. Oregon State University Computer Science Department.

Doyle, J. (1985). Expert systems and the "myth" of symbolic reasoning. *IEEE Transactions on Software Engineering*, SE-11:1386–1390.

Dreyfus, H. L. (1981). From micro-worlds to knowledge representation: AI at an impasse. In Haugeland, J., editor, *Mind Design*, pages 161–204. MIT Press, Cambridge, Massachusetts.

Egan, D. E. and Schwartz, B. J. (1979). Chunking and recall of symbolic drawings. *Memory and Cognition*, 7:149–158.

Elstein, A. S., Shulman, L. S., and Sprafka, S. A. (1978). *Medical Problem Solving: An Analysis of Clinical Reasoning*. Havard University Press, Cambridge, Massachusetts.

Ericsson, K. A. and Simon, H. A. (1984). *Protocol Analysis: Verbal Reports as Data*. MIT Press, Cambridge, Massachusetts.

Eshelman, L., Ehret, D., McDermott, J., and Tan, M. (1987). MOLE: A tenacious knowledge-acquisition tool. *International Journal of Man–Machine Studies*, 26:41–54.

Feigenbaum, E. A. (1977). The art of artificial intelligence: I. Themes and case studies of knowledge engineering. In *Proceedings of the Fifth International Joint Conference on Artificial Intelligence*, pages 1014–1029, Cambridge, Massachusetts.

Feigenbaum, E. A. (1984). Knowledge engineering: The applied side of artificial intelligence. *Annals of the New York Academy of Sciences*, 246:91–107.

Feinstein, A. R. (1983). An additional basic science for clinical medicine: II. The limitations of randomized trials. *Annals of Internal Medicine*, 99:544–550.

Feltovich, P. J. and Barrows, H. S. (1984). Issues of generality in medical problem solving. In *Tutorials in Problem-Based Learning: A New Direction in Teaching the Health Professions*, pages 128–142. Van Gorcum, Maastricht, The Netherlands.

Fitts, P. M. (1964). Perceptual-motor skill learning. In Melton, A., editor, *Categories of Human Learning*. Academic Press, New York.

Flavell, J. H. and H. M. Wellman, H. (1977). Metamemory. In *Perspectives on the Development of Memory and Cognition*, pages 3–33. Lawrence Erlbaum, Hillsdale, New Jersey.

Fodor, J. A. (1968). The appeal of tacit knowledge in psychological explanation. *Journal of Philosophy*, 65:627–640.

Fox, J., Myers, C. D., Greaves, M. F., and Pegram, S. (1985). Knowledge acquisition for expert systems: Experience in leukemia diagnosis. *Methods of Information in Medicine*, 24:65–72.

Frake, C. O. (1972). The ethnographic study of cognitive systems. In Spradley, J. P., editor, *Culture and Cognition: Rules, Maps, and Plans*, pages 191–205. Chandler, New York.

Freiling, M. J. and Alexander, J. H. (1984). Diagrams and grammars: Tools for mass producing expert systems. In *The First Conference on Artificial Intelligence Applications*, pages 537–543, Denver, Colorado. IEEE Computer Society Press.

Freiling, M. J. and Jacobson, C. (1988). Sythesizing an effective control strategy for acquired doman knowledge. In *Proceedings of the Third Knowledge Acquisition for Knowledge-Based Systems Workshop*, Banff, Alberta, Canada.

Friedland, P. (1979). *Knowledge-Based Experiment Design in Molecular Genetics*. PhD thesis, Stanford University, Stanford, California. Report CS-79-771.

Friedland, P. E. and Iwasaki, Y. (1985). The concept and implementation of skeletal plans. *Journal of Automated Reasoning*, 1:161–208.

Friedman, R. B., Entine, S. M., and Carbone, P. P. (1983). Experience with an automated cancer protocol surveillance system. *American Journal of Clinical Oncology*, 6:583–592.

Friedman, R. H. and Frank, A. D. (1983). Use of conditional rule structure to automate clinical decision support: A comparison of artificial intelligence and deterministic programming techniques. *Computers and Biomedical Research*, 16:378–394.

Gaines, B. R. and Shaw, M. L. G. (1980). New directions in the analysis and interactive elicitation of personal construct systems. *International Journal of Man–Machine Studies*, 13:81–116.

Gale, W. A. (1987). Knowledge-based knowledge acquisition for a statistical consulting system. *International Journal of Man–Machine Studies*, 26:55–64.

Georgeff, M. P. and Bonollo, U. (1983). Procedural expert systems. In *Proceedings of the Eighth International Joint Conference on Artificial Intelligence*, pages 151–157, Tokyo, Japan.

Gerring, P. E., Shortliffe, E. H., and van Melle, W. (1982). The Interviewer/Reasoner model: An approach to improving system responsiveness in interactive AI systems. *AI Magazine*, 3:24–27.

Gevarter, W. B. (1987). The nature and evaluation of commercial expert system building tools. *Computer*, 20:24–41.

Goldberger, H. A. and Schwenn, P. (1983). Man–machine symbiosis in the assistance and training of rural health workers: A proposal. In *Meeting the Challenge: Informatics and Medical Education*, pages 295–306. Elsevier Science Publications.

Greeno, J. G. (1983). Conceptual entities. In *Mental Models*, pages 227–252. Lawrence Erlbaum Associates, Hillsdale, New Jersey.

Gruber, T. R. and Cohen, P. (1987). Design for acquisition: Principles of knowledge-system design to facilitate knowledge acquisition. *International Journal of Man–Machine Studies*, 26:143–159.

Gruber, T. R. (1988). Acquiring strategic knowledge from experts. *International Journal of Man–Machine Studies*, 29:579–597.

Hall, L. O. and Bandler, W. (1985). Relational knowledge acquisition. In *Proceedings of the Second Conference on Artificial Intelligence Applications*, pages 509–513, Miami Beach, Florida. IEEE Computer Society.

Hasling, D. W., Clancey, W. J., and Rennels, G. D. (1984). Strategic explanations for a diagnostic consultation system. In Coombs, M. J., editor, *Developments in Expert Systems*, pages 117–133. Academic Press, New York.

Hickam, D. H., Shortliffe, E. H., Bischoff, M. B., Scott, A. C., and Jacobs, C. D. (1985). A study of the treatment advice of a computer-based cancer chemotherapy protocol advisor. *Annals of Internal Medicine*, 101:928–936.

Hickam, D. H., Shortliffe, E. H., M. B. Bischoff, M., and Jacobs, C. D. (1984). The effect of enhancing cancer chemotherapy protocol guidelines with expert knowledge in a computer-based treatment consultant. *Medical Decision Making*, 4:533. (abstract).

Hubbard, S. M., Henney, J. E., and DeVita, V. T. (1987). A computer database for information on cancer treatment. *New England Journal of Medicine*, 316:315–318.

Hutchins, E. L., Hollan, J. D., and Norman, D. L. (1986). Direct manipulation interfaces. In *User Centered System Design*, pages 87–124. Lawrence Erlbaum Associates, Hillsdale, New Jersey.

Huth, E. J. (1984). Microcomputer software for medical applications. *Annals of Internal Medicine*, 100:607.

Jacob, R. J. K. (1985). A state transition diagram language for visual programming. *Computer*, 18:51–59.

Jacoby, L. and Witherspoon, D. (1982). Remembering without awareness. *Canadian Journal of Psychology*, 36:300–324.

Johnson, P. E. (1983). What kind of expert should a system be? *Journal of Medicine and Philosophy*, 8:77–97.

Kahn, G., Nowlan, S., and McDermott, J. (1985). Strategies for knowledge acquisition. *IEEE Transactions on Pattern Analysis and Machine Intelligence*, PAMI-7:511–522.

Kahn, M. G., Ferguson, J. C., Shortliffe, E. H., and Fagan, L. M. (1985). Representation and use of temporal information in ONCOCIN. In Ackerman, M. J., editor, *Proceedings of the Ninth Annual Symposium on Computer Applications in Medical Care*, pages 172–176, Baltimore, Maryland. IEEE Computer Society.

Karbach, W., Voss, A., and Tong, X. (1988). Filling in the knowledge acquisition gap: Via KADS' models of expertise to ZDEST-2's expert systems. In *Proceedings of the European Knowledge Acquisition Workshop*, Bonn, Federal Republic of Germany. Available as Technical Report Number 143, German Research Institute for Mathematics and Data Processing (GMD), St. Augustin, FRG.

Kassirer, J. P., Kuipers, B. J., and Gorry, G. A. (1982). Toward a theory of clinical expertise. *American Journal of Medicine*, 73:251–258.

Kearsley, G. (1982). Authoring systems in computer based education. *Communications of the ACM*, 25:429–437.

Keller, A. M. (1986). The role of semantics in translating view updates. *Computer*, 19:63–73.

Kelly, G. A. (1955). *The Psychology of Personal Constructs*. Norton, New York.

Kent, D. L., Shortliffe, E. H., Carlson, R. W., Bischoff, M. B., and Jacobs, C. D. (1985). Improvements in data collection through physician use of a computer-based chemotherapy treatment consultant. *Journal of Clinical Oncology*, 3:1409–1417.

King, C., Manire, L., Strong, R. M., and Goldstein, L. (1984). Data management systems in clinical research. In Blum, B. I., editor, *Information Systems for Patient Care*, pages 404–415. Springer-Verlag, New York.

Kitto, C. M. (1988). Progress in automated knowledge acquisition tools: How close are we to replacing the knowledge engineer? In *Proceedings of the Third Knowledge Acquisition for Knowledge-Based Systems Workshop*, Banff, Alberta, Canada.

Klinker, G., Boyd, C., Genetet, S., and McDermott, J. (1987a). A KNACK for knowledge acquisition. In *Proceedings AAAI-87*, pages 488–493, Seattle, Washinghton. American Association for Artificial Intelligence.

Klinker, G., Bentolila, J., Genetet, S., and McDermott, J. (1987b). KNACK: Report-driven knowledge acquisition. *International Journal of Man–Machine Studies*, 26:65–79.

Klinker, G. (1988). KNACK: Sample-driven knowledge acquisition for reporting systems. In Marcus, S., editor, *Automating Knowledge Acquisition for Expert Systems*, pages 125–174. Kluwer Academic, Boston.

Klinker, G., Boyd, C., Dong, D., Maimon, J., McDermott, J., and Schnelbach, R. (1988). Building expert systems with knack. In *Proceedings of the Third Knowledge Acquisition for Knowledge-Based Systems Workshop*, Banff, Alberta, Canada.

Knatterud, G. L. (1981). Methods of quality control and of continuous adit procedures for controlled clinical trials. *Controlled Clinical Trials*, 1:327–332.

Komorowski, H. J. and Maluszynski, J. (1986). Logic programming and rapid prototyping. Technical Report TR-01-86, Center for Research in Computing Technology, Harvard University, Cambridge, Massachusetts.

Koretz, M. M., Jackson, P. M., Torti, F. M., and Carter, S. K. (1983). A comparison of the quality of participation of community affiliates and that of universities in the Northern California Oncology Group. *Journal of Clinical Oncology*, 1:640–644.

La France, M. (1987). The knowledge acquisition grid: A method for training knowledge engineers. *International Journal of Man–Machine Studies*, 26:245–255.

Lane, C. D. (1986). Ozone reference manual. Technical Report KSL-86-40, Knowledge Systems Laboratory, Stanford University, Stanford, California.

Lane, C. D., Walton, J. D., and E. H. Shortliffe, E. (1986). Graphical access to medical expert systems: II. Design of an interface for physicians. *Methods of Information in Medicine*, 25:143–150.

Layhad, M. W. and McShane, D. J. (1983). Applications of MEDLOG, a microcomputer-based system for time-oriented clinical data. In *Proceedings of the Seventh Annual Symposium on Computer Applications in Medical Care*, pages 731–734, Washington, D.C. IEEE Computer Society.

Lenat, D., Prakash, M., and Shepherd, M. (1986). CYC: Using common sense knowledge to overcome brittleness and knowledge acquisition bottlenecks. *AI Magazine*, 6:65–85.

Lenhard, R. E., Blum, B. I., and McColligan, E. E. (1984). An information system for oncology. In Blum, B., editor, *Information Systems for Patient Care*, pages 385–403. Springer-Verlag, New York.

Levesque, H. J. and Brachman, R. J. (1985). A fundamental tradeoff in knowledge representation and reasoning. In *Readings in Knowledge Representation*, pages 41–70. Morgan Kaufmann Publishers, Los Altos, California.

Loftus, E. F. (1979). *Eyewitness Testimony*. Harvard University Press, Cambridge, Massachusetts.

Lyons, W. (1986). *The Disappearance of Introspection*. MIT Press, Cambridge, Massachusetts.

Majchrzak, A., Tien-Chien, C., Barfield, W., Eberts, R., and Salvendy, G. (1987). *Human Aspects of Computer-Aided Design*. Taylor and Francis, Philadelphia.

Marcus, S., McDermott, J., and Wang, T. (1985). Knowledge acquisition for constructive systems. In *Proceedings of the Ninth International Joint Conference on Artificial Intelligence*, pages 637–639, Los Angeles, California.

Marcus, S. (1988). SALT: A knowledge acquisition tool for propose-and-revise systems. In Marcus, S., editor, *Automating Knowledge Acquisition for Expert Systems*, pages 81–121. Kluwer Academic, Boston.

Masand, B. M. (1982). A cancer protocol writer's assistant. Master's thesis, Massachusetts Institute of Technology, Boston, Massachusetts.

McCarthy, J. (1968). Programs with common sense. In Minsky, M., editor, *Semantic Information Processing*, pages 403–418. MIT Press, Cambridge, Massachusetts.

McCarthy, J. and Hayes, P. J. (1969). Some philosophical problems from the standpoint of artificial intelligence. In *Machine Intelligence*, volume 4, pages 463–502. Edinburgh University Press, Edinburgh, U.K.

McDermott, J. (1986). Making expert systems explicit. In Kugler, H.-J., editor, *Information Processing 86*, pages 539–544, Dublin, Ireland. International Federation of Information Processing Societies, Elsevier Science Publishers B.V. (North Holland).

McDermott, J. (1988). Preliminary steps toward a taxonomy of problem-solving methods. In Marcus, S., editor, *Automating Knowledge Acquisition for Expert Systems*, pages 225–256. Kluwer Academic, Boston.

McGuire, C. H. (1985). Medical problem-solving: A critique of the literature. *Journal of Medical Education*, 60:587–595.

Meinert, C. L. (1982). Funding for clinical trials. *Controlled Clinical Trials*, 3:165–171.

Michalski, R. S., Carbonell, J. G., and Mitchell, T. M., editors (1983). *Machine Learning: An Artificial Intelligence Approach*. Tioga Publishing Company, Palo Alto, California.

Michalski, R. S., Carbonell, J. G., and Mitchell, T. M., editors (1986). *Machine Learning: An Artificial Intelligence Approach, Volume II*. Morgan Kaufman Publishers, Los Altos, California.

Michalski, R. S. and Chilausky, R. L. (1980). Knowledge acquisition by encoding expert rules versus computer induction from examples: A case study involving soybean pathology. *International Journal of Man–Machine Studies*, 12:63–87.

Miller, P. L. (1983). Critiquing anesthetic management: The 'ATTENDING' computer system. *Anesthesiology*, 53:362–369.

Miller, P. L., Blumenfrucht, S. J., Rose, J. R., Rothschild, M., Swett, H. A., Weltin, G., and Maars, N. J. I. (1987). HYDRA: A knowledge acquisition tool for expert systems which critique medical workup. *Medical Decision Making*, 7:12–21.

Miller, R. A., Pople, H. E., and Myers, J. D. (1982). INTERNIST-1: An experimental computer-based diagnostic consultant for general internal medicine. *New England Journal of Medicine*, 307:468–476.

Minsky, M. (1975). A framework for representing knowledge. In Winston, P. H., editor, *The Psychology of Computer Vision*, pages 211–277. McGraw-Hill, New York.

Miyake, N. and Norman, D. A. (1978). To ask a question, one must know enough to know what is not known. Technical Report 7802, Center for Human Information Processing, University of California, San Diego.

Morik, K. (1987). Acquiring domain models. *International Journal of Man–Machine Studies*, 26:93–104.

Mosteller, F., Gilbert, J. P., and McPeek, B. (1983). Controversies in design and analysis of clinical trials. In *Clinical Trials: Issues and Approaches*, volume 46 of *Statistics: Textbooks and Monographs*, pages 13–64. Marcel Dekker, New York.

Mulsant, B. and Servan-Schreiber, D. (1984). Knowledge engineering: A daily activity on a hospital ward. *Computers and Biomedical Research*, 17:71–91.

Musen, M. A., Langlotz, C. P., Fagan, L. M., and Shortliffe, E. H. (1985). Rationale for knowledge base redesign in a medical advice system. In *Proceedings of AAMSI Congress 85*, pages 197–201, San Francisco, California. American Association for Medical Systems and Informatics.

Musen, M. A., Rohn, J. A., Fagan, L. M., and Shortliffe, E. H. (1986). Knowledge engineering for a clinical trial advice system: Uncovering errors in protocol specification. In *Proceedings of AAMSI Congress 86*, pages 24–27, Anaheim, California. American Association for Medical Systems and Informatics. Reprinted in *Bulletin du Cancer* (Paris), 1987,74:291–296.

Musen, M. A., Fagan, L. M., Combs, D. M., and Shortliffe, E. H. (1987). Use of a domain model to drive an interactive knowledge-editing tool. *International Journal of Man–Machine Studies*, 26:105–121.

Musen, M. A., Combs, D. M., Walton, J. D., Shortliffe, E. H., and Fagan, L. M. (1988a). OPAL: Toward the computer-aided design of oncology advice systems. In Miller, P. L., editor, *Selected Topics in Medical Artificial Intelligence*, pages 166–180. Springer-Verlag, New York.

Musen, M. A., Fagan, L. M., and Shortliffe, E. H. (1988b). Graphical specification of procedural knowledge for an expert system. In Hendler, J., editor, *Expert Systems: The User Interface*, pages 15–35. Ablex, Norwood, New Jersey.

Musen, M. A. (1988). Conceptual models of interactive knowledge-acquisition tools. In *Proceedings of the European Knowledge Acquisition Workshop*, Bonn, Federal Republic of Germany. Available as Technical Report Number 143, German Research Institute for Mathematics and Data Processing (GMD), St. Augustin, FRG.

Naeymi-Rad, F., Koschmann, T., Trace, D., Kepic, T., R., C., Weil, M. H., and Evens, M. (1986). Expert knowledge base designed using ER-modeling technique. In *Proceedings of MEDINFO 86*, pages 51–55, Washington, D.C. Fifth World Congress on Medical Informatics.

Neufeld, V. R., Norman, G. R., Feightner, J. W., and Barrows, H. S. (1981). Clinical problem-solving by medical students: A cross-sectional and longitudinal analysis. *Medical Education*, 15:315–321.

Neves, D. M. and Anderson, J. R. (1981). Knowledge compilation: Mechanisms for automatization of cognitive skills. In Anderson, J., editor, *Cognitive Skills and Their Acquisition*, pages 57–84. Lawrence Erlbaum Associates, Hillsdale, New Jersey.

Newell, A. (1982). The knowledge level. *Artificial Intelligence*, 18:87–127.

Nilsson, N. J. (1981). The interplay between theoretical and experimental methods in artificial intelligence. *Cognition and Brain Theory*, 4:69–74.

Nisbett, R. E. and Wilson, T. D. (1977). Telling more than we can know: Verbal reports on mental processes. *Psychological Review*, 84:231–259.

Norman, D. A. (1983). Some observations on mental models. In Genter, D. and Stevens, A. L., editors, *Mental Models*, pages 7–14. Lawrence Erlbaum, Hillsdale, New Jersey.

Norman, G. R., Jacoby, L. L., Feightner, J. W., and Campbell, E. J. M. (1979). Clinical experience and the structure of memory. In *Proceedings of the Eighteenth Annual Conference on Research in Medical Education*, pages 214–218, Washington, DC. American Association of Medical Colleges.

Parsaye, K. (1988). Acquiring and verifying knowledge automatically. *AI Expert*, 3:48–63.

Partsch, H. and Steinbruggen, R. (1983). Program transformation systems. *Computing Surveys*, 15:199–236.

Patel, V. L., Groen, G. J., and Frederiksen, C. H. (1986). Differences between medical students and doctors in memory for clinical cases. *Medical Education*, 20:3–9.

Patel, V. L., HoPingKong, H., and Mark, V. C. (1984). Role of prior knowledge in comprehension of medical information by medical students and physicians. In *Proceedings of the Twenty-third Annual Conference on Research in Medical Education*, pages 127–132, Washington, DC. American Association of Medical Colleges.

Phillips, B., Messick, S. L., Freiling, M. J., and Alexander, J. H. (1985). INKA: The INGLISH knowledge acquisition interface for electronic instrument troubleshooting systems. In *The Second Conference on Artificial Intelligence Applications*, pages 676–681, Miami, Florida. IEEE Computer Society Press.

Pollak, M. N. (1983). Computer-aided information management systems in clinical trials: A physician's perspective. *Computer Programs in Biomedicine*, 16:243–252.

Prerau, D. S. (1987). Knowledge acquisition in the development of a large expert system. *AI Magazine*, 8:43–51.

Rappaport, A. and Gaines, B. R. (1988). Integration of acquisition and performance systems. In *Proceedings of the Third Knowledge Acquisition for Knowledge-Based Systems Workshop*, Banff, Alberta, Canada.

Reboh, R. (1981). Knowledge engineering techniques and tools in the Prospector environment. Technical Report 243, SRI International, Menlo Park, California.

Regoczei, S. and Plantinga, E. P. O. (1987). Creating the domain of discourse: Ontology and inventory. *International Journal of Man–Machine Studies*, 27:235–250.

Rumelhart, D. E. and Norman, D. A. (1983). Representation in memory. Technical Report CHIP 116, Center for Human Information Processing, University of California, San Diego, California.

Ryle, G. (1949). *The Concept of Mind*. Barnes and Noble, New York.

Salzberg, B. (1986). Third normal form made easy. *SIGMOD Record*, 15:2–18.

Samuel, A. L. (1967). Some studies in machine learning using the game of checkers. II Recent progress. *IBM Journal of Research and Development*, 11:601–617.

Schank, R. C. and Abelson, R. (1977). *Scripts, Plans, Goals, and Understanding*. Lawrence Erlbaum Associates, Hillsdale, New Jersey.

Schechter, M. T. and Sheps, S. B. (1984). Grading clinical research: A midterm report card. *Canadian Medical Association Journal*, 131:1025–1027.

Schmidt, R. (1985). The responsibility for the study protocol in a drug trial. *Journal of Clinical Pharmacology, Therapy, and Toxicity*, 23:158–160.

Shaw, M. L. G., editor (1981). *Recent Advances in Personal Construct Technology*. Academic Press, New York.

Shaw, M. L. G. and Gaines, B. R. (1987). KITTEN: Knowledge initiation and transfer tools for experts and novices. *International Journal of Man–Machine Studies*, 27:251–280.

Shiffrin, R. M. and Dumais, S. T. (1981). Development of automatism. In Anderson, J. R., editor, *Cognitive Skills and Their Acquisition*, pages 111–140. Lawrence Erlbaum Associates, Hillsdale, New Jersey.

Shneiderman, B. (1983). Direct manipulation: A step beyond programming languages. *Computer*, 16:57–69.

Shortliffe, E. H., Scott, A. C., Bischoff, M. B., van Melle, W., and Jacobs, C. D. (1981). ONCOCIN: An expert system for oncology protocol management. In *Proceedings of the Seventh International Joint Conference on Artificial Intelligence*, pages 876–881, Vancouver, British Columbia.

Shortliffe, E. H. (1986). Medical expert systems: Knowledge tools for physicians. *Western Journal of Medicine*, 145:830–839.

Silverman, H. (1975). A digitalis therapy advisor. Technical Report TR-143, Project MAC, Massachusetts Institute Technology, Cambridge, Massachusetts.

Simon, H. A. (1975). The functional equivalence of problem solving skills. *Cognitive Psychology*, 7:268–288.

Slovic, P. (1969). Analyzing the expert judge: A descriptive study of a stockbroker's decision process. *Journal of Applied Psychology*, 53:255–263.

Slovic, P. and Lichtenstein, S. (1971). Comparison of Bayesian and regression approaches to the study of information processing in judgment. *Organizational Behavior and Human Performance*, 6:649–744.

Smith, J. W. (1985). *RED: A Classificatory and Abductive Expert System*. PhD thesis, Ohio State University, Columbus, Ohio.

Spang, S., editor (1987). The new AI pioneers: The knowledge merchants. *Spang Robinson Report on AI*, 3:1–8.

Spradley, J. P. (1979). *The Ethnographic Interview*. Holt, Rinehart and Winston, New York.

Stefik, M. (1981). Planning with constraints. *Artificial Intelligence*, 16:111–139.

Stefik, M. and Bobrow, D. G. (1986). Object-oriented programming: Themes and variations. *AI Magazine*, 6:40–62.

Stoy, J. E. (1977). *Denotational Semantics: The Scott–Strachey Approach to Programming Language Theory*. MIT Press, Cambridge, Massachusetts.

Swartout, W. and Balzer, R. (1982). On the inevitable intertwining of specification and implementation. *Communications of the ACM*, 25:438–440.

Swartout, W. R. (1981). *Producing Explanations and Justifications of Expert Consulting Programs*. PhD thesis, Massachusetts Institute of Technology, Cambridge, Massachusetts. MIT/LCS/TR-251.

Sylvester, R. J., Pinedo, H. M., de Pauw, M., Staquet, M. J., Buyse, M. E., Renard, J., and Bonadonna, G. (1981). Quality of institutional participation in multicenter clinical trials. *New England Journal of Medicine*, 305:852–855.

Thomas, L. (1979). Medical lessons from history. In *The Medusa and the Snail*, pages 158–175. Viking Press, New York.

Tu, S. W., Kahn, M. G., Musen, M. A., Ferguson, J. C., Shortliffe, E. H., and Fagan, L. M. (1989). Episodic monitoring of time-oriented data for heuristic skeletal-plan refinement. *Communications of the ACM* (in press).

Tuhrim, S. and Reggia, J. A. (1986). Feasibility of physician-developed expert systems. *Medical Decision Making*, 6:23–26.

Tuhrim, S., Reggia, J. A., and Floor, M. (1988). Expert system development: Letting the domain specialist directly author knowledge bases. In Hendler, J., editor, *Expert Systems: The User Interface*, pages 37–56. Ablex, Norwood, New Jersey.

Tversky, A. and Kahneman, D. (1974). Judgment under uncertainty: Heuristics and biases. *Science*, 184:1124–1131.

Uhr, L. and Vossler, C. (1963). A pattern-recognition program that generates, evaluates, and adjusts its own operators. In *Computers and Thought*, pages 251–268. McGraw-Hill, New York.

van Melle, W. (1979). A domain-independent production-rule system for consultation programs. In *Proceedings of Sixth International Joint Conference on Artificial Intelligence*, pages 923–925.

Walton, J. D., Musen, M. A., Combs, D. M., Lane, C. D., Shortliffe, E. H., and Fagan, L. M. (1987). Graphical access to medical expert systems: III. Design of a knowledge acquisition environment. *Methods of Information in Medicine*, 26:78–88.

Wasserman, A. I. (1985). Extending state transition diagrams for the specification of human–computer interaction. *IEEE Transactions on Software Engineering*, SE-11:699–713.

Waterman, D. A. and Hayes-Roth, F. (1983). An investigation of tools for building expert systems. In *Building Expert Systems*, pages 169–215. Addison-Wesley, Reading, Massachusetts.

Watts, M. S. M., editor (1986). Medical Informatics (special issue). *Western Journal of Medicine*, 145:742–924.

Weiss, S. M. and Kulikowski, C. A. (1979). EXPERT: A system for developing consultation models. In *Proceedings of the Sixth International Joint Conference on Artificial Intelligence*, pages 942–947, Tokyo, Japan.

Whitehead, S. F. and Bilofsky, H. (1980). CLINFO–a clinical research data management and analysis system. In *Proceedings of the Fourth Annual Symposium on Computer Applications in Medical Care*, Washington, D.C. IEEE Computer Society.

Wiederhold, G. (1981). *Databases for Health Care*. Springer-Verlag, New York.

Wiederhold, G. (1983). *Database Design*. McGraw-Hill, New York, 2nd edition.

Wilkins, D. C. (1986). Knowledge base debugging using apprenticeship learning techniques. In *Proceedings of the Knowledge Acquisition for Knowledge-Based Systems Workshop*, Banff, Alberta, Canada. American Association for Artificial Intelligence.

Winograd, T. (1975). Frame representations and the declarative/procedural controversy. In *Representation and Understanding: Studies in Cognitive Science*, pages 185–210. Academic Press, New York.

Winograd, T. and Flores, F. (1986). *Understanding Computers and Cognition: A New Foundation for Design*. Ablex, Norwood, New Jersey.

Wirtschafter, D., Carpenter, J. T., and Mesel, E. (1979). A consultant-extender system for breast cancer adjuvant chemotherapy. *Annals of Internal Medicine*, 90:396–401.

Wirtschafter, D., Scalise, M., Henke, C., and Gams, R. A. (1981). Do information systems improve the quality of clinical research? results of a randomized trial in a cooperative multi-institutional cancer group. *Computers and Biomedical Research*, 14:78–90.